AF597557

SOLITUDE

ERIK CHMIL

FOR ANTONIA & MATTEO

Petra Giloy-Hirtz

»THEY PAVED PARADISE AND PUT UP A PARKING LOT«[1]

SOLITUDE
Zu den Fotografien von Erik Chmil

I

Die Welt als Parkplatz. An den zentralen Orten und den entlegenen: ob inmitten der Megapolis, an den Rändern der Vorstädte oder in der Abgeschiedenheit des Dorfes, der Einsamkeit des Waldes, der Ödnis der Wüste, entlang des Ozeans oder hoch in den Gebirgen, ubiquitär: Parking Lots. In New York, Los Angeles, Chicago, Miami, in Buenos Aires, Hongkong, Dubai oder Kapstadt, in Australien, an der Pazifikküste Südamerikas, in europäischen Städten wie Barcelona, Oslo, Marseille: Tiefgaragen in gleißendem Licht, Paläste unter der Erde, über der Erde, Bunker oder Dächer, unter Brücken; zugepflastert, teergedeckt, voller Müll oder antiseptisch clean, bisweilen in futuristischer Architektur oder nach lokalem Geschmack.

Eine Serie von Fotografien, entstanden über beinahe zwanzig Jahren hinweg von einem, der auszog, Automobile zu fotografieren und dabei ein anderes für sich entdeckte: den Parkplatz. Sein aufmerksamer Blick erlöst diesen Ort von seiner Banalität. Erik Chmil ist fasziniert von der Ästhetik jener normalen Erscheinung, und so wächst sein Interesse an diesem Ort, der mehr verheißt als nur formale Variation. Weg von der Werbung und ihren glamourösen Bildern und ohne Vorgaben oder kommerzielle Erwartungen seiner Auftraggeber lässt er sich von seiner Neugierde und Entdeckerlust treiben und begibt sich auf die Spur jener oft verzweifelt gesuchten und zugleich übersehenen Orte. Die Bilder danken sich also keiner schnellen Idee. Das Vorhaben entwickelt sich über einen langen Zeitraum, wird ihm zur inneren Notwendigkeit und hat Konsequenzen. *In Freiheit* sind diese Fotografien gemacht, sie werden zum Vehikel, eine künstlerische Sprache zu entwickeln und die eigenen Vorstellungen umzusetzen, motiviert durch das Verlangen, *das Medium Fotografie spannend zu halten*.[2] So ist diese Serie auch lebensgeschichtlich bedeutsam und Ausdruck eines neuen Selbstverständnisses. Für diesen Band hat Erik Chmil aus dem großen Konvolut von Fotografien knapp hundert ausgewählt, eine subjektive Wahl, die in einigen Fällen auch biografisch motiviert ist, wie die in Leverkusen und Köln entstandenen Arbeiten, Städte, die für ihn mit Kindheit und Lebensmittelpunkt verbunden sind.

Was ist all diesen Fotografien gemeinsam, über das Motiv des Parkplatzes hinaus? Zunächst erscheint jedes Bild anders, der Zyklus als ein Spektrum unendlicher Möglichkeiten, ohne strengen konzeptuellen Rahmen, weder einem chronologischen noch einem geografischen System unterworfen. Und doch gibt es durchaus Ordnungsprinzipien. Die Leere, sie fällt zuerst ins Auge: kein Mensch, keine Maschine. In den Zeiten des Schlafs inmitten der Nacht, antizyklisch zu den Routinen des Lebens, im Morgengrauen und am späten Abend, sind diese Bilder gemacht. Und in das Erstaunen über die Unberührtheit jener Orte drängt sich die Vorstellung eines anderen Zustands, jenen von Überfüllung, Getriebe, Verkehr, Aktion. Das Ungewohnte enthält sein Gegenteil, die Gewöhnlichkeit alltäglicher Nutzung. So finden wir, geben wir uns der Betrachtung und dem Fluss der Bilder hin, Traumwelten jenseits der Turbulenz des Alltags und der Spuren des Gebrauchs.

Der Titel der jeweiligen Arbeit bezeichnet den Ort, an dem sie entstanden ist. Der ist bisweilen offenkundig, etwa die Skyline von Hongkong, und es mag ein Vergnügen sein für den Betrachter, ihn zu erraten: Köln! Wie sich dort eine kleine Spitze des Domes noch über dem Parkdeck erhebt! Die frühen Arbeiten sind analog mit der Großbildkamera gemacht, in exzellenter Qualität der hohen Auflösung der Details. Und auch wenn Chmil später digital fotografiert, bleiben die Bilder *echt*, sind sie nicht am Computer generiert oder verfremdet oder neu komponiert, wie etwa die späteren Arbeiten von Andreas Gursky.

Erik Chmil bewertet nicht. Eher scheint er fasziniert von der Vielfalt der Erscheinungsweisen seines Sujets. Die Fotografien zeugen von der Lust am Bild, an der Komposition, an der möglichen narrativen Struktur, an den Imaginationen, die es im Betrachter freisetzen mag. Dabei sind sie nicht inszeniert wie bei Jeff Wall etwa oder Gregory Crewdson, der mit immensem Aufwand hyperrealistische Tableaus arrangiert, um so etwas wie Rätselhaftigkeit und übernatürliche Suggestivkraft zu entfalten. Das Erzählerische scheint in Chmils Aufnahmen dem vorgefundenen Ort inhärent. Insbesondere die Nachtbilder laden ein zu Geschichten im Kopf: das Unheimliche der Szenerie, Scheinwerferlicht, im Dickicht der Pflanzen verborgen ein Haus. Das ist, wie David Lynch über seine »Factory Photographs« sagt, *a setting for the narrative*.

Die Oberflächen der Plätze: regennass spiegelnd, laubbedeckt, von Schneemassen verborgen, der Teer unter der Hitze geplatzt, glatter Belag, versiegelt, poliert; eingebettet in die Umgebung oder isoliert aus jeglichem Kontext, manchmal wie eine Bühne, gerade auch in der Beleuchtung. Nachtblauer Himmel, geometrische Flächen: wie Bilder, wie Malerei wirken die Linien, die rechtwinkligen Felder, die Farbe – abstrakt, minimal, Color Field. Ein tiefgrauer Himmel oder eine Front von Fassaden als Pendant zum Grau des Betons.

Die Bilder verstehen sich nicht als politisches Manifest und nicht als Dokumentation über den Zustand der Welt. Und doch bebildern sie, wenn vielleicht auch jenseits der Intention des Autors, die Eroberung der Welt durch das Auto. Liegt mit diesem Band nicht eine Kulturgeschichte des Parkplatzes vor? Indem er den Blick paradigmatisch auf die Besetzung des Territoriums richtet, erzählt er von der Geschichte unserer Städte, Landschaften und Länder und von modernen Lebensformen. Der Titel »Solitude«, Einsamkeit, hat zweifelsohne auch eine ironische Komponente. Ausgerechnet der Parkplatz als Oase der Ruhe, der Erholung, des Mit-sich-allein-Seins. Zudem: Die Leere, das Stille, Friedliche und Unberührte, sie tragen das Gegenteil in sich, die Hektik und Dynamik, das Inhumane, die Wunden, die in Stadt und Natur geschlagen sind. So erscheint die Serie dokumentarisch und erzählerisch zugleich, sachlich und poetisch; sie sucht das analytische Auge und das fantasiebegabte Hirn.

II

Schon einmal hat sich, sehr prominent, ein Künstler mit seiner Kamera den Parkplätzen gewidmet: Ed Ruscha. Aus der Luft, vom Helikopter sind sie fotografiert, sonntags, und so auch menschenleer und ohne ein einziges Auto. Schwarz-Weiß, neutral erscheinen die Strukturen, die Raster und Gitter von oben, die *Zeichnungen*, grafische Abstraktionen, wie sie in der späteren Malerei des Künstlers wiederzufinden sind. Seine Wahrnehmung von Los Angeles, der vom Auto geprägten Stadt überhaupt, der Tankstellen, Parkplätze, Garagen und Freeways wie auch der Apartments und Swimmingpools fasziniert in der Serialität der Bilder, in den strikten Ordnungsprinzipien und der außerordentlichen Präsentationform als Buch. Ed Ruschas »Thirtyfour Parking Lots« (1967) gehört neben »Twentysix Gasoline Stations« (1963) oder »Every Building on the Sunset Strip« (1966) zu den herausragenden und einflussreichen Arbeiten in der zeitgenössischen Kunst und gilt wegen der konzeptuellen und analytischen Annäherung an *bebaute Landschaft* als Meilenstein in der Entwicklung der Fotografie: *His subject matter was neither purely documentary nor solely artistic, in fact it was stereotypical and banal, with motifs drawn from the car-dominated western landscape. That rebellious material, along with his serial presentation, made for a mythical road-movie or photo-novel effect with Beat Generation overtones.*[3]

Typologien von industriellen Bauten hatten Bernd und Hilla Becher – anknüpfend an die Repräsentanten der Neuen Sachlichkeit der zwanziger Jahre wie besonders Karl Blossfeldt, August Sander und Albert Renger-Patzsch – zusammengetragen und damit eine internationale Schule von Fotografen begründet. Wie Archäologen inventarisierten sie die Vielfalt der Formen im Industriezeitalter, zum Beispiel Hochöfen, Gasbehälter, Wassertürme. Durch Distanz zum Gegenstand und Präzision, durch strikte Regeln der Anordnung und visuelle Klarheit haben sie ganze Archive der industriellen Kultur aufgebaut. Sie waren als einzige Europäer unter den zehn Künstlern der legendären 1976 in New York eröffneten Ausstellung »New Topographics. Photographs of a Man-Altered Landscape«, ein Wendepunkt in der Geschichte der Fotografie, die gegen eine Romantisierung und Idealisierung der Landschaft den Blick auf ihre Zerstörung durch die Industrialisierung richtete, die gegenüber dem Spektakulären eine Ästhetik des Banalen, des Alltäglichen entfaltete. Robert Adams gehörte dazu und Lewis Baltz, der in einer Serie von Schwarz-Weiß-Bildern in minutiösen Details die beängstigend anonyme Gesichtslosigkeit moderner Industriebauten in den USA festgehalten hat – »The new Industrial Parks near Irvine,

California« (1974) – und, später in Farbe, sterile, menschenleere Innenräume – »Sites of Technology« (1989–1991). Die Arbeiten jener Fotografen reflektieren die unkontrolliert wachsende Urbanisierung der Natur durch die Siedlungen der Vorstädte, durch Straßen, Trailer Parks, Shopping Malls … Ihre Dokumentation von Uniformität, Standardisierung, Anonymität und kommerzieller Überformung sowie die Auslöschung des Restes von *wilderness* war die klare politische Botschaft ihrer Werke. Unter ihnen ist Stephen Shore übrigens der Einzige, der in Farbe fotografierte (und der erste lebende Künstler, der, 1971 im Alter von 23 Jahren, eine Einzelausstellung im Metropolitan Museum of Art erhielt). Er war es, dem zusammen mit William Eggleston zu danken ist, dass die Farbfotografie als Kunst anerkannt wurde; sein Buch »Uncommon Places« (1982) war Bibel für die folgende Generation: *Like Robert Frank and Walker Evans before him, Shore discovered a hitherto unarticulated vision of America via highway and camera. Approaching his subjects with cool objectivity, Shore in these images retains precise internal systems of gestures in composition and light, through which a parking lot emptied of people, a hotel bedroom, or a building on a side street assumes both an archetypical aura and an ambiguously personal importance.*[4]

Eine Nähe zur Haltung jener amerikanischen Fotografie, wie sie auch Joel Meyerowitz und Richard Misrach verkörpern oder Alec Soth mit seinen *large-scale American projects* im Mittleren Westen der USA oder Joel Sternfeld mit seiner Serie »American Prospects« aus dem Jahr 1987, haben die Bilder, die der deutsche Fotograf Olaf Otto Becker in der Antarktis gemacht hat: Sie alle dokumentieren die veränderte Landschaft, die Spuren des Menschen, die er zum Schaden des Planeten hinterlassen hat. Vielfach ist beides in diesen Fotografien angelegt – wie bei Robert Adams, der über mehr als vierzig Jahre den amerikanischen Westen fotografiert hat: die Schönheit und deren Fragilität, Affirmation und die Trauer über den Verlust von Raum und Stille, von Hoffnung und der Verzweiflung über den Zustand der Erde.

III

Was zeigen Erik Chmils Fotografien, über was geben sie Auskunft, wie lassen sie sich deuten über ihre ästhetische Attraktivität hinaus?

Das Aufregende der Fotografie, welches sie zum prominenten künstlerischen Medium der Gegenwart macht, liegt wohl darin, dass sie Welt nicht abbildet, sondern Vorstellungen von Welt offeriert. Dass sie, selbst wenn sie konzentriert ist auf das Reale und die Aufmerksamkeit des Betrachters auf den Gegenstand richtet, doch noch eine andere Welt spürbar werden lässt: *Photographien generieren Realität, sie erschaffen Wiedererzählungen, sie transportieren und erzeugen Ideen und Deutungen der Welt*, sagt Thomas Demand, einer der bedeutenden Fotokünstler der Gegenwart. Fotografien verweisen auf das *Reale* und das *Imaginäre*. Sie sind Projektionsfläche für den Betrachter. Wenn er Glück hat, bieten sie ihm *Modelle für (sein eigenes) Erleben, Erkennen, Werten und Handeln* an, wie es Vilém Flusser in seiner berühmten Schrift »Für eine Philosophie der Fotografie« formuliert.

Betrachten wir die hier versammelten Fotografien als Bild: die Konturen und Farben, Licht und Schatten, das Verhältnis des zentralen Motivs zur Peripherie, das jeweils spezifisch Atmosphärische, die Stimmungen, die Darstellungsformen, die von Sachlichkeit bis zur Romantik reichen, von Purismus zu Nostalgie und bis hin zum Spiel mit Klischees … Das Buch trägt nicht den Titel *Hundert Parkplätze*, es heißt »Solitude«. Es geht Erik Chmil nicht um kühle Inventarisierung, sondern um Poetisierung, um die Aura der Orte und ihre narrative Qualität: *Wenn ich aussteige, erzählt dieser Ort mir was: im eigentlichen von Menschen. Trennung, einander finden, dunkle Geschäfte … absurde Zufälligkeit … an diesem einen Ort. Eine Entdeckung ohne Aufdeckung. Sichtbares und Verborgenes halten sich auf stimmungsvolle Weise die Waage.*[5] Und dennoch: Wenngleich diese Fotografien eher durch den visuellen Reiz ins Schauen locken, als ein politisches Manifest sein zu wollen, zeigen sie doch vielfältig auch die globale, postindustrielle, spätkapitalistische Gesellschaft, die Konzentration von Macht und Reichtum und ihr Gegenteil sowie gerade die Marginalisierung von »Solitude«.

Wie sieht unsere Welt aus und wie könnte sie aussehen? Was verraten Parkplätze über unser Leben? Unbegrenzte Mobilität, individuelle Freiheit? Gibt es eine Alternative zur Besetzung immer weiterer Flächen, sind kollektive Rituale des Fahrens im Kontext von Arbeit und Konsum bald obsolet? Kann

Beweglichkeit neu gedacht werden, erledigt sich der Fetisch Auto und sind so vielleicht jene Bilder in absehbarer Zeit anachronistisch, überholte Reminiszenz an ein Zeitalter von Lärm und Chaos – und somit auch historische Zeugnisse?

DON'T IT ALWAYS SEEM TO GO
THAT YOU DON'T KNOW WHAT YOU'VE GOT
TILL IT'S GONE
THEY PAVED PARADISE
AND PUT UP A PARKING LOT
Joni Mitchell

Inspiriert von den französischen Strukturalisten und insbesondere von Michel Foucault, stellt der Künstler Peter Halley die Verbindung her zwischen seiner geometrischen Malerei und der Geometrisierung des sozialen Raumes in der Welt, in der wir leben. In seinem Essay »The Deployment of the Geometric« (1984) beschreibt er die Transformation der Landschaft, der Gesellschaft und des Denkens durch die Geometrie als Reglementierung. Er spricht von einer Korrespondenz zwischen der *geometrization of the landscape* und der *geometrization of thought. Space is divided into discrete, isolated cells [...] reached through complex networks of corridors and roadways that must be traveled at prescribed speeds and prescribed times.*[6]

Auf wie vielen Ebenen lassen sich Erik Chmils Parking Lots lesen! In erster Linie versammelt »Solitude« eine Fülle opulenter Bilder großartiger Landschaften und spektakulärer Architekturen und die Faszination der Orte überträgt sich leicht auf den Betrachter. Der Band nimmt ihn mit auf eine Reise durch die Welt. So repräsentieren diese Fotografien auch den Wunsch nach individueller Mobilität: Ausbrechen aus der Enge der Städte in die Weite der Natur, dem Stillstand und Druck entfliehen. Welch ein Gefühl der Befreiung! Und so scheint es, wird mancher gepflasterte Platz in ein Paradies zurückverwandelt.

[1] *Zeile aus dem Lied von Joni Mitchell, »Big Yellow Taxi«, 1970.*
[2] *Erik Chmil im Gespräch mit der Autorin in München am 17. Mai 2017.*
[3] *Margit Rowell, »Ed Ruscha. Photographer«, Göttingen 2006.*
[4] *»Uncommon Places. The Complete Works. Photographs by Stephen Shore«, mit einem Essay von Stephan Schmidt-Wulffen, New York 2015.*
[5] *Erik Chmil im Gespräch mit Jürgen Opel am 26. April 2017.*
[6] *Peter Halley, »The Crisis in Geometry« (1984), in: ders., »Collected Essays«. 1981–1987, Edition Gallery Bruno Bischofberger, Zürich u. a. 1988, S. 80.*

Petra Giloy-Hirtz

»THEY PAVED PARADISE AND PUT UP A PARKING LOT«[1]

SOLITUDE
On the Photographs of Erik Chmil

I

The world as a parking lot, not just in central locations but also in remote places: whether in the middle of the big city or on the outskirts of the suburbs, in the seclusion of the village, the loneliness of the forest, the barrenness of the desert, along the shoreline of the ocean or high up in the mountains: parking lots are ubiquitous. In New York, Los Angeles, Chicago, Miami, in Buenos Aires, Hong Kong, Dubai, or Cape Town, in Australia, on the Pacific coast of South America, in European cities such as Barcelona, Oslo, Marseille: parking garages bathed in glaring light, palaces under and above ground, bunkers or roofs, under bridges; paved over, filled with garbage or antiseptically clean, sometimes boasting futuristic architecture or following regional tastes.

A series of photographs created over a period of almost twenty years by an artist who set out to photograph automobiles and, in the process, discovered a different subject: the parking lot. His attentive gaze delivers this place from its banality. Erik Chmil came to be fascinated with the aesthetic of this common phenomenon and his interest in this place, which promises more than just formal variation, grew. Away from advertising and its glamorous images and without any specific demands or commercial expectations of his clients, he let his curiosity and joy of discovery guide him and embarked on a search for these often difficult-to-find and easily overlooked places. The images are, in other words, not the result of a quick idea. The project evolved over a longer period of time, became an inner need of his, and had consequences. These photographs were taken *in freedom*; they became a vehicle to develop an artistic language and realize his own ideas, motivated by a desire to *keep the medium of photography exciting*.[2] As a result, this series is also important in terms of his personal history and the expression of a new self-conception.

Erik Chmil has selected just under a hundred photographs from this large body of work for this volume, a subjective selection that, in some cases, is also biographically motivated, as in the case of the photographs taken in Leverkusen and Cologne, cities he associates with childhood and long-time residence.

What do all these photographs have in common beyond the subject of the parking lot? At first each picture appears different and the series seems like a spectrum of infinite possibilities, without a rigid conceptual framework, subject to neither chronological nor geographical order. And yet there are organizing principles. What first strikes the eye is the emptiness: no human beings, no machines. These pictures were taken when people were asleep in the dead of night, at dawn and late in the evening, anticyclical to the routines of life. Yet the amazement at the unspoiled state of these places is punctuated with the notion of a different state, one of overcrowding, bustle, traffic, action. The unfamiliar contains its opposite: the normality of everyday use. When we indulge in contemplation and in the flow of images, we thus find dream worlds beyond the turbulence of everyday life and the traces of use.

The title of a work refers to the place where it was created. Sometimes this is obvious, as with the skyline of Hong Kong, and sometimes it may be fun for the viewer to guess. Note the tiny spire of the cathedral that rises just above the parking deck: Cologne! The early photographs are analog, taken with a large-format camera; they are of excellent quality with the high resolution bringing out a lot of detail. And even later on, when Chmil uses digital photography, the pictures remain *real*; they are not computer-generated, distorted, or re-composed like, say, the later works of Andreas Gursky.

Erik Chmil does not evaluate. He seems to be fascinated with the many different guises his subject takes. The photographs reflect delight in the image, in composition, in potential narrative structure, in the imaginings it may spark in the viewer. Yet they are not staged, as they are in the case of Jeff Wall or of Gregory Crewdson, who arranges immensely elaborate, hyper-realistic tableaux to unfold a mysteriousness and supernatural evocativeness of sorts. In Chmil's photographs, the narrative element seems to be inherent in the existing place. The nocturnal images in particular suggest stories in viewers' heads: the uncanny scenery, floodlit, a house hidden in the thicket of plants. This is what David Lynch says about his Factory Photographs: *a setting for the narrative.*

The surfaces of the parking lots: wet with rain and reflective; covered with leaves; hidden under snow; cracks in the asphalt due to heat; the pavement surface smooth, sealed, polished; embedded in the surroundings or isolated from any context; sometimes like a stage, especially with the lighting. Dark blue night sky, geometric surfaces: the lines, the rectangular fields, the colors appear like painting–abstract, Minimal, Color Field. A dark gray sky or a phalanx of façades to match the gray of the concrete.

The pictures are not intended as a political manifesto or as a documentation of the state of the world. And yet they illustrate–even if, perhaps, beyond the author's intention–how the automobile has conquered the world. Does this volume not present a cultural history of the parking lot? By focusing the gaze paradigmatically on the occupation of territory, it tells the story of our cities, landscapes and countries and of modern lifestyles. The title, »Solitude«, doubtless has ironic overtones: the parking lot of all places as an oasis of peace, of respite, of being by oneself. Moreover, the emptiness, the quiet, the peacefulness and unspoiled atmosphere, they all carry their opposites within them: the rush and dynamic, the inhumanity, the wounds that have been inflicted on city and nature. In this sense there seems to be both a documentary, factual quality as well as a narrative, poetic one to the series; it seeks the analytical eye and the imaginative brain.

II

Once before an artist, Ed Ruscha, famously pointed his camera at parking lots. They are photographed from above, from a helicopter, on Sundays, and so they, too, are deserted and without a single car. In black and white, the structures, the grids appear neutral from above, like abstract *drawings* of the kind we encounter in the artist's later paintings. His view of Los Angeles, the car-dominated city par excellence, with its gas stations, parking lots, garages, and freeways, as well as its apartments and swimming pools, is fascinating for the seriality of the pictures, their strict organizing principles, and their unusual presentation in the form of a book. Along with his »Twentysix Gasoline Stations« (1963) and »Every Building on the Sunset Strip« (1966), »Ruscha's Thirtyfour Parking Lots« (1967) ranks among the most prominent and influential works of contemporary art and is considered a milestone in the development of photography on account of its conceptual and analytical approach to the *built landscape: His subject matter was neither purely documentary nor solely artistic, in fact it was stereotypical and banal, with motifs drawn from the car-dominated western landscape. That rebellious material, along with his serial presentation, made for a mythical road-movie or photo-novel effect with Beat Generation overtones.*[3]

Drawing on photographers of New Objectivity–notably Karl Blossfeldt, August Sander, and Albert Renger-Patzsch–Bernd and Hilla Becher had compiled typologies of industrial buildings and founded an international school of photography in the process. In the manner of archaeologists they inventoried the variety of forms in the age of industry, such as blast furnaces, gas tanks, water towers. By being precise, photographing objects from an invariable distance and following strict rules of pictorial organization and visual clarity, they built up entire archives of industrial culture. They were the only Europeans among the ten artists included in the legendary exhibition »New Topographics. Photographs of a Man-Altered Landscape«, which opened in New York in 1975–a turning point in the history of photography–rejected any romanticizing and idealizing of the landscape and instead focused on its destruction through industrialization, countering the spectacular with an aesthetic of the mundane, the everyday. Robert Adams was included, as was Lewis Baltz, who captured the frighteningly anonymous facelessness of modern industrial buildings in the U.S. in a series of black-and-white pictures titled »The new Industrial Parks near Irvine, California« (1974) and later on, in color, sterile, deserted interiors (Sites of Technology, 1989–91). The works of these photographers reflect the uncontrolled sprawling urbanization of nature by suburban settlements, streets, trailer parks, shopping malls … The obvious political message of their works consisted in their documentation of uniformity, standardization, anonymity, and commercial transformation as well as the obliteration of any remaining *wilderness*. Stephen Shore was, by the way, the only one among them who photographed in color (and the first living artist to be the subject of a solo exhibition at the Metropolitan Museum of Art at the age of 23, in 1971). It is thanks to him, and William Eggleston, that color photography came to be recognized as art. His 1982 book *Uncommon Places* became the bible of the next generation: *Like Robert Frank and Walker Evans before him, Shore discovered a hitherto unarticulated vision of America via highway and camera. Approaching his subjects with cool objectivity, Shore in these images retains precise internal systems of gestures in composition and light, through which a parking lot emptied of people, a hotel bedroom, or a building on a side street assumes both an archetypical aura and an ambiguously personal importance.*[4]

An affinity to the approach of that type of American photography–epitomized also by the likes of Joel Meyerowitz and Richard Misrach, by Alec Soth with his *large-scale American projects* in the American Midwest and Joel Sternfeld with his 1987 series »American Prospects«–is also evident in the pictures the German photographer Olaf Otto Becker took in the Antarctic: they all document the transformed landscape, the marks man has made to the detriment of the planet. Often both are contained in these photographs, as they are in the work of Robert Adams who for more than forty years photographed the American West: its beauty and its fragility, affirmation and grief at the loss of space and peacefulness, hope and despair over the state of the earth.

III

What do Erik Chmil's photographs show; what do they provide information about; how are they to be read beyond their aesthetic appeal?

What probably makes photography so compelling, and such a prominent artistic medium of our day, is that, rather than representing the world, it offers conceptions of the world: even when it is focused on the real and draws the viewer's attention to the object, it still provides a sense of a different world. As Thomas Demand, one of the most important photo artists of today, explains: *Photographs generate reality; they create retellings; they transport and generate ideas and interpretations of the world.* Photographs point to the *real* and the *imaginary*. They are projection surfaces for the viewer. If lucky, they provide viewers *with models for (their own) experience, perception, evaluation and conduct*, as Vilém Flusser put it in his famous essay »Towards a Philosophy of Photography«.

Let us look at the photographs assembled here in pictorial terms: the contours and colors, light and shade, the way the central subject relates to the periphery, the particular atmospheric quality, the moods, the modes of representation which range from objectivity to romanticism, from purism to nostalgia to a play with clichés … The book is not titled *One Hundred Parking Lots*–it is called *Solitude*. Erik Chmil is not interested in coolly compiling an inventory; he is interested in poeticizing, in the aura of the places and their narrative quality: *When I get out of the car, this place tells me something–really about people. Separation, finding one another, dark transactions … absurd coincidence … all of that in this one place. Discovery without uncovering. The visible and the hidden balance one another in a manner that is full of atmosphere.*[5] And even though these photographs, rather than aiming to be a political manifesto, tempt us to look on account of their visual appeal, they do show at the same time in many ways the global postindustrial, late capitalist society, the concentration of power and wealth and its flip side, and the very marginalization of »Solitude«.

What does our world look like and what could it look like? What do parking lots tell us about our lives? Unlimited mobility, individual freedom? Is there an alternative to the occupation of ever more terrain; will collective rituals of driving related to work and consumption soon be obsolete? Is it possible to rethink mobility; will the fetish *car* be dispensed with and will those images perhaps be anachronistic in the foreseeable future, reminiscent of a bygone era of noise and chaos and, consequently, historical documents?

DON'T IT ALWAYS SEEM TO GO
THAT YOU DON'T KNOW WHAT YOU'VE GOT
TILL IT'S GONE
THEY PAVED PARADISE
AND PUT UP A PARKING LOT
Joni Mitchell

Inspired by the French Structuralists and especially by Michel Foucault, the artist Peter Halley establishes a connection between his geometric paintings and the geometrization of social space in the world we live in. In his 1984 essay »The Deployment of the Geometric« he describes the transformation of the landscape, society, and thought through geometry as regimentation. He points to the correspondence between the *geometrization of the landscape and the »geometrization of thought«. Space is divided into discrete, isolated cells … reached through complex networks of corridors and roadways that must be traveled at prescribed speeds and prescribed times.*[6]

Erik Chmil's parking lots can be read on so many levels. »Solitude« primarily assembles a wealth of opulent images of magnificent landscapes and spectacular architectures and the fascination of the places is readily passed on to the viewers. The volume takes them along on a journey around the world. And so these photographs also represent the desire for individual mobility: for escaping the confinement of the cities out into the vastness of nature, fleeing the gridlock and the pressure. What a feeling of liberation! And in this way, it seems, many a paved parking lot is converted back into a paradise.

[1] *Joni Mitchell, »Big Yellow Taxi«, 1970.*
[2] *Erik Chmil in conversation with the author in Munich, 17 May 2017.*
[3] *Margit Rowell, »Ed Ruscha. Photographer« (Göttingen: Steidl, 2006).*
[4] *Uncommon Places. »The Complete Works. Photographs by Stephen Shore«, new expanded edition, with an essay by Stephan Schmidt-Wulffen (New York: Aperture, 2015).*
[5] *Erik Chmil in conversation with Jürgen Opel, 26 April 2017.*
[6] *Peter Halley, »The Crisis in Geometry« (1984), in Halley, »Collected Essays«. 1981–1987 (Zurich et al.: Edition Gallery Bruno Bischofberger, 1988), p. 80.*

01———2006 ATACAMA, CHILE

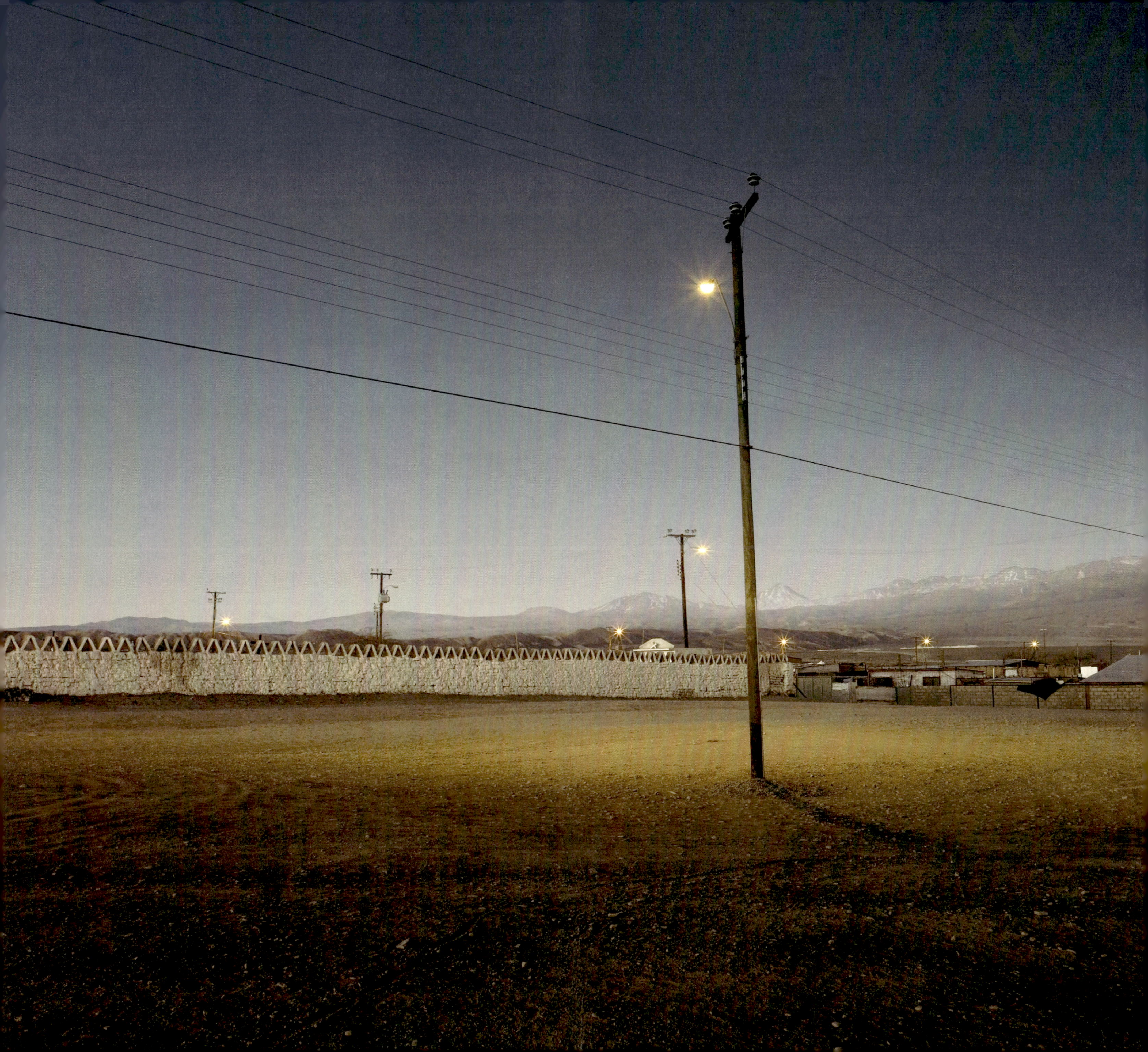

02 _____ 2013 DALLAS, USA

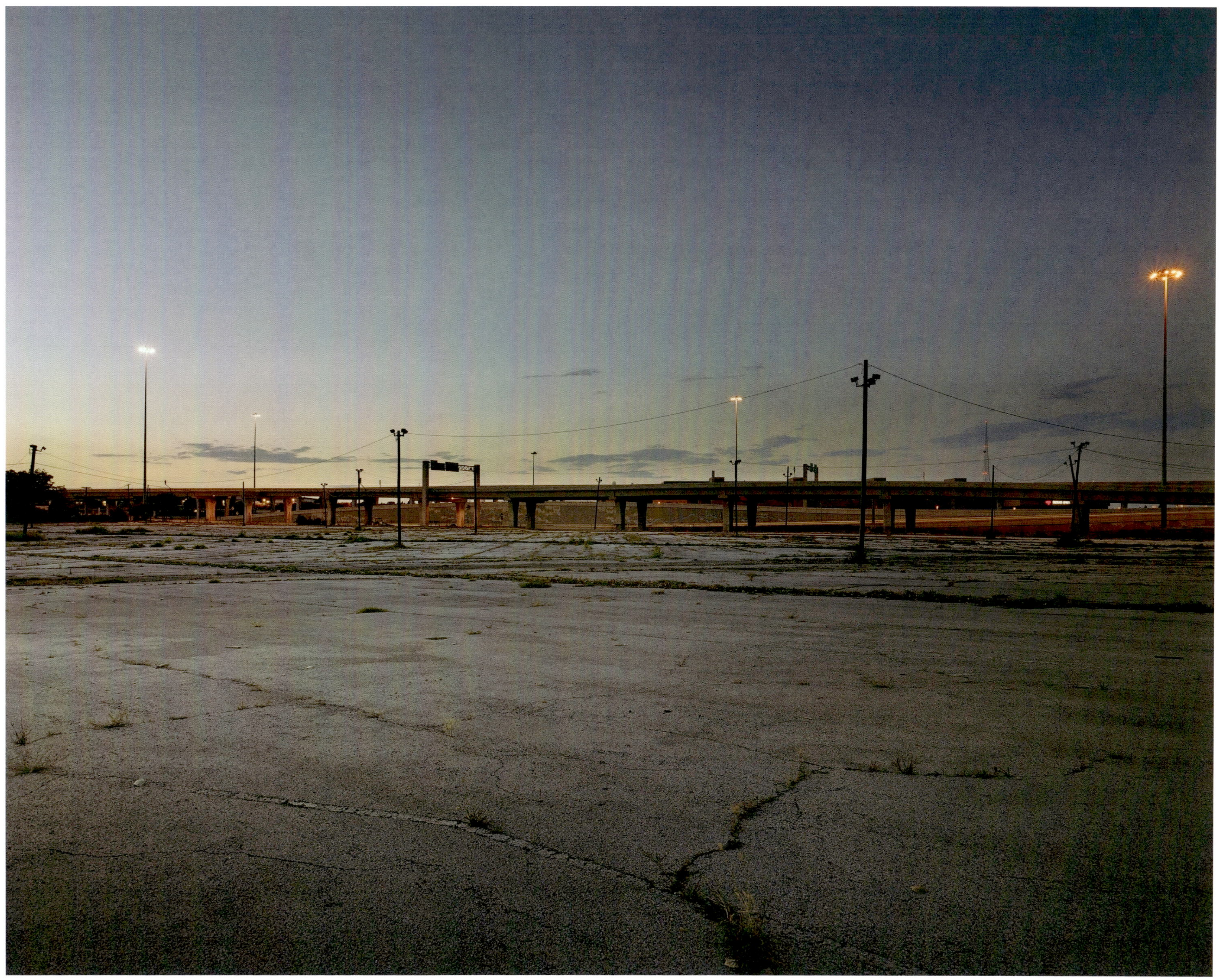

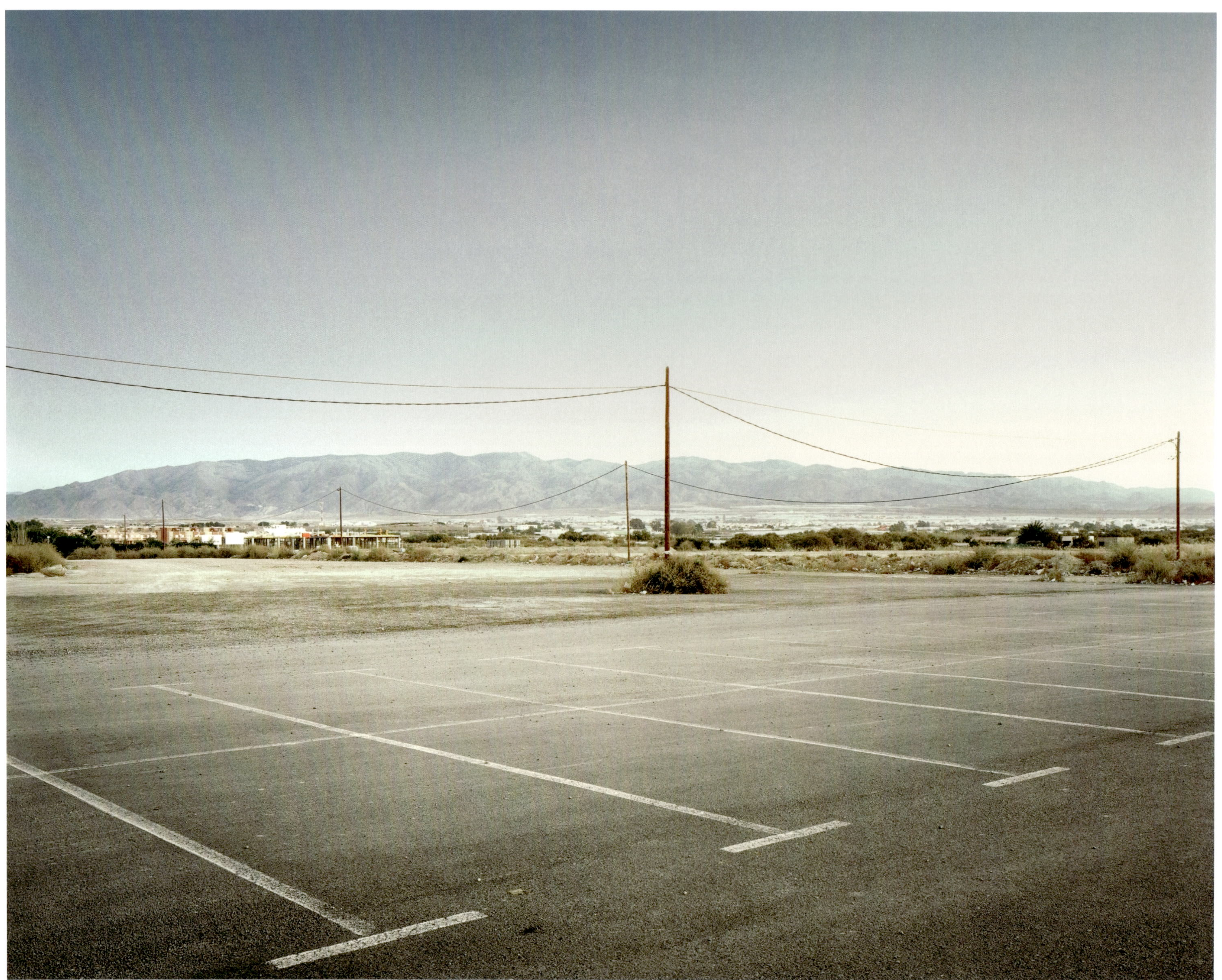

04 ——— 2006 SAN FRANCISCO, USA

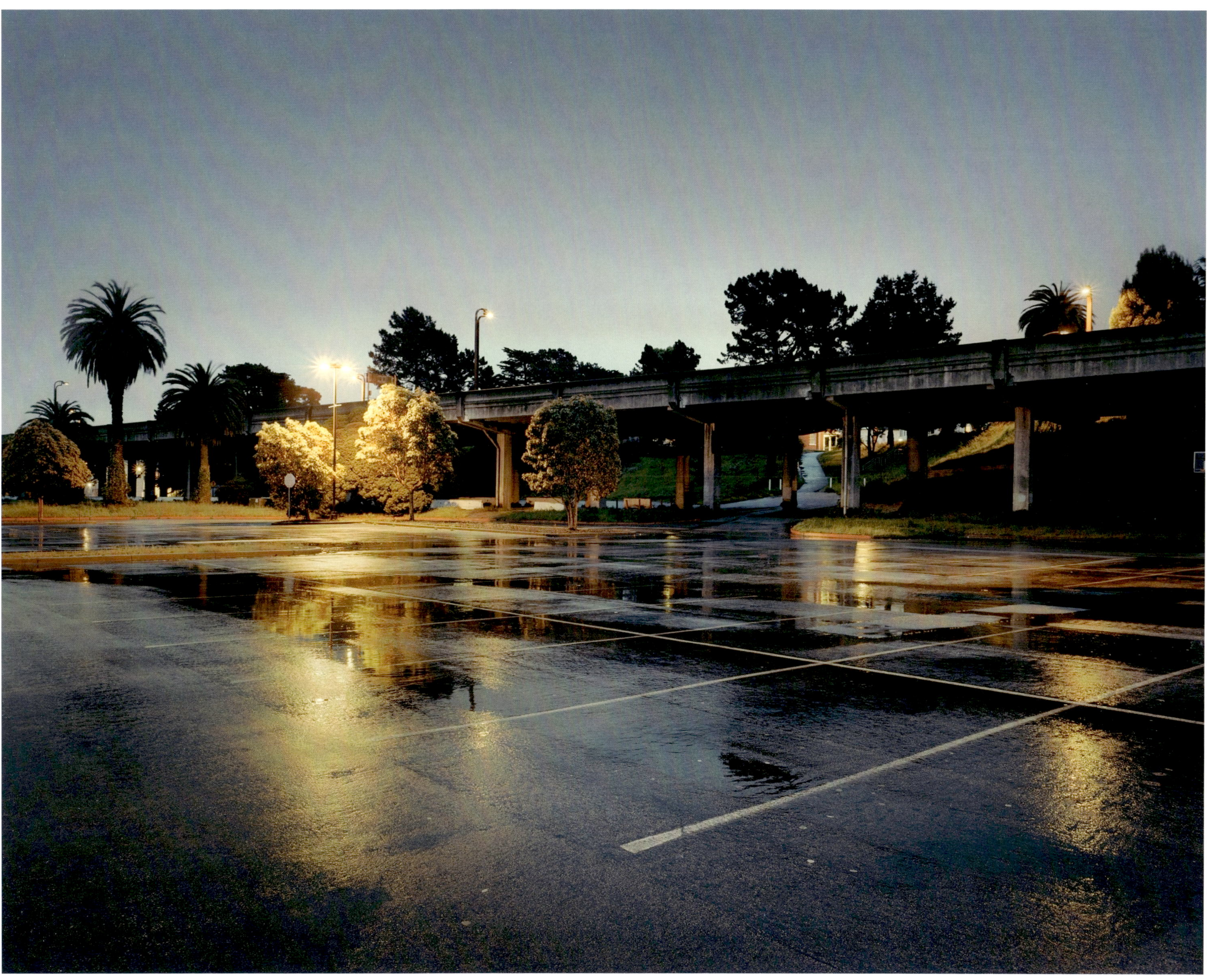

05——2006 SAN FRANCISCO, USA

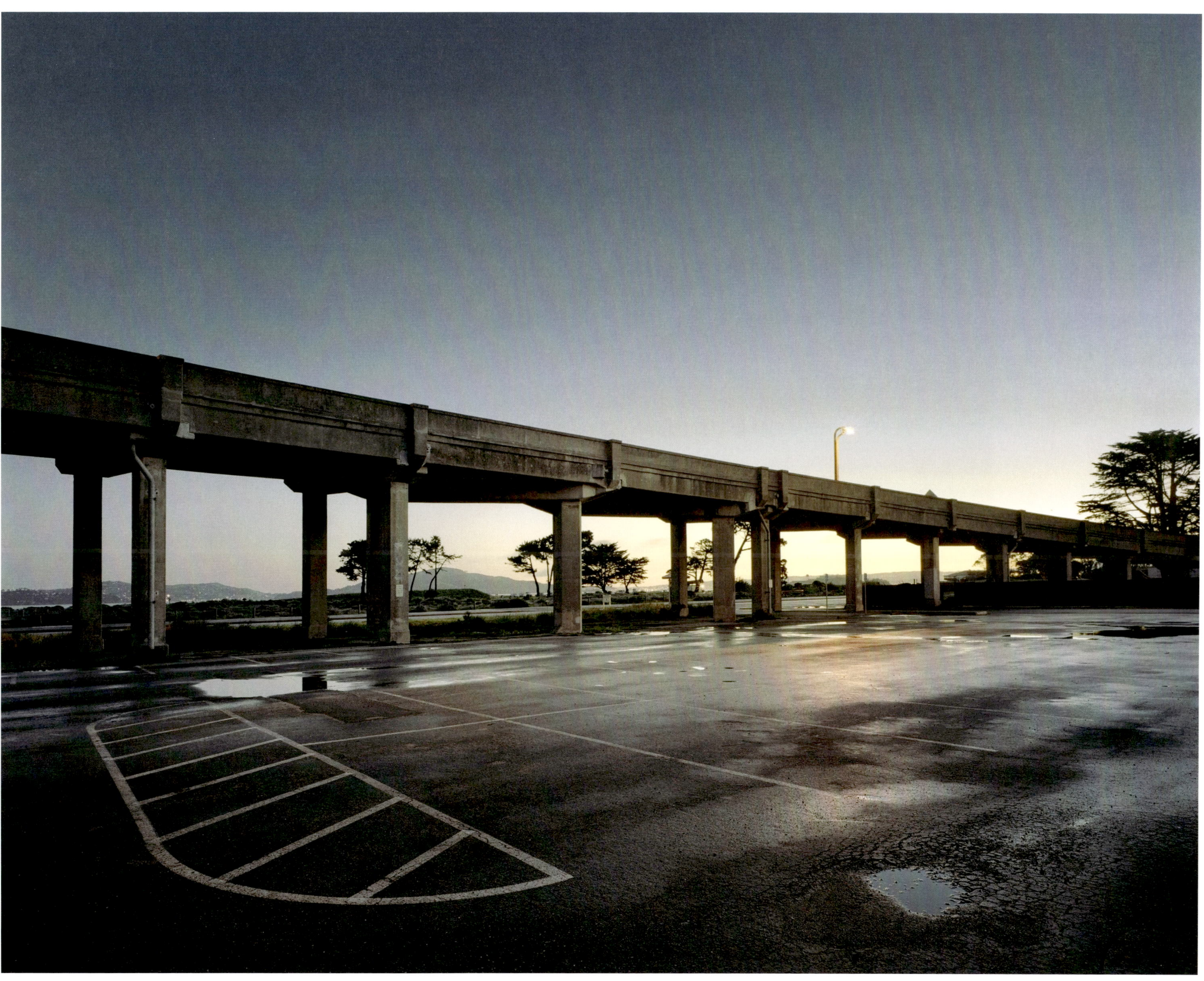

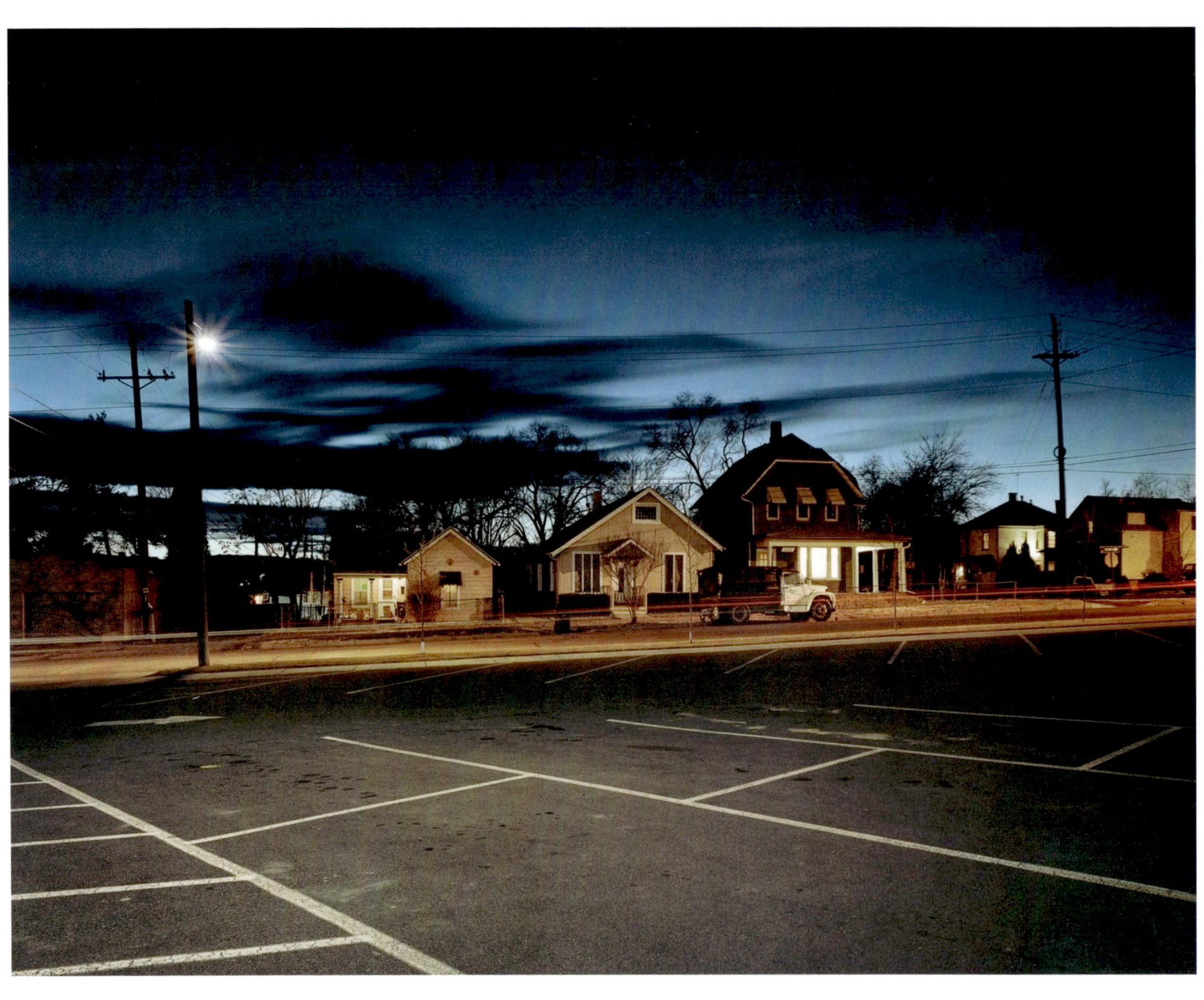

06——2008 PUEBLO, USA
07——2008 PUEBLO, USA

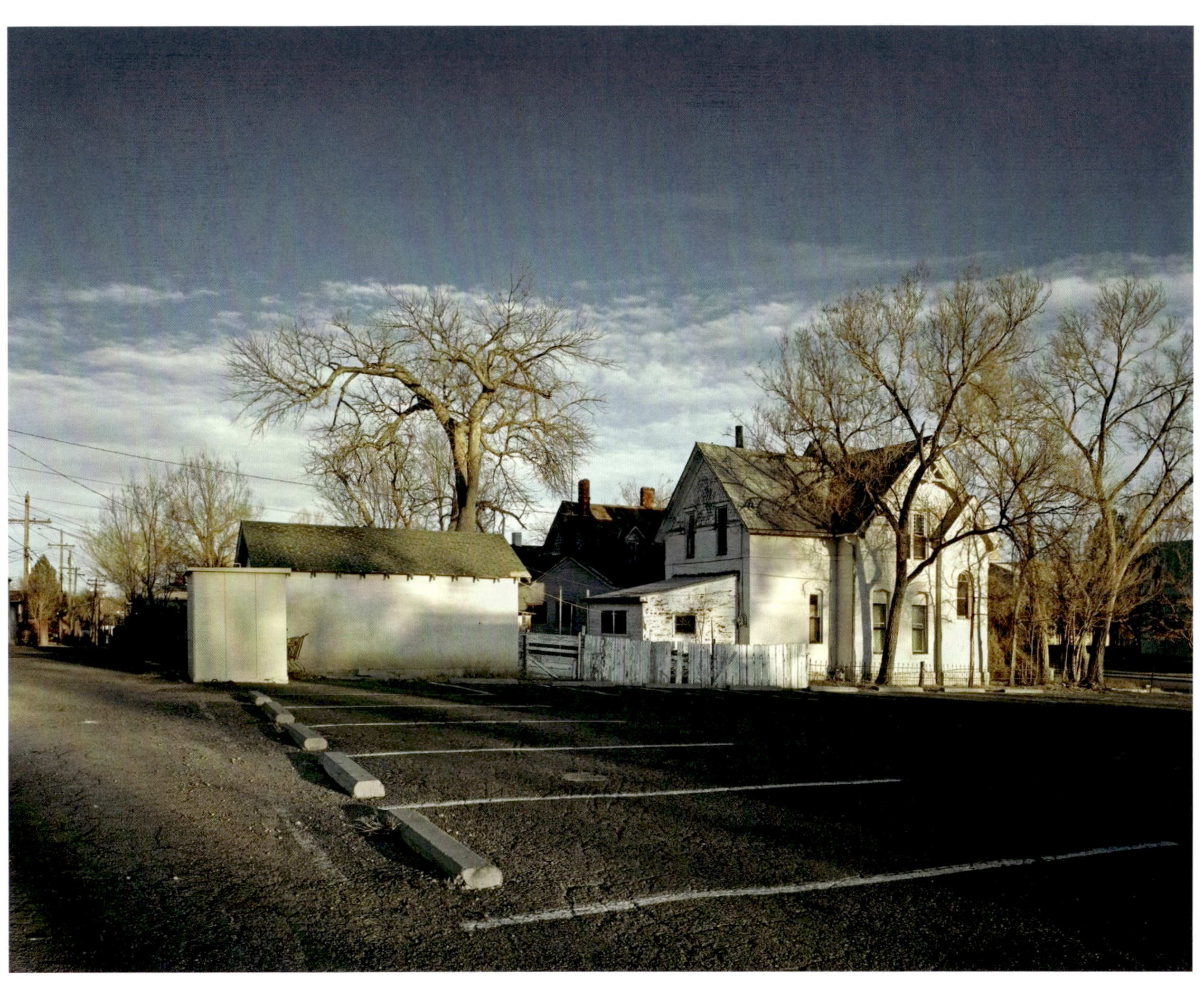

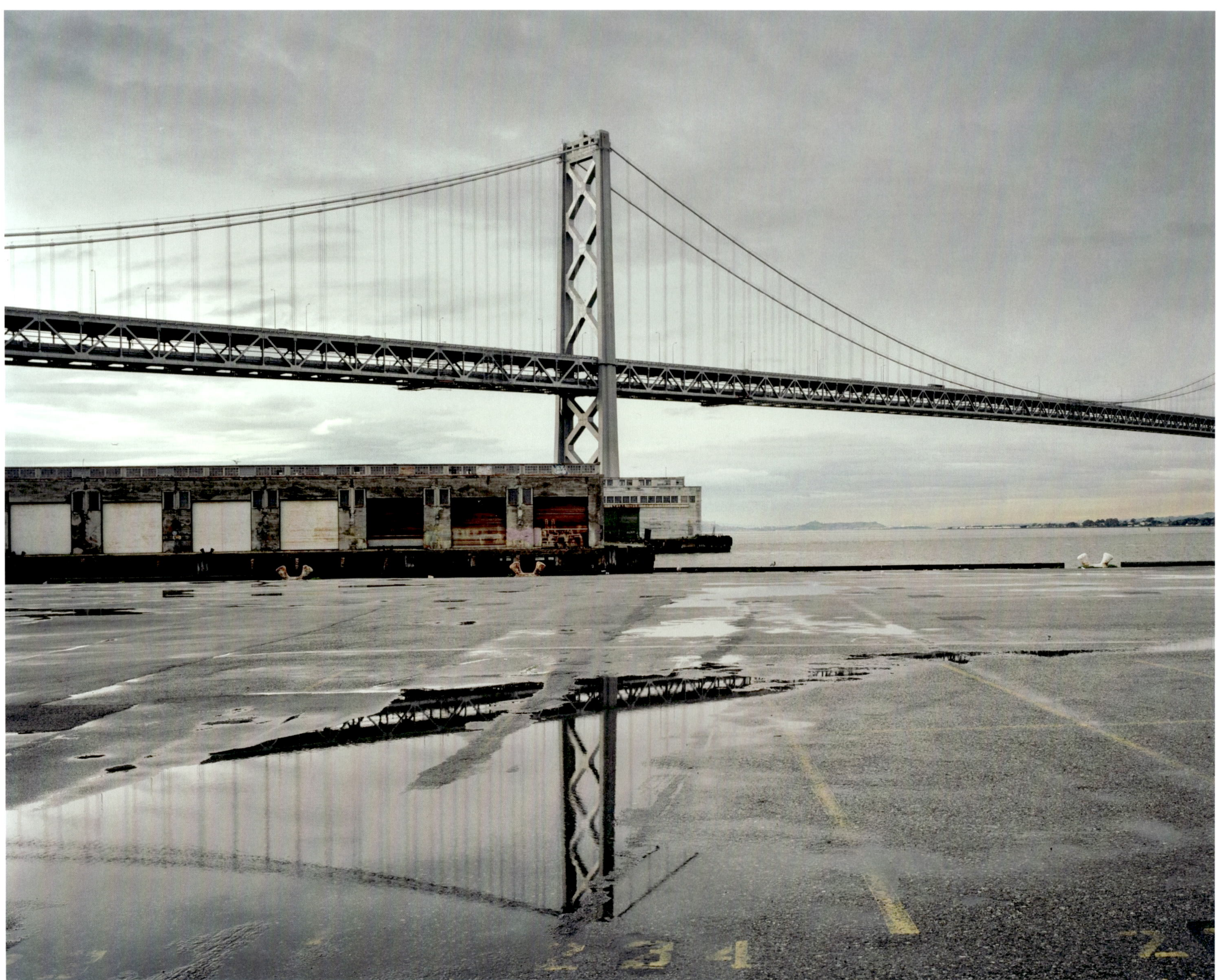

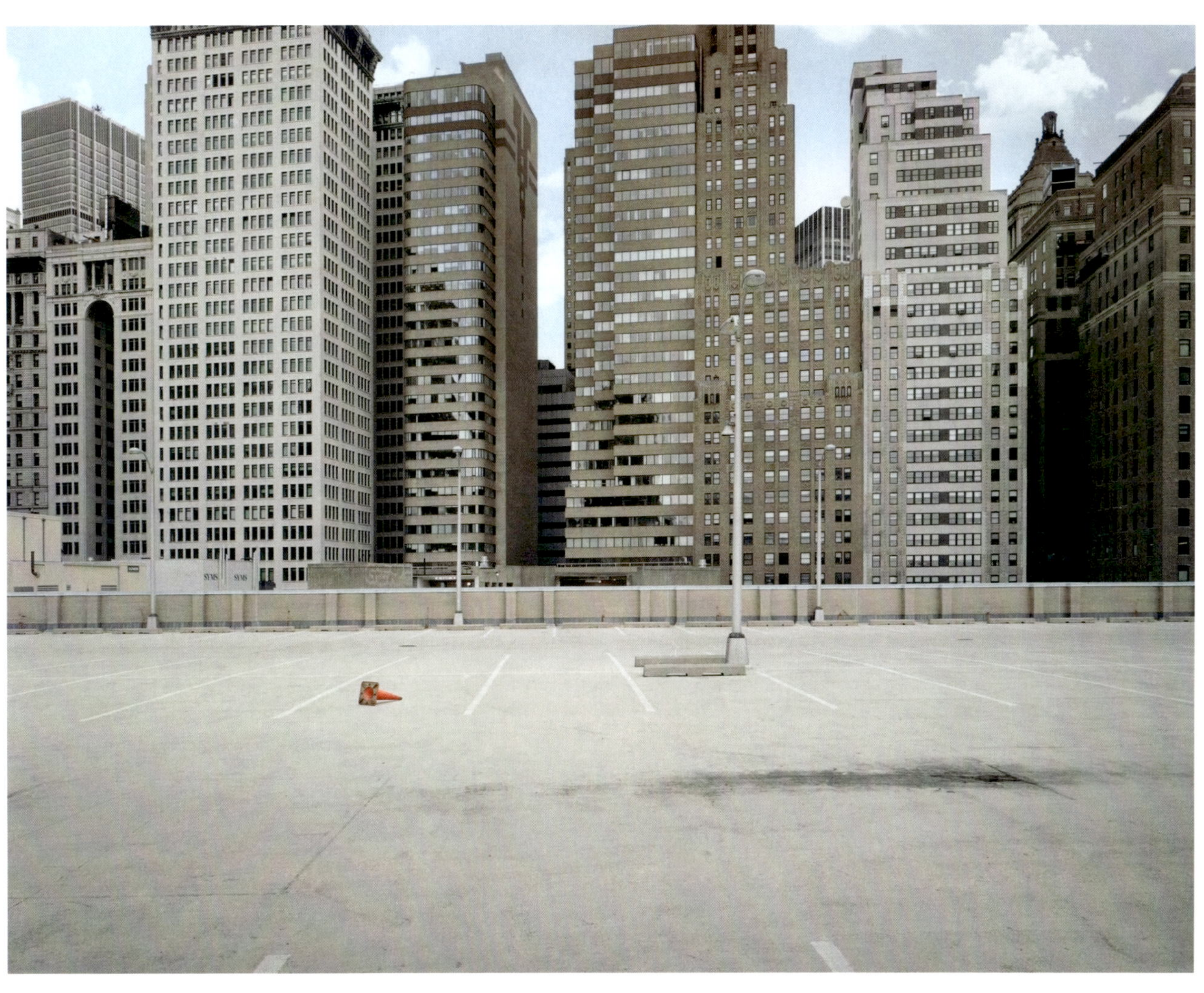

SAN FRANCISCO, USA 2006 ——— 08
NEW YORK, USA 2004 ——— 09

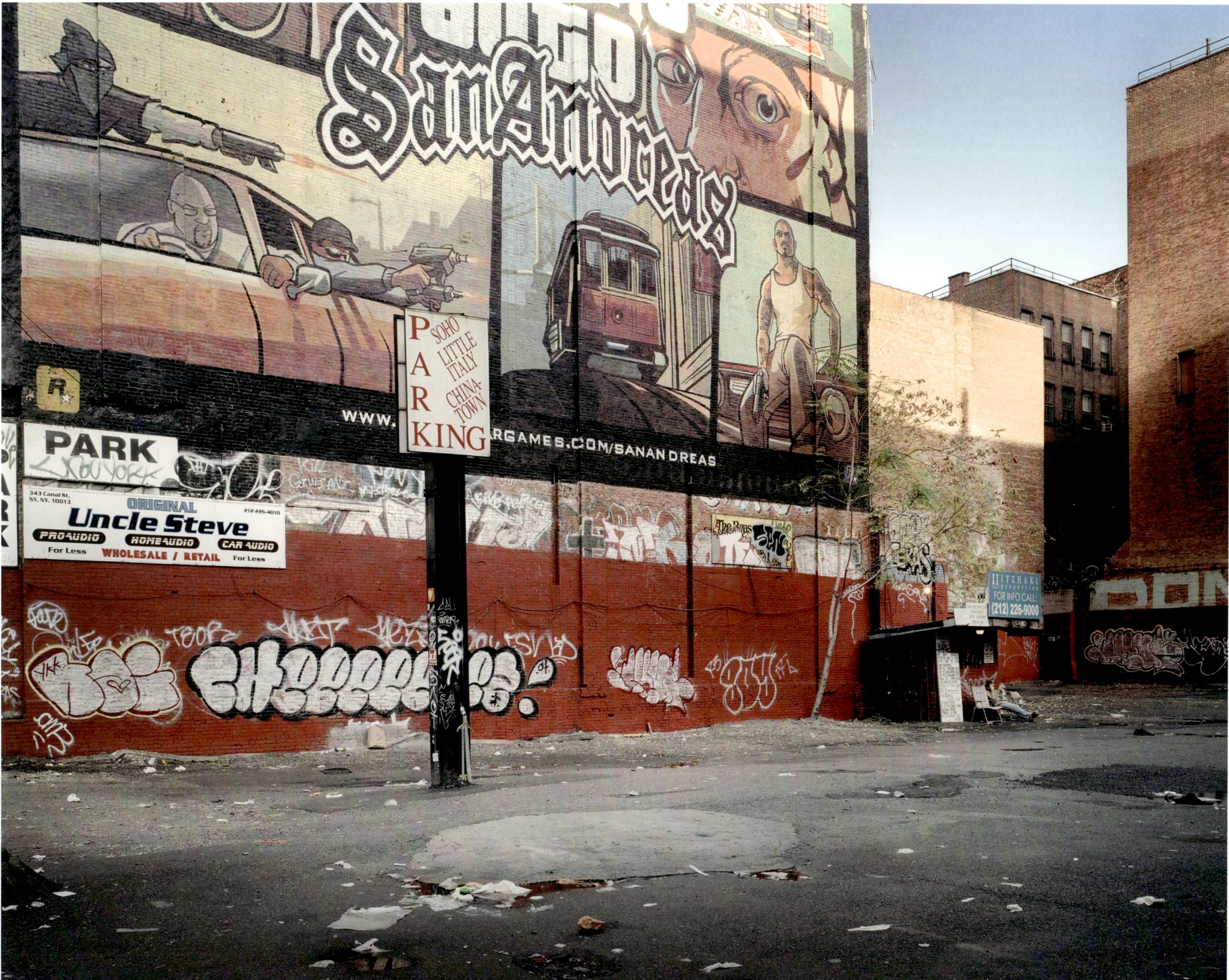
San Andreas
PARKING
SOHO
LITTLE ITALY
CHINA-TOWN
WWW.
RGAMES.COM/SANANDREAS
PARK
343 Canal St.
NY, NY. 10013
212-226-4010
ORIGINAL
Uncle Steve
PROAUDIO
HOMEAUDIO
CAR AUDIO
For Less
WHOLESALE / RETAIL
For Less
FOR INFO CALL:
(212) 226-9000

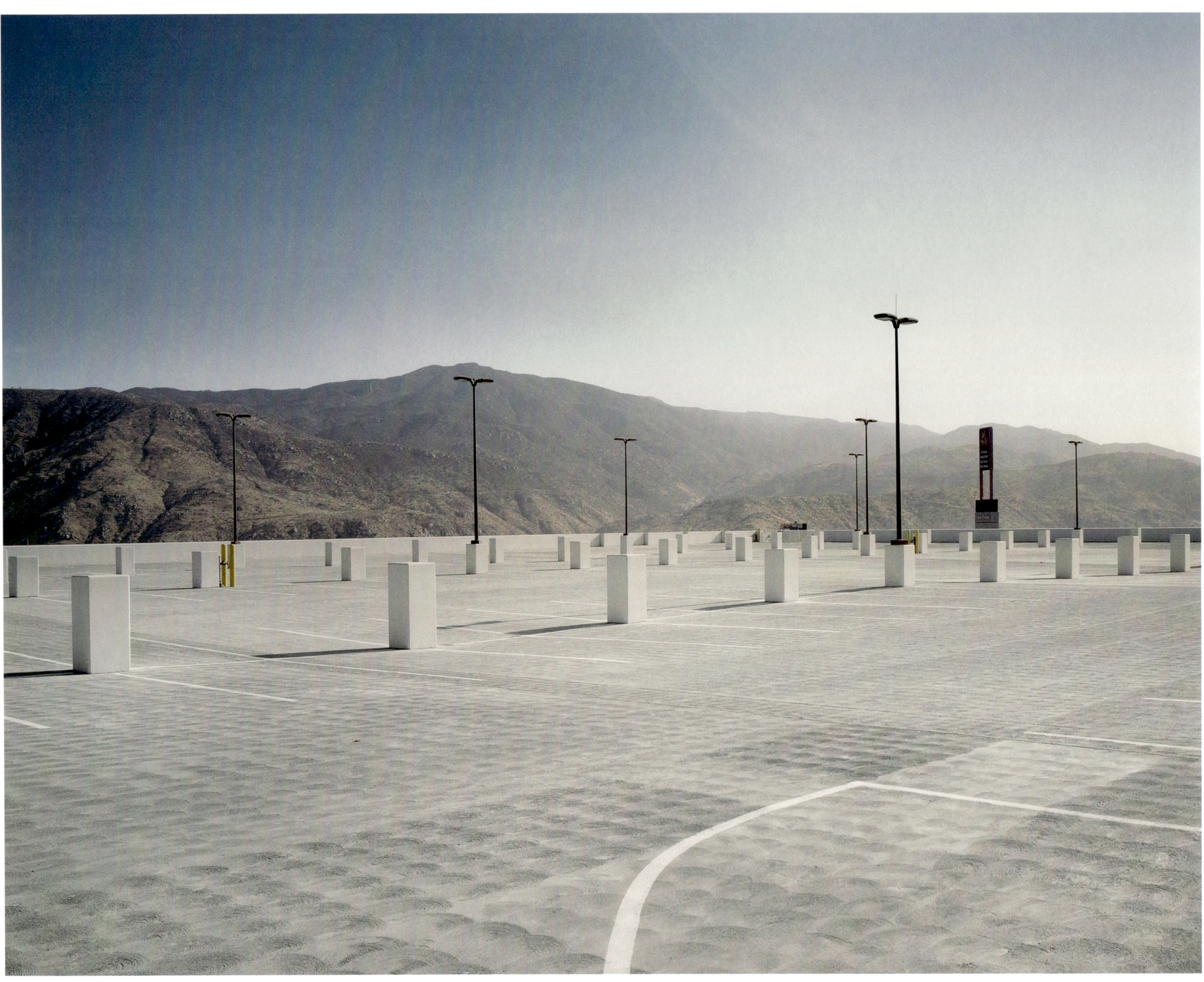

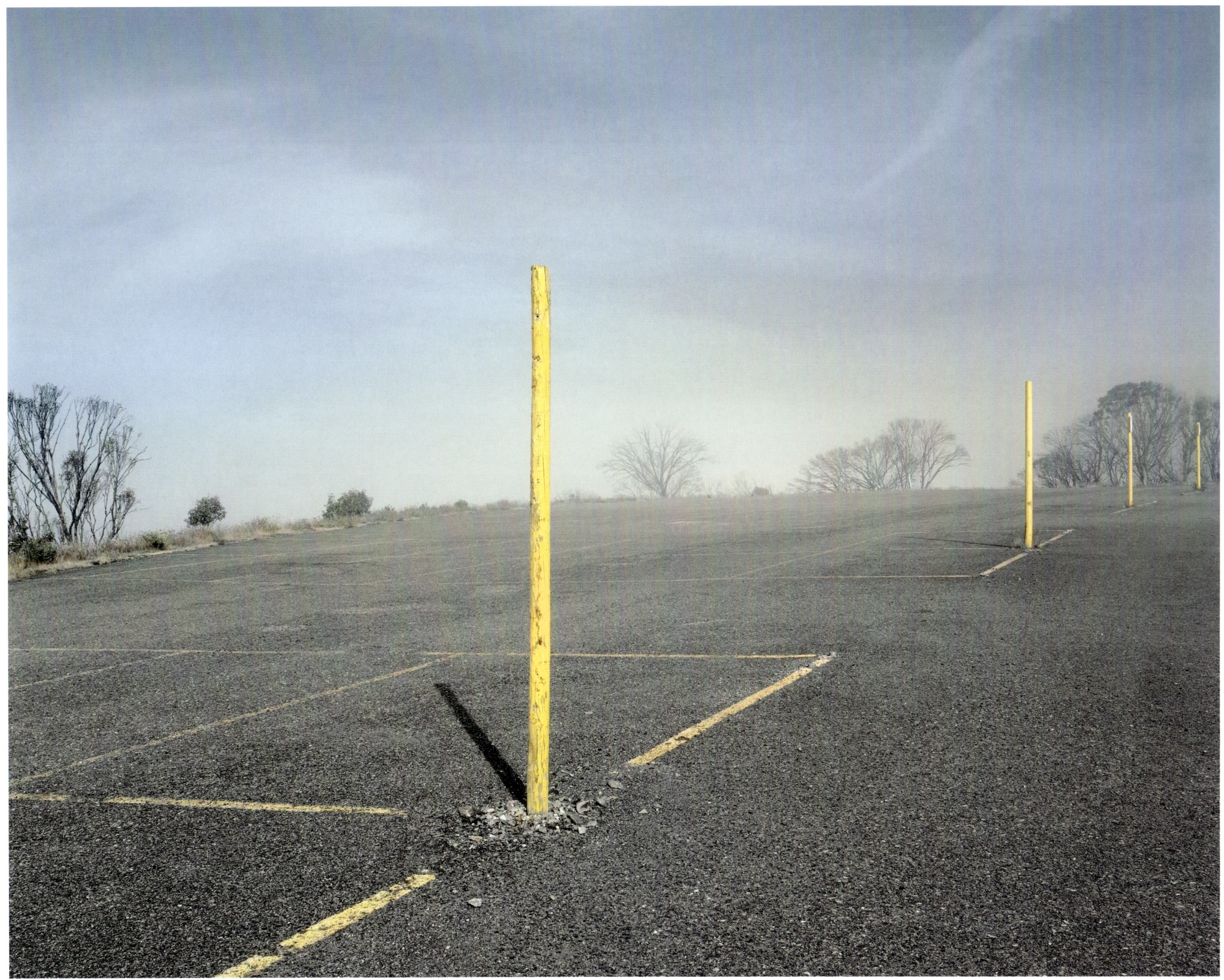

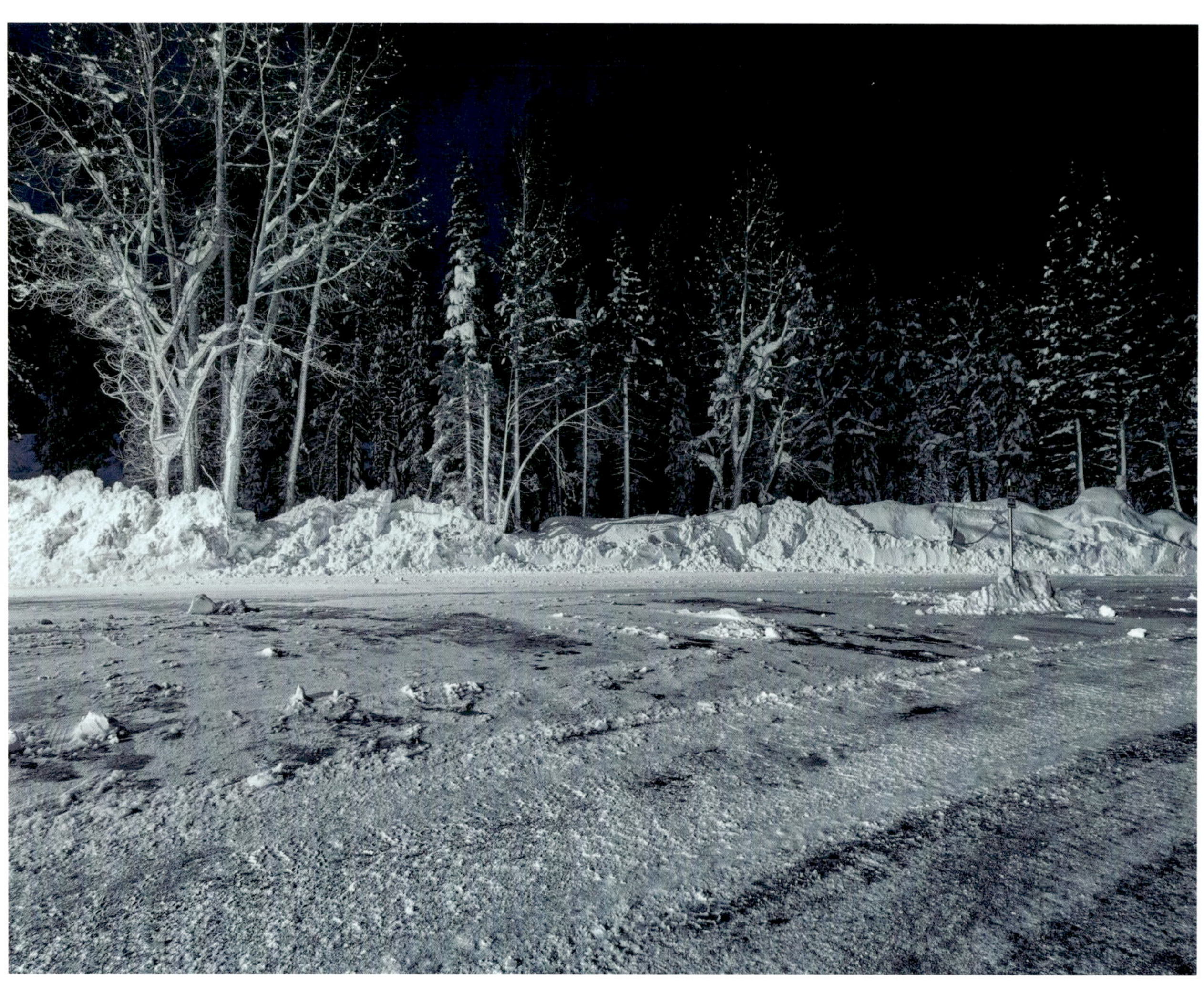

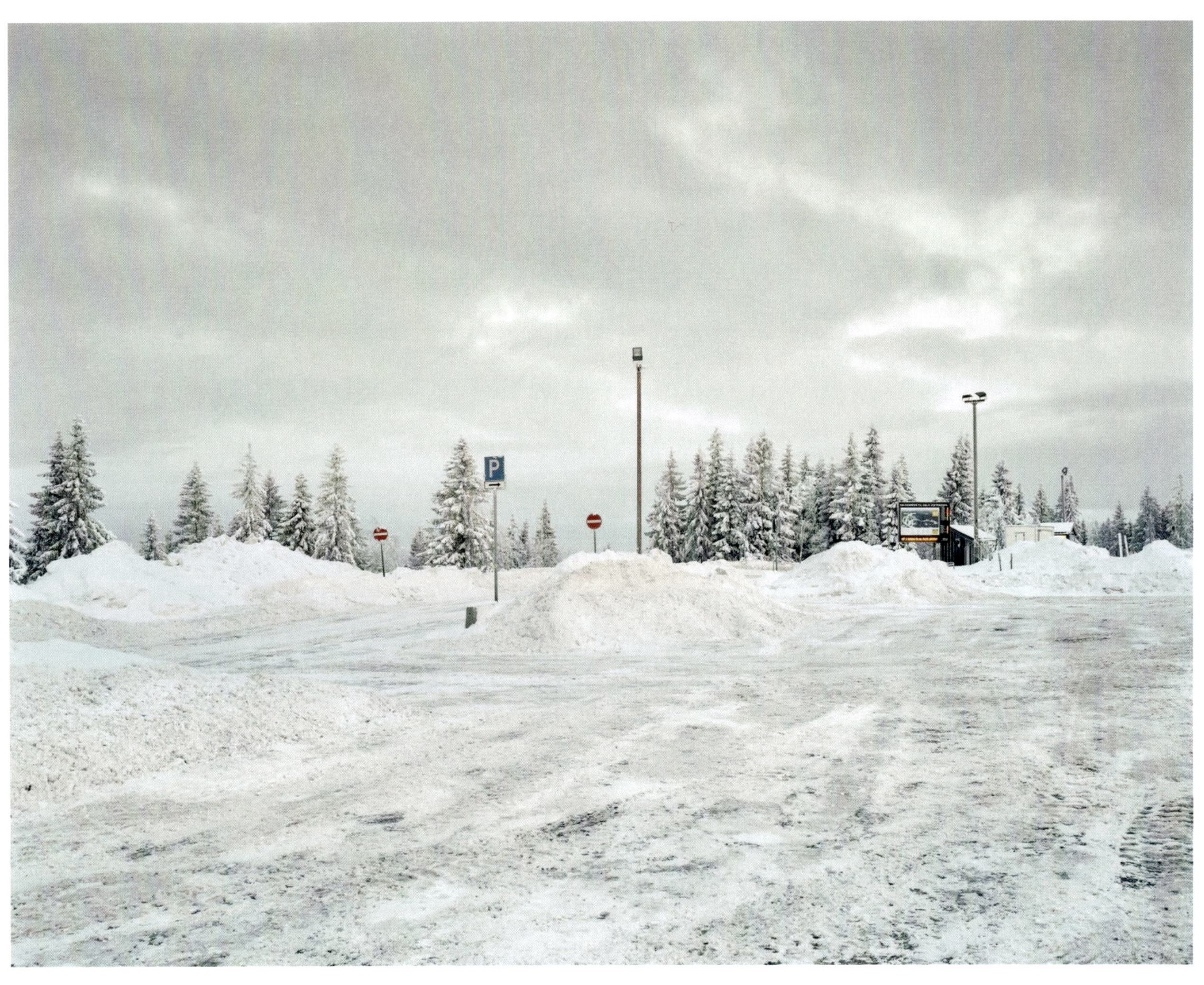

15——2006 TRE CIME, ITALY

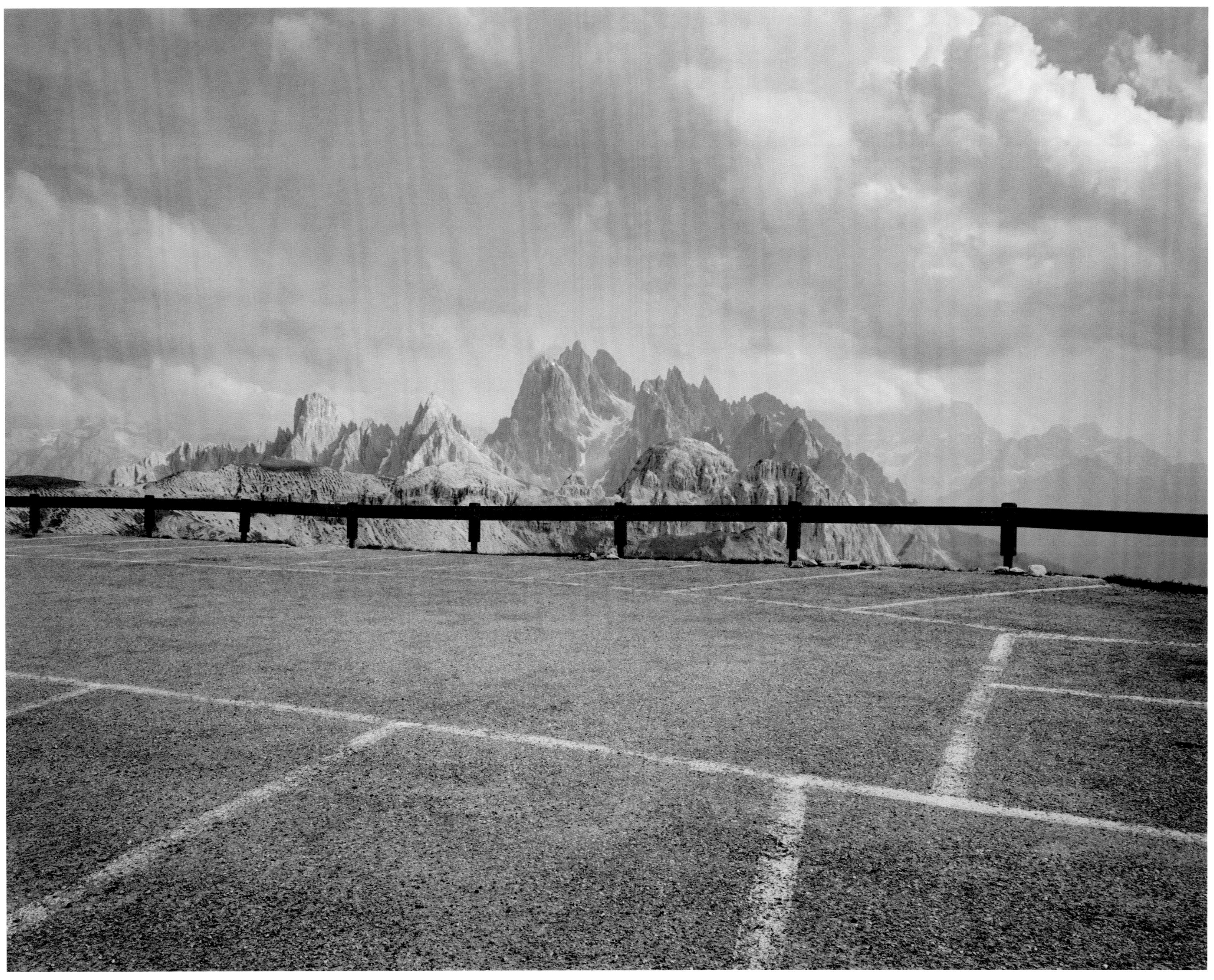

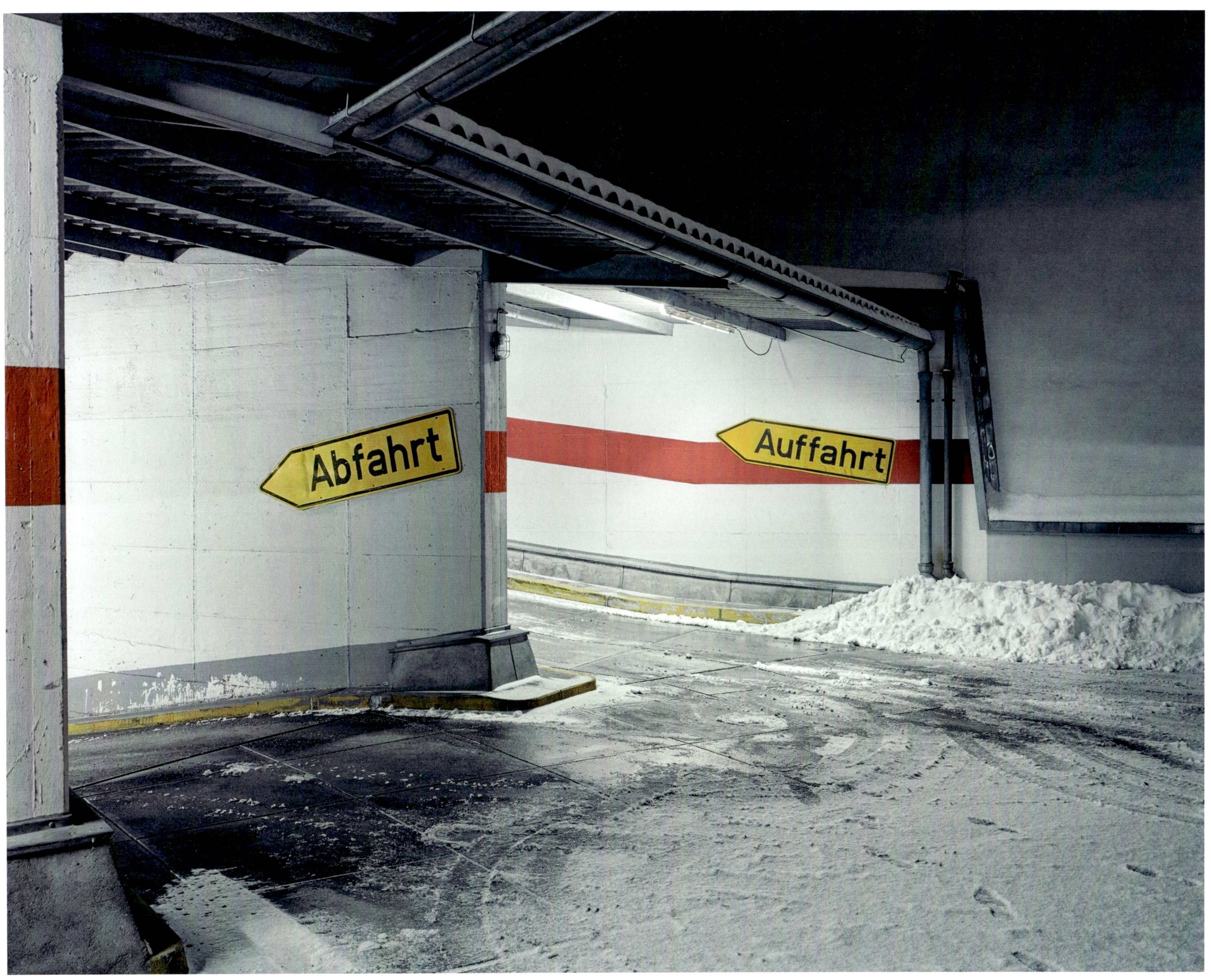
Abfahrt
Auffahrt

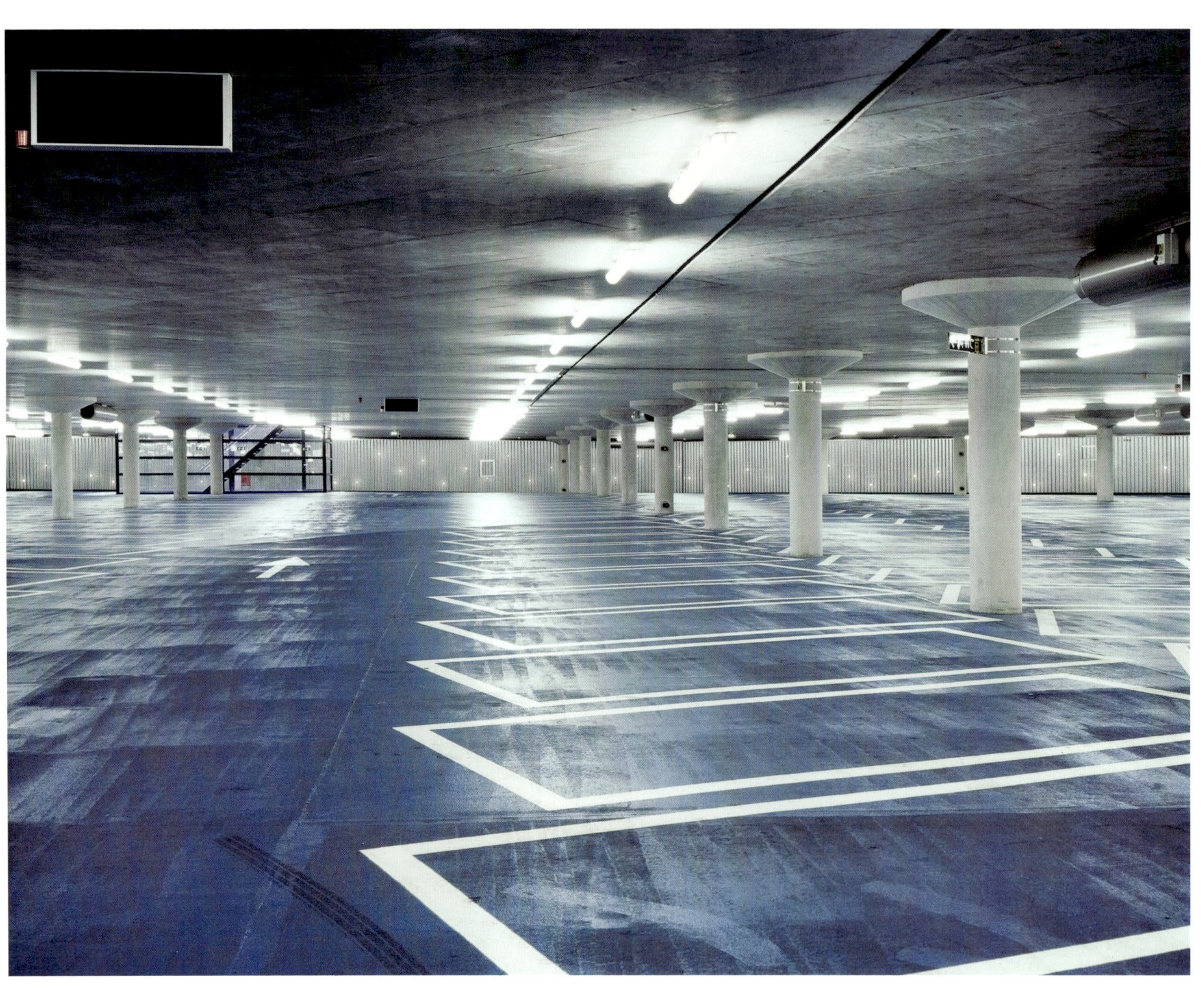

17———2003 BREDA, NETHERLANDS
18———2006 BEIJING, CHINA

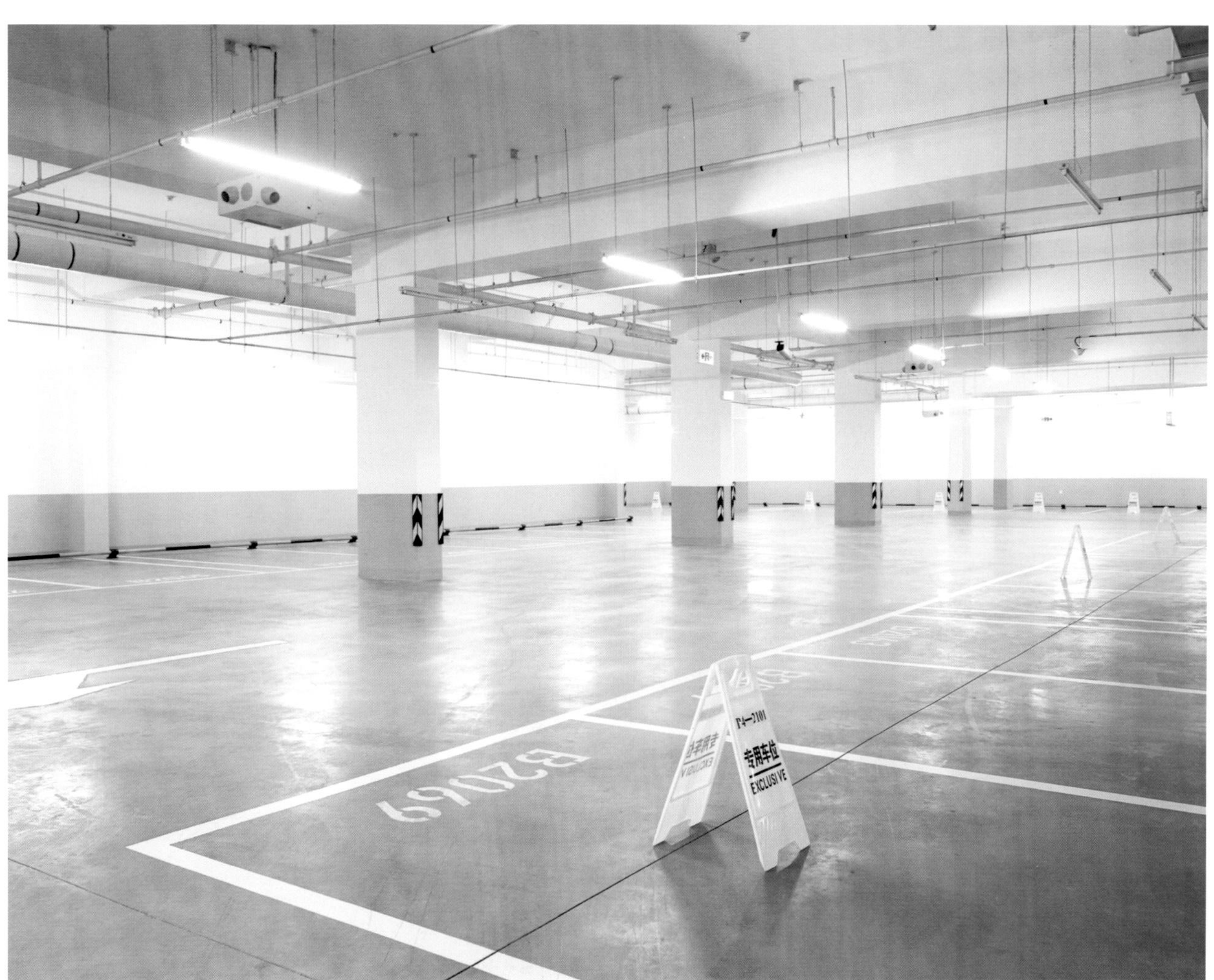
B2069
专用车位
EXCLUSIVE

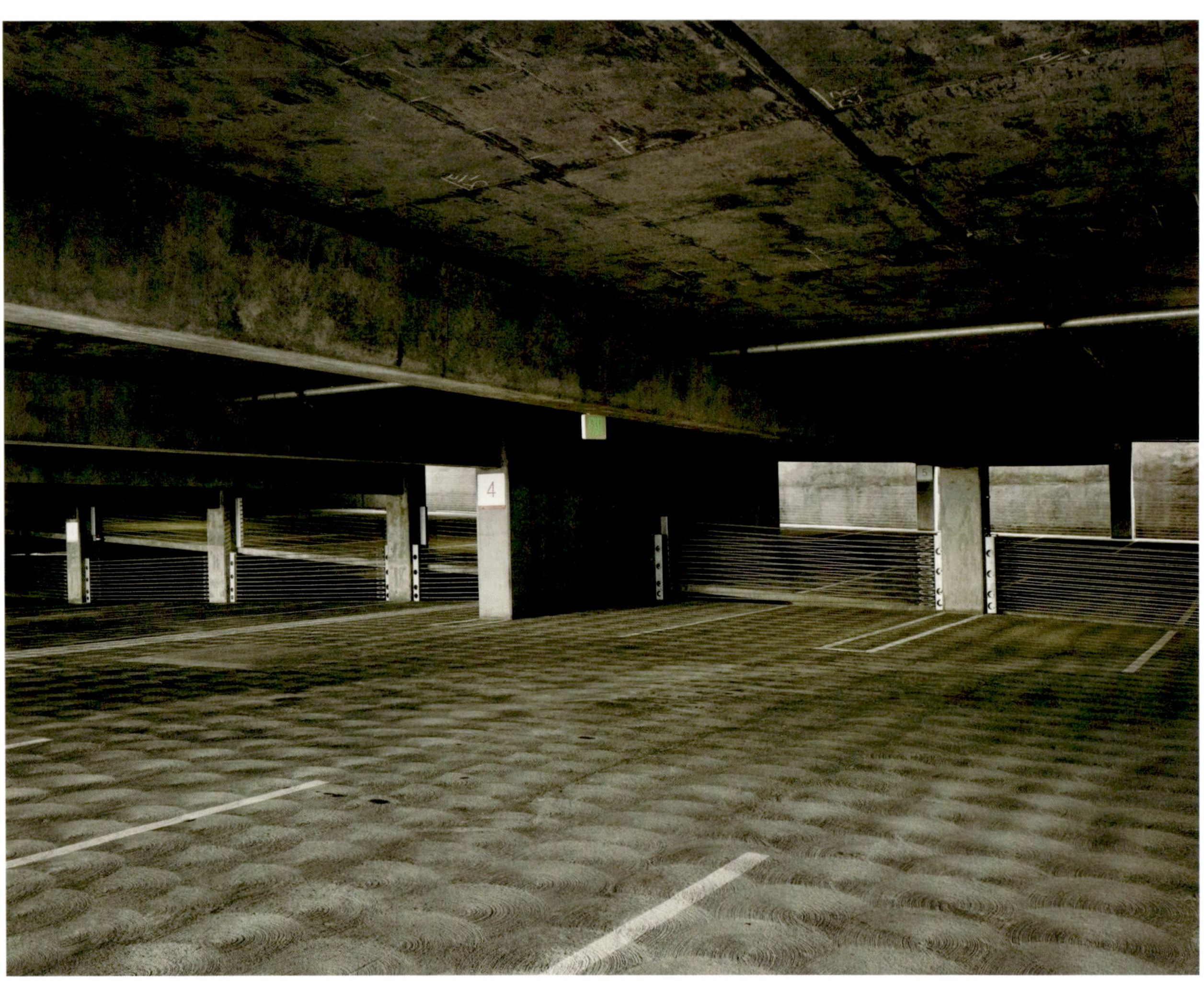
4

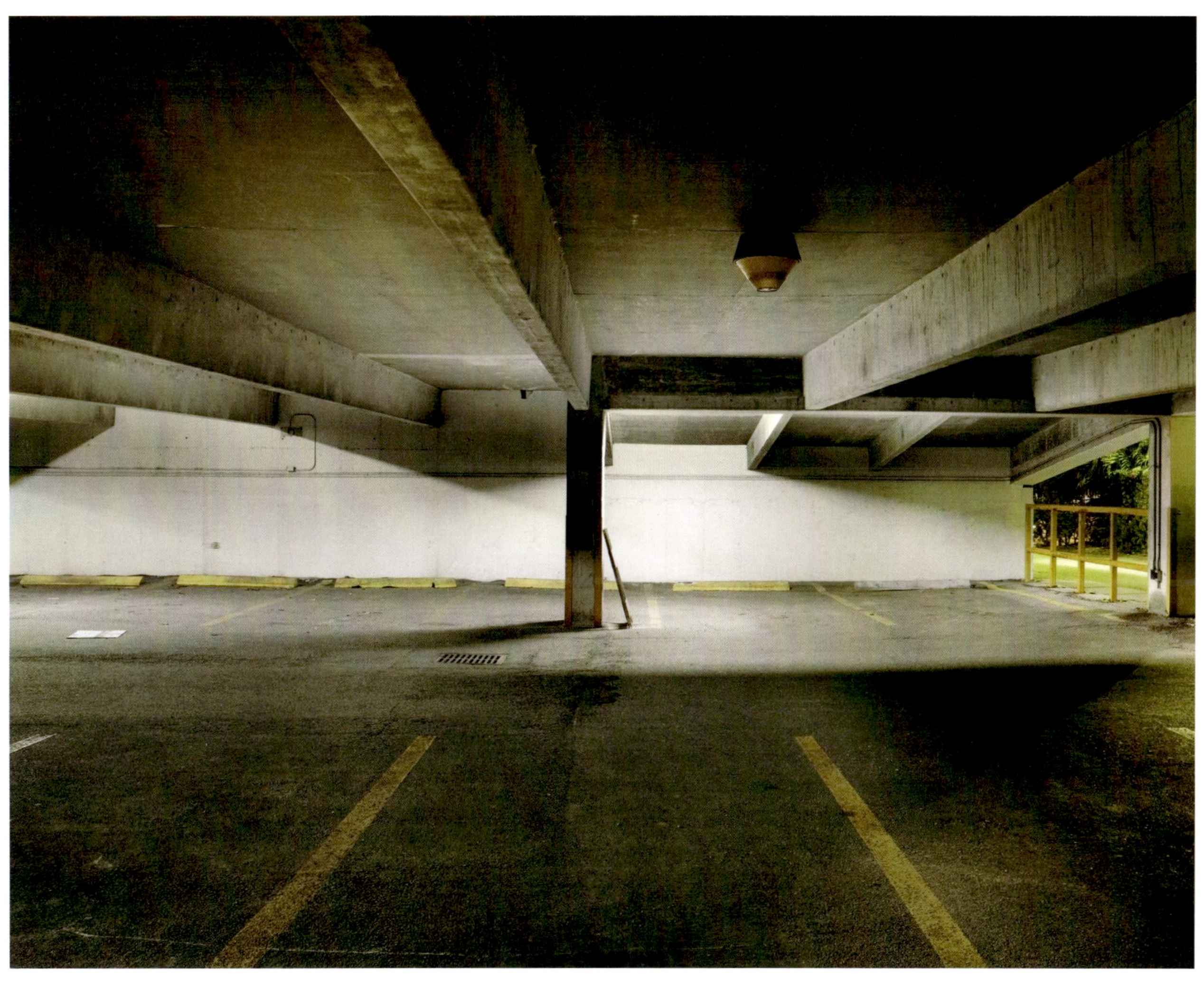

SAN FRANCISCO, USA 2012 ——— 19
MIAMI, USA 2014 ——— 20

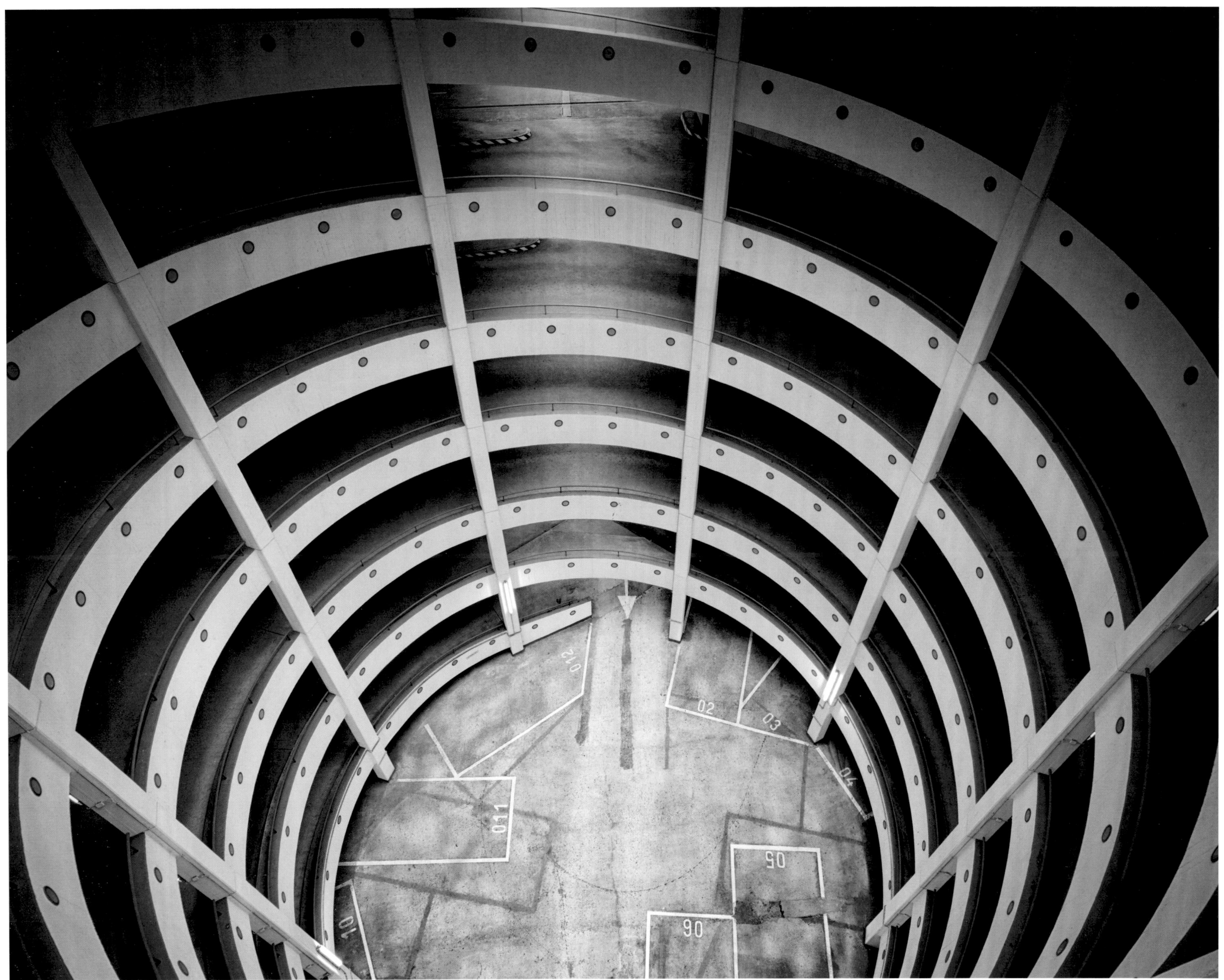
012
02
03
04
011

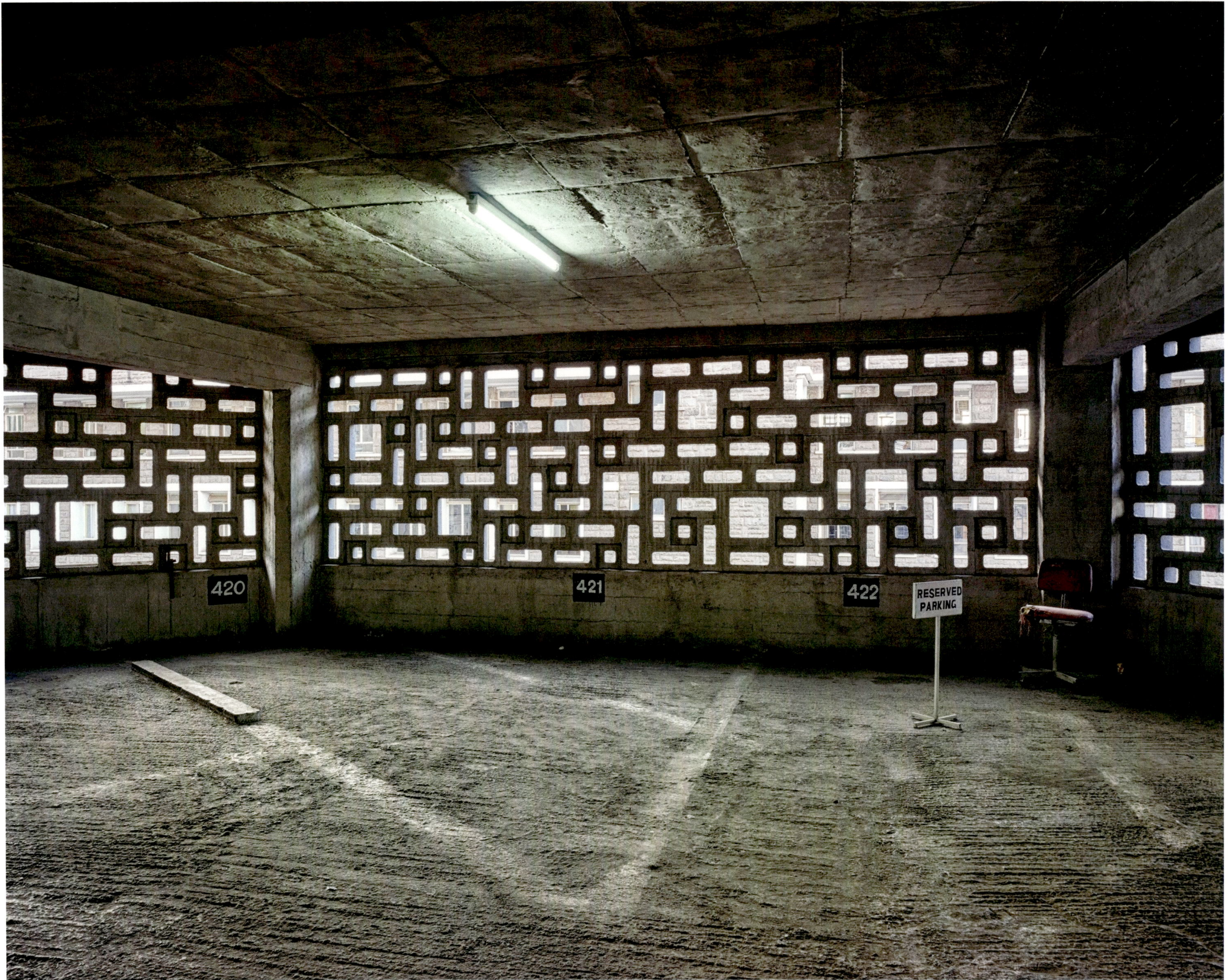
420
421
422
RESERVED
PARKING

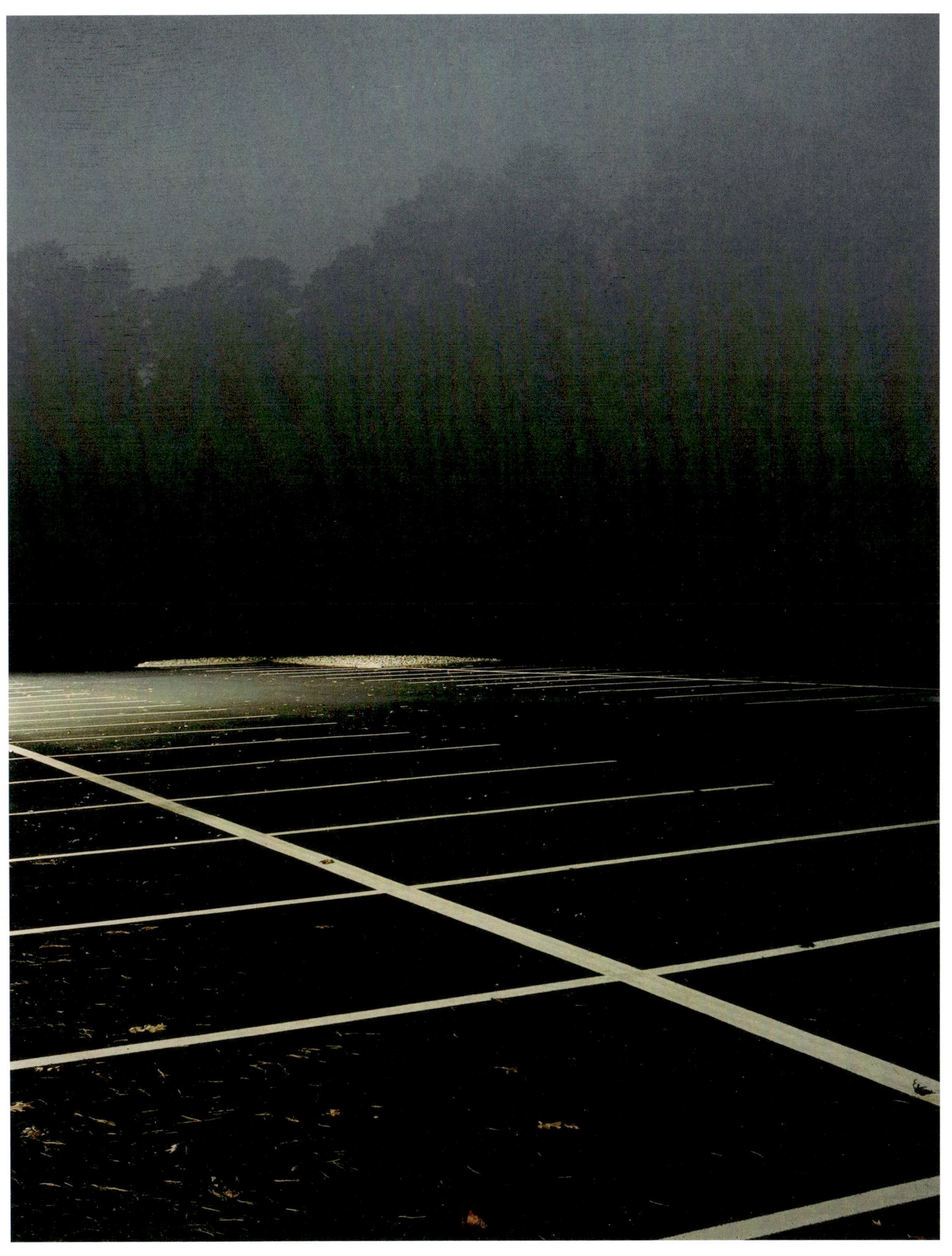

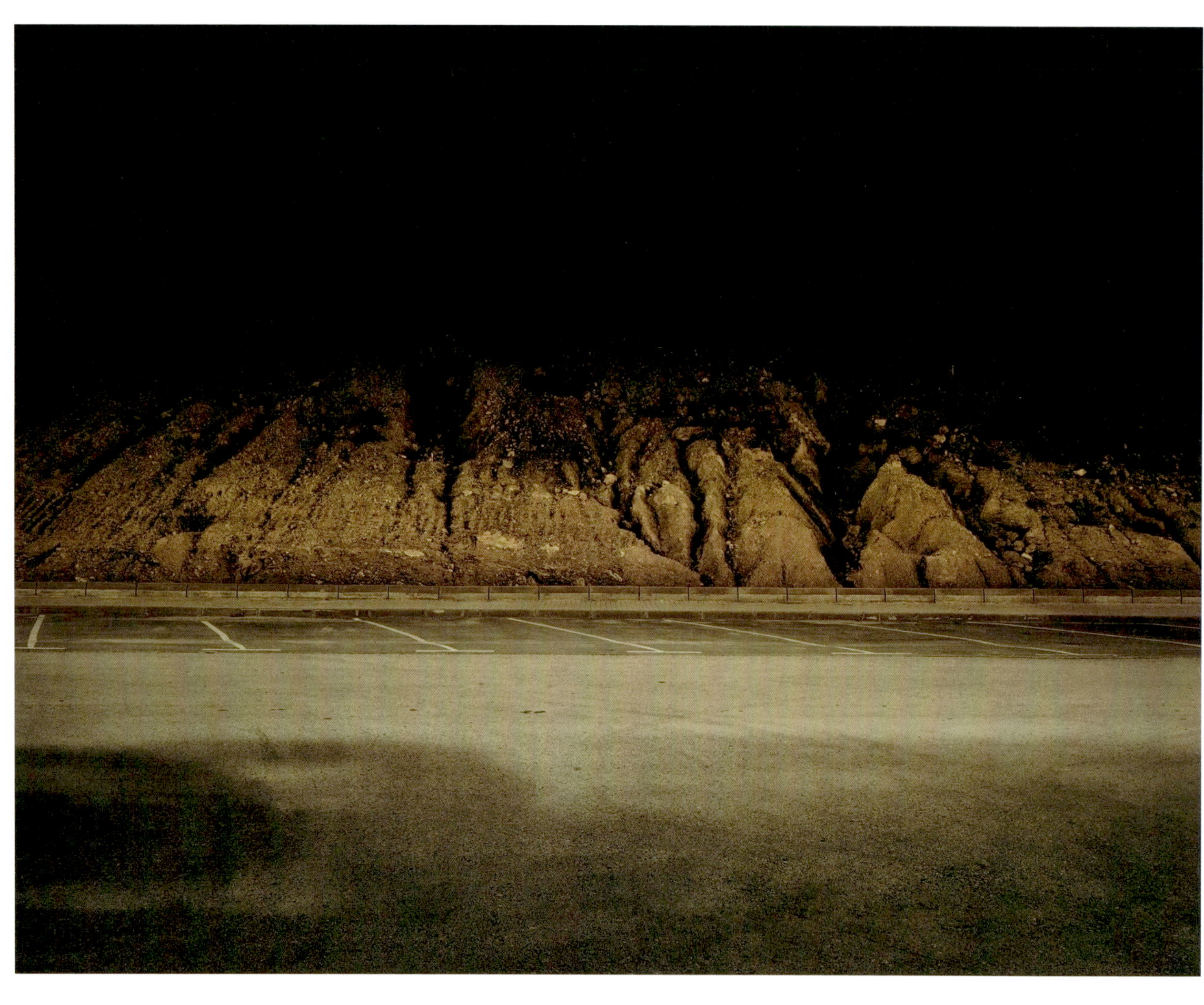

24——2005 JEREZ, SPAIN
25——2005 CAPE TOWN, SOUTH AFRICA

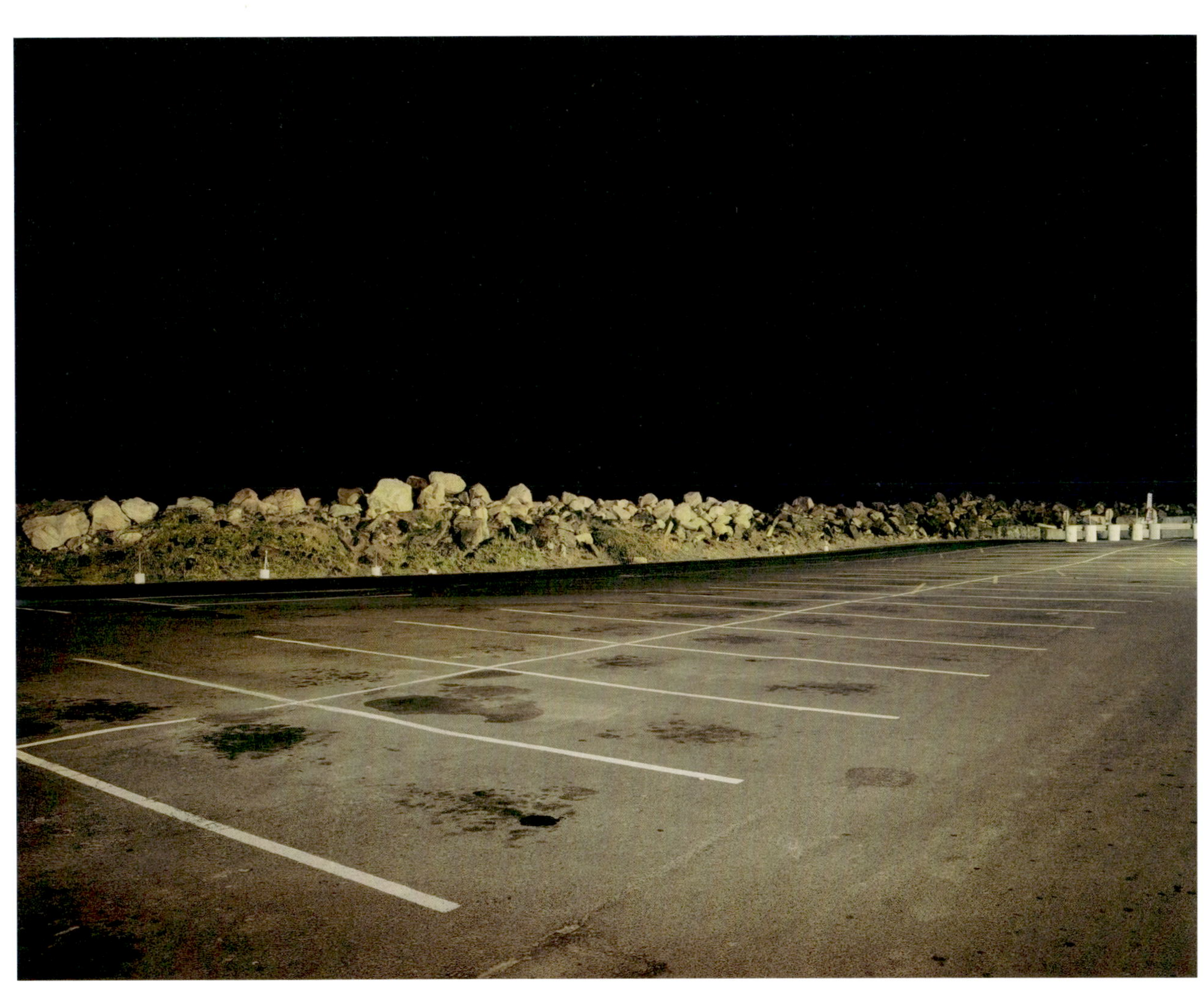

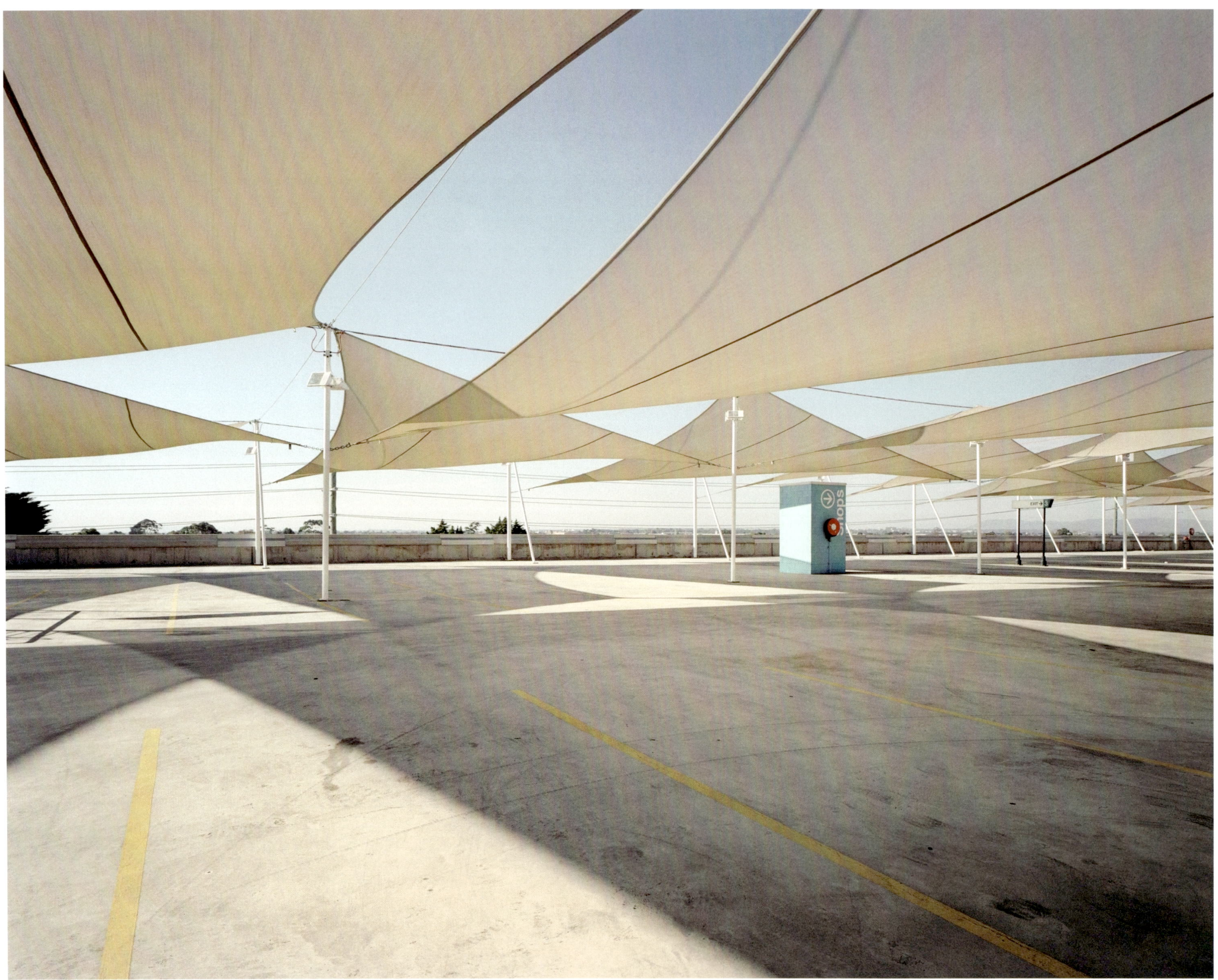
shops
EXIT 3

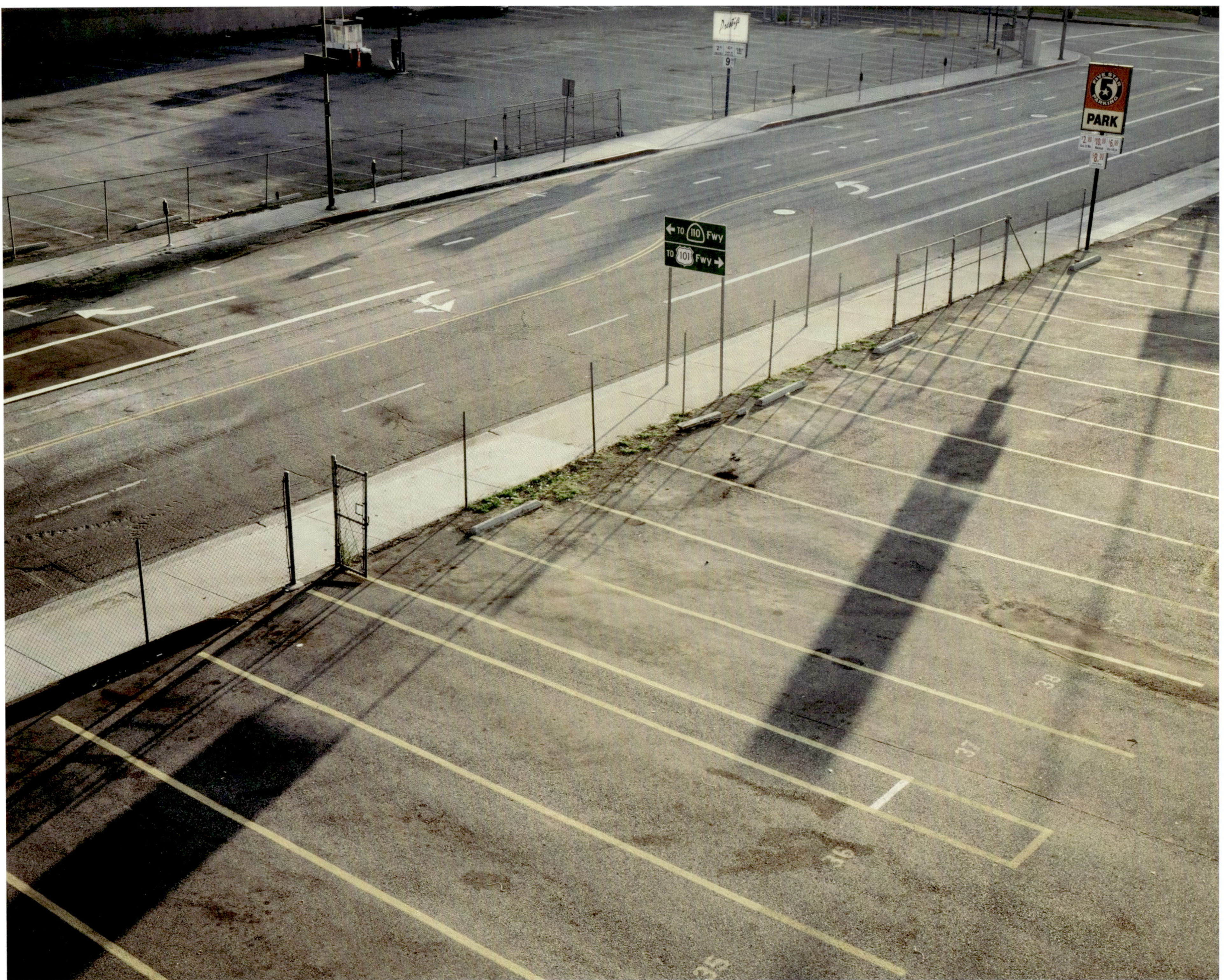
TO 110 Fwy
TO 101 Fwy
PARK

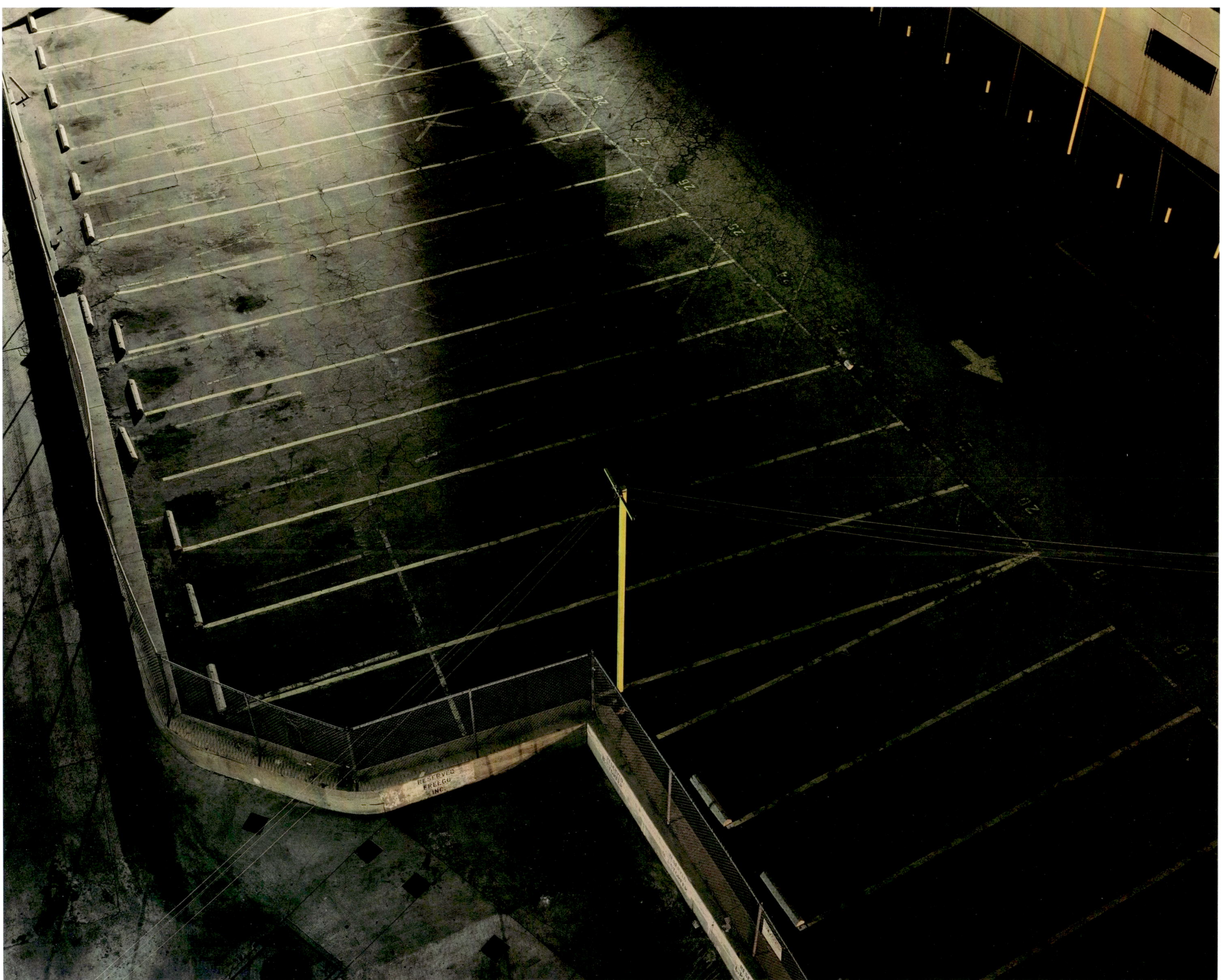
RESERVED
FREEGO
INC.

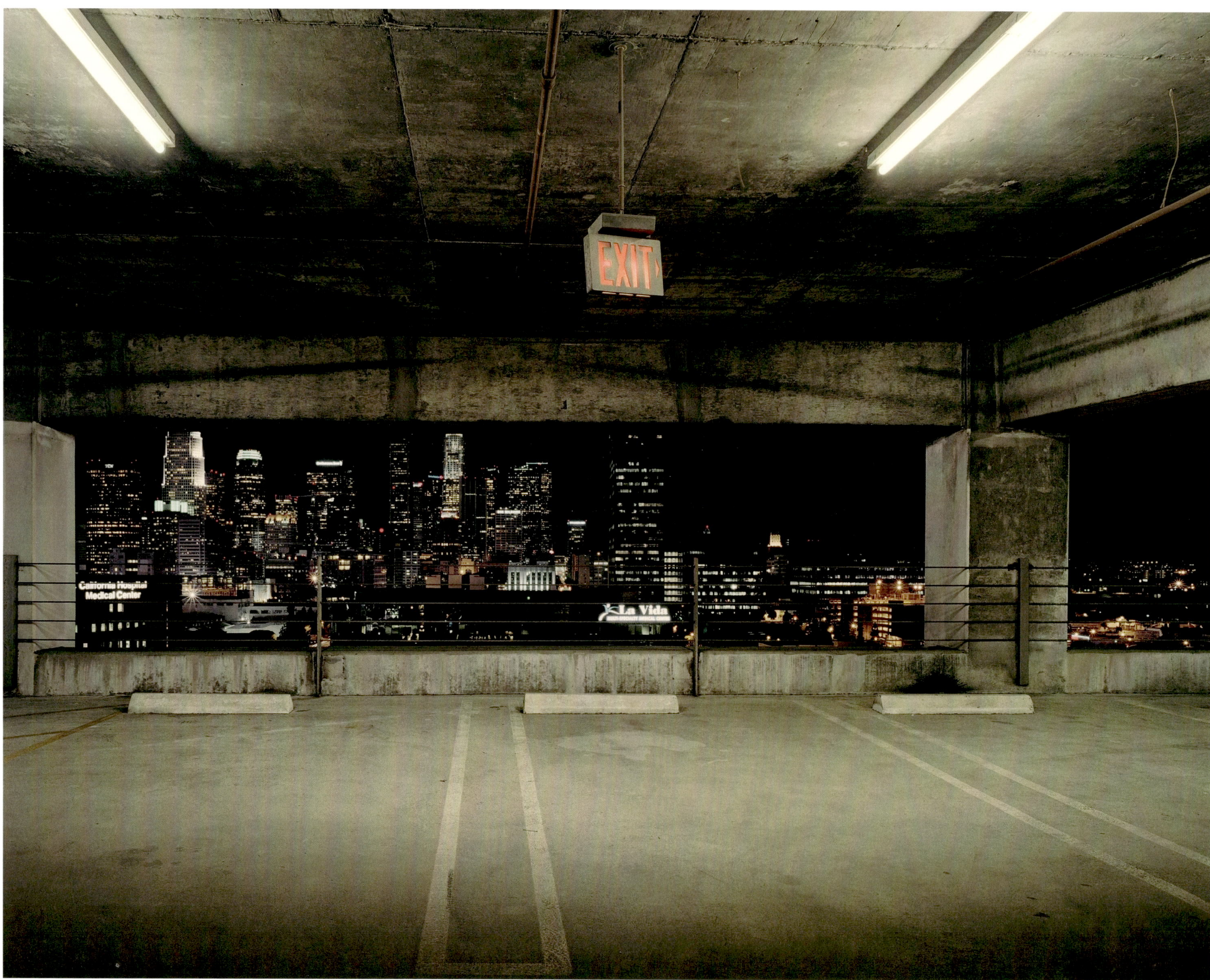
EXIT
California Hospital
Medical Center
La Vida

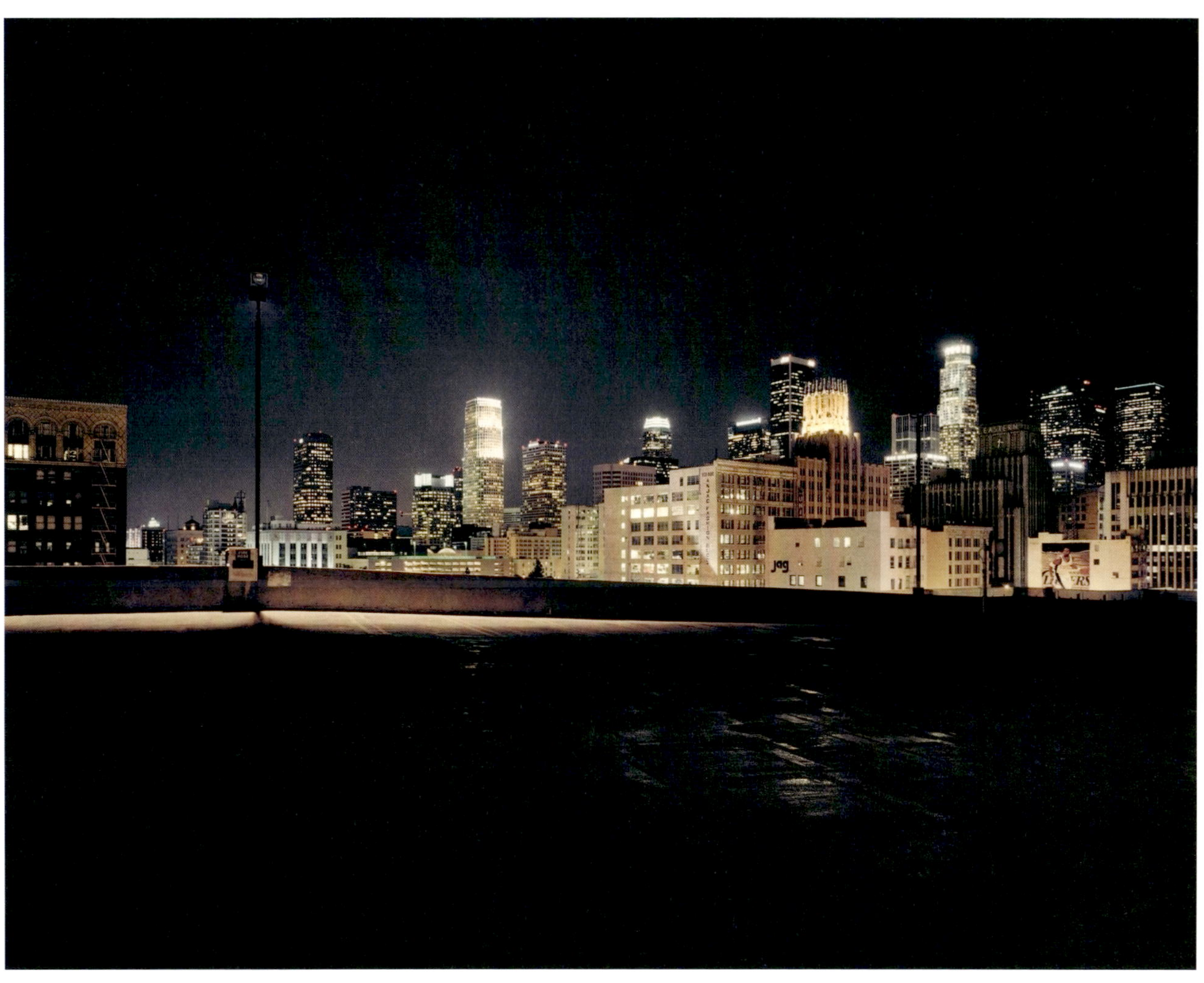

LOS ANGELES, USA 2006——29
LOS ANGELES, USA 2006——30

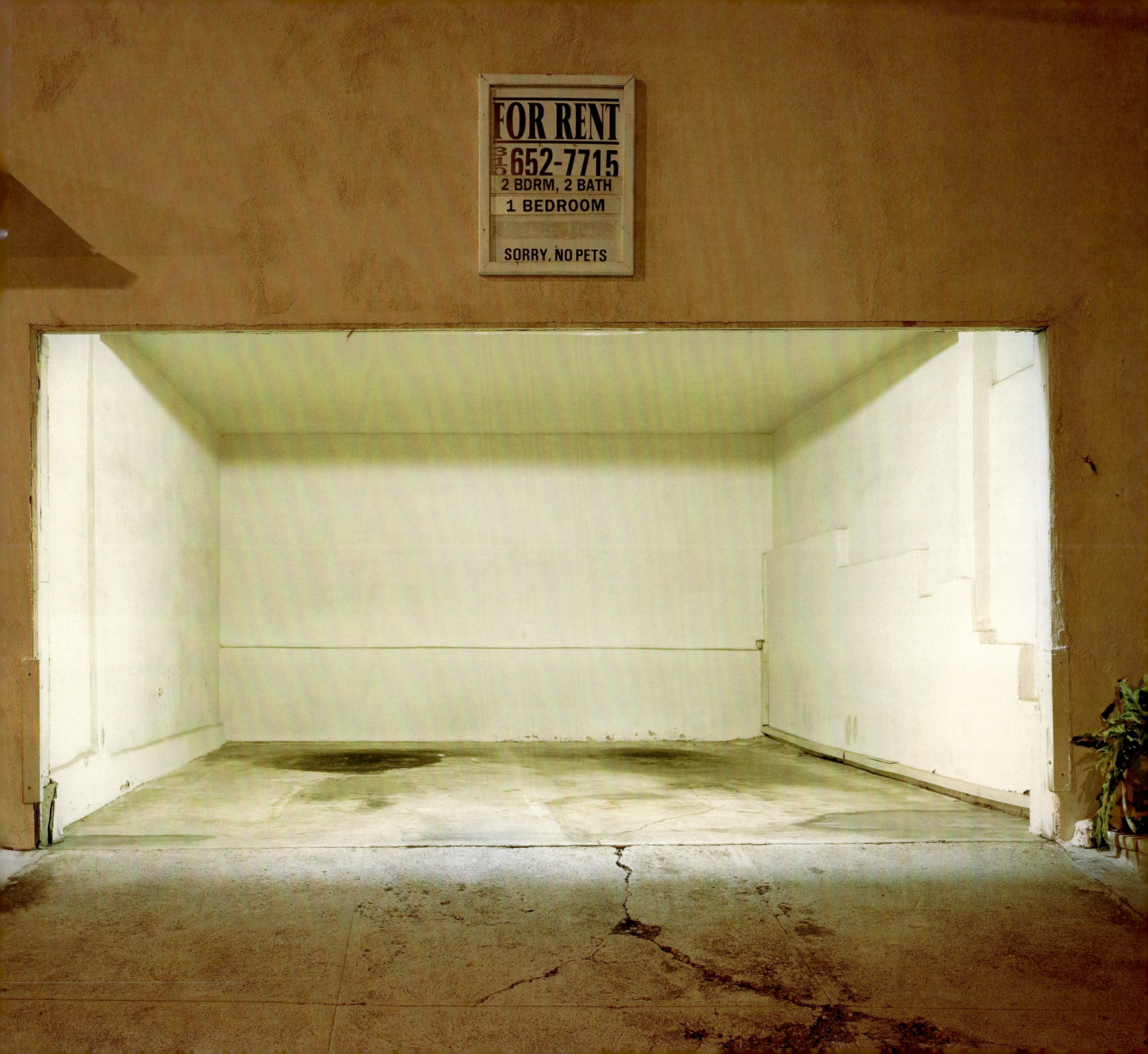
FOR RENT
310
652-7715
2 BDRM, 2 BATH
1 BEDROOM
SORRY, NO PETS

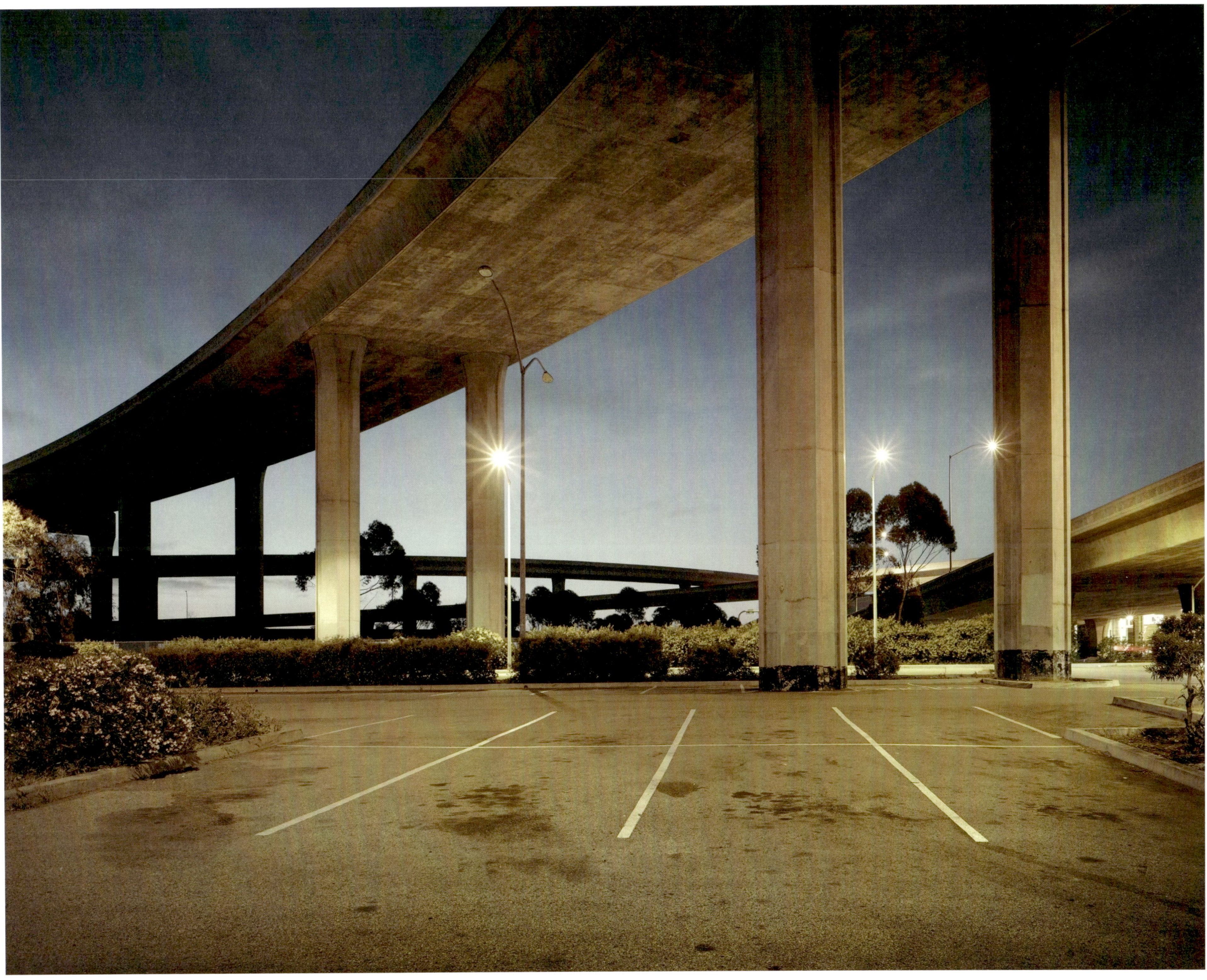

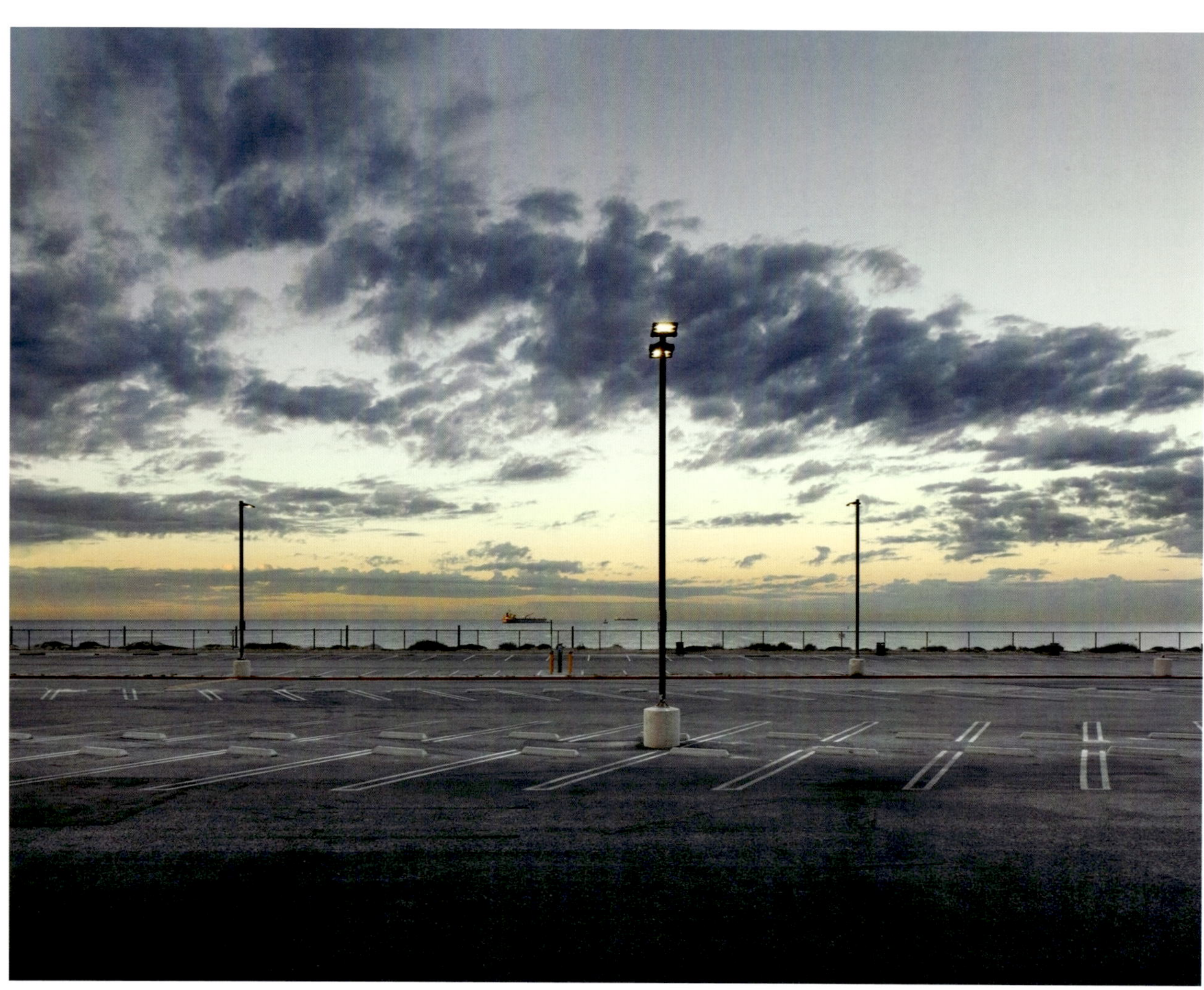

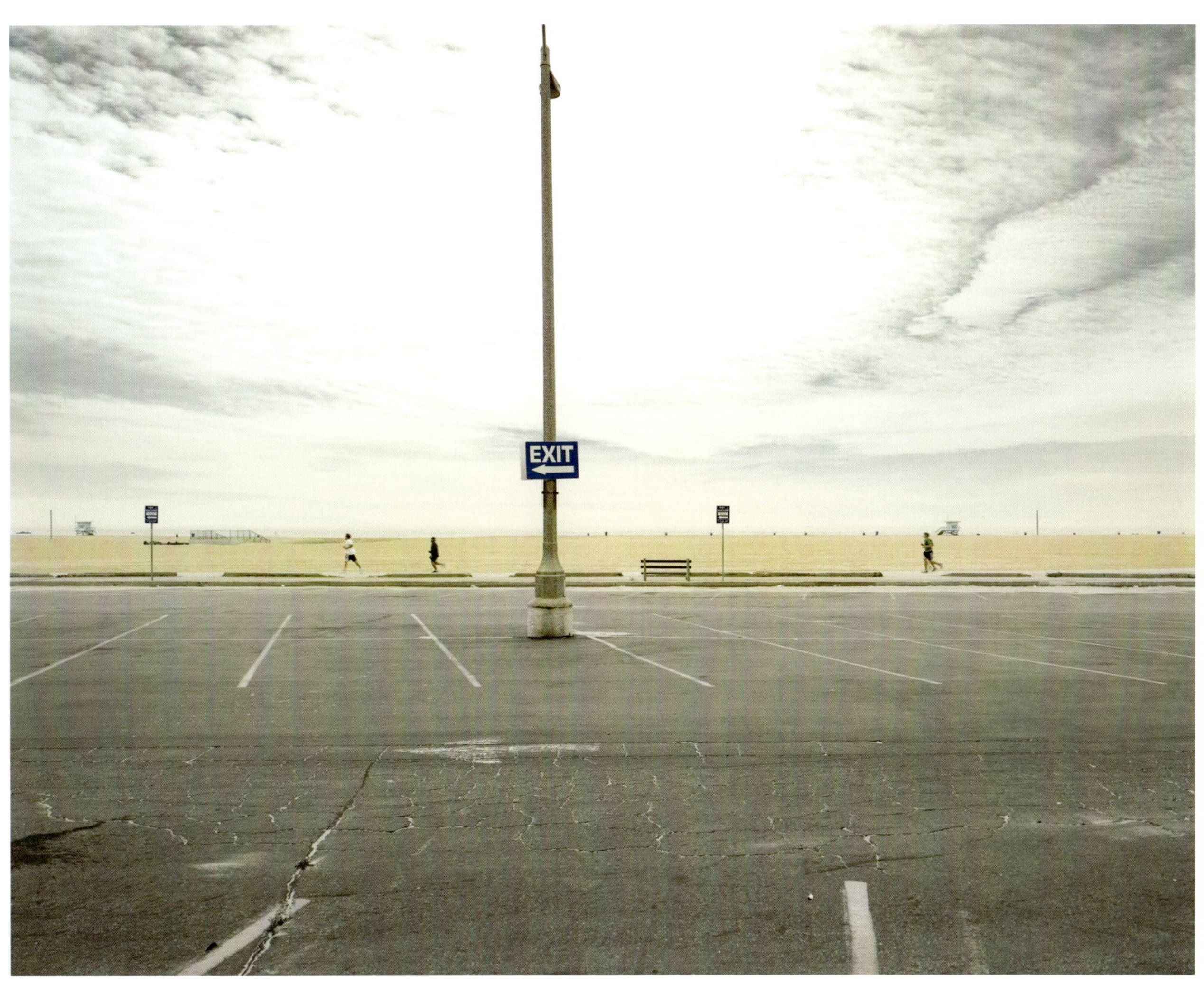

EL SEGUNDO, USA 2014 —— 33
SANTA MONICA, USA 2012 —— 34

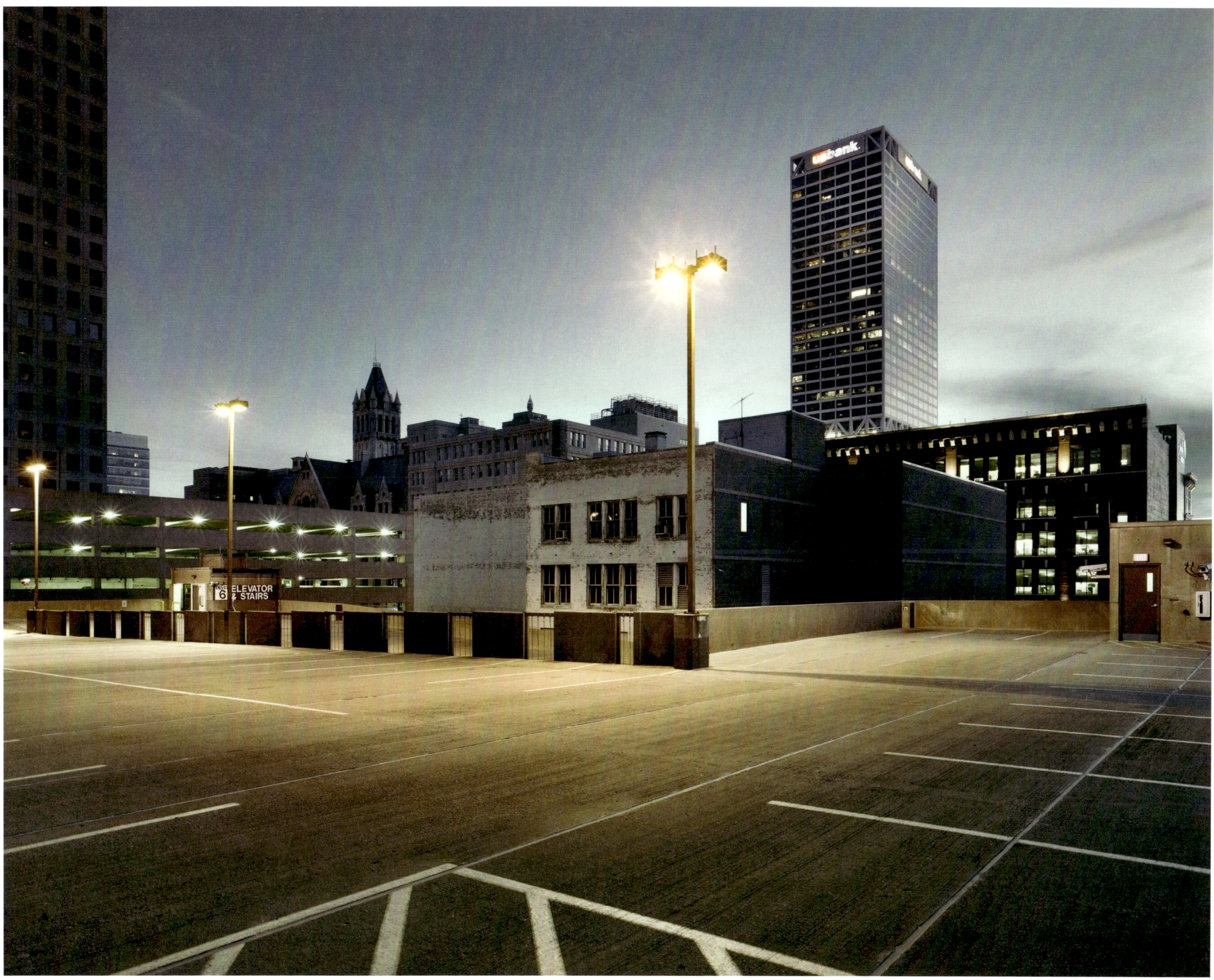
6
ELEVATOR
& STAIRS

2013 LAKE POWELL, USA

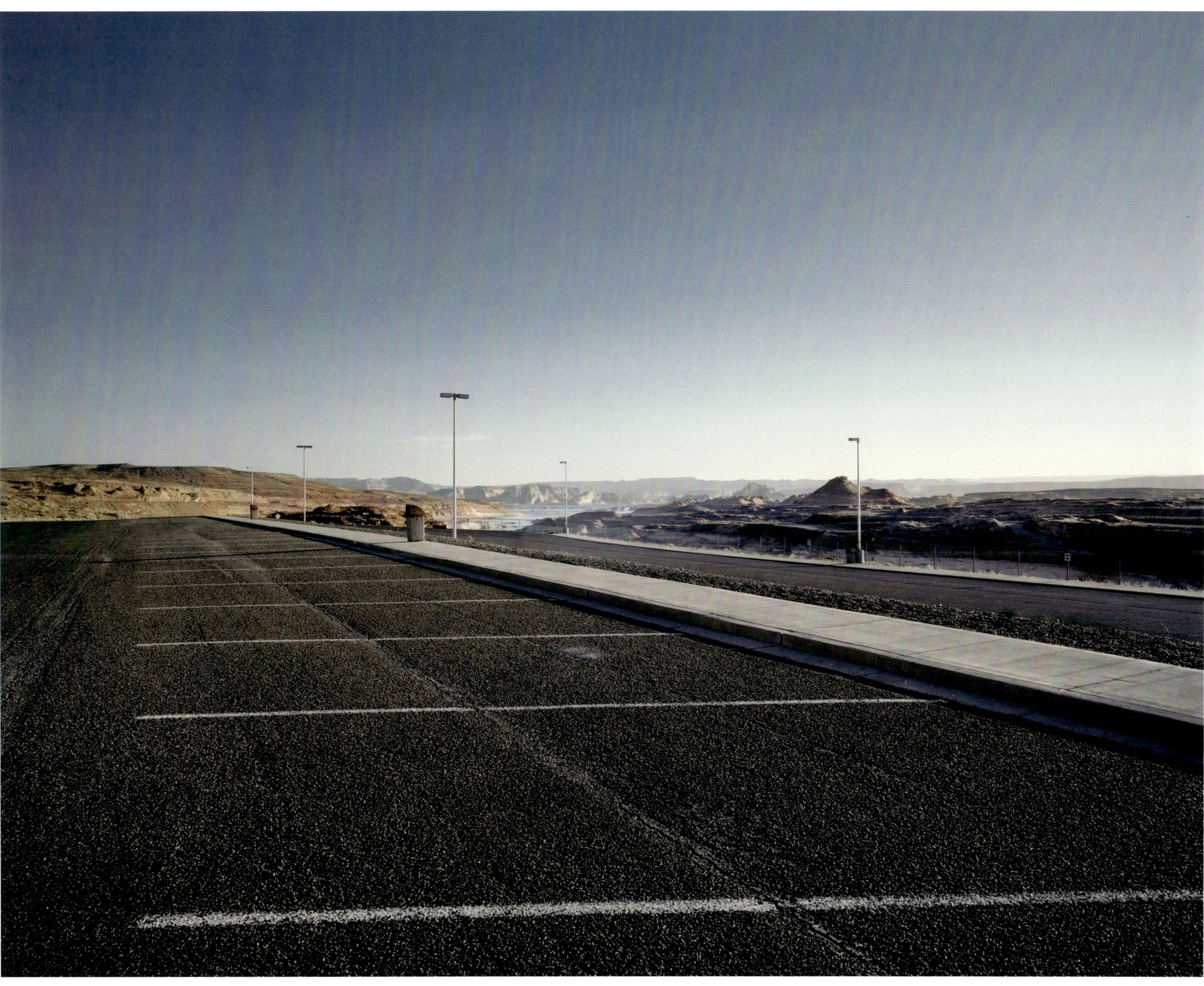

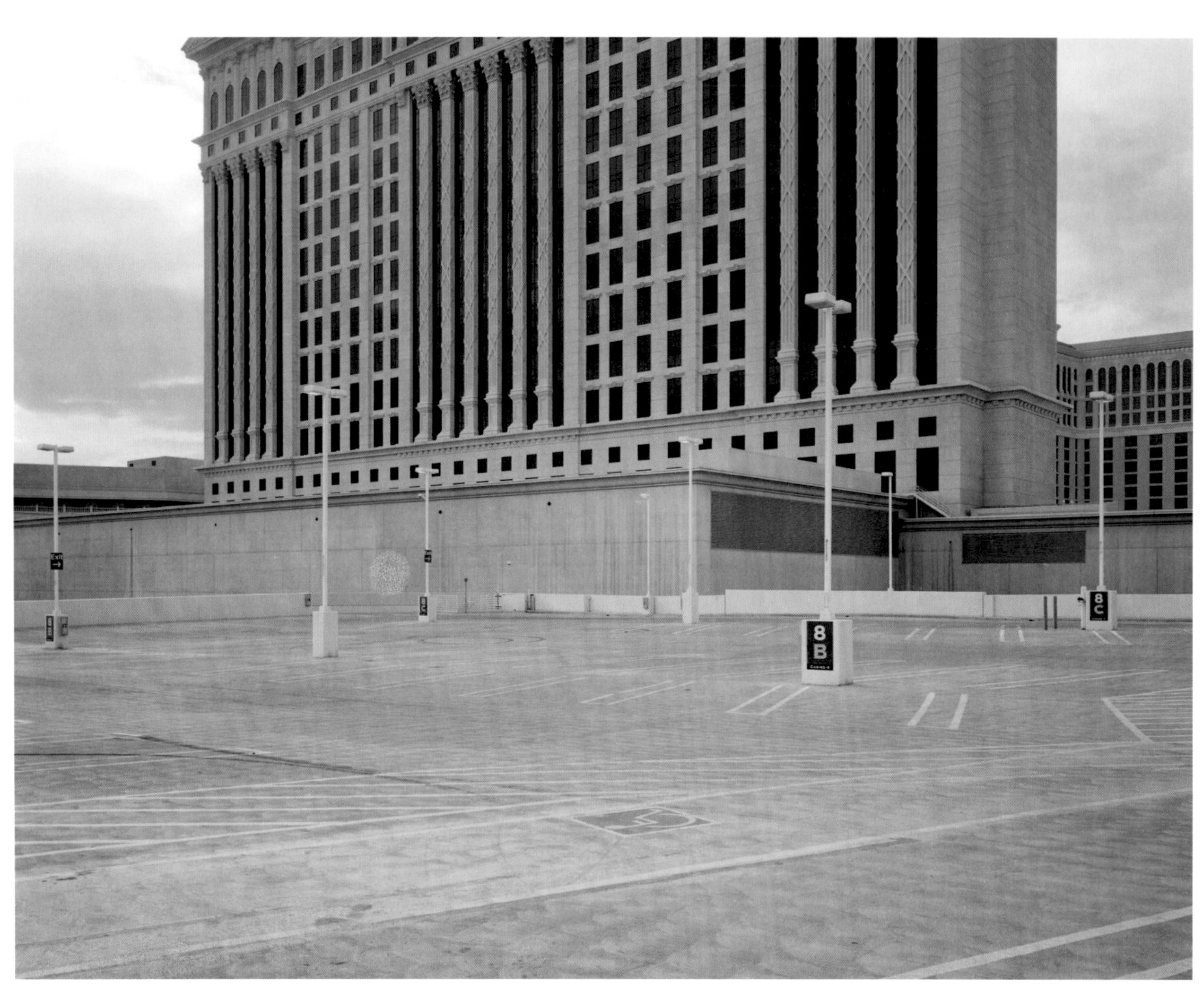

37———2006 LAS VEGAS, USA
38———2006 LAS VEGAS, USA

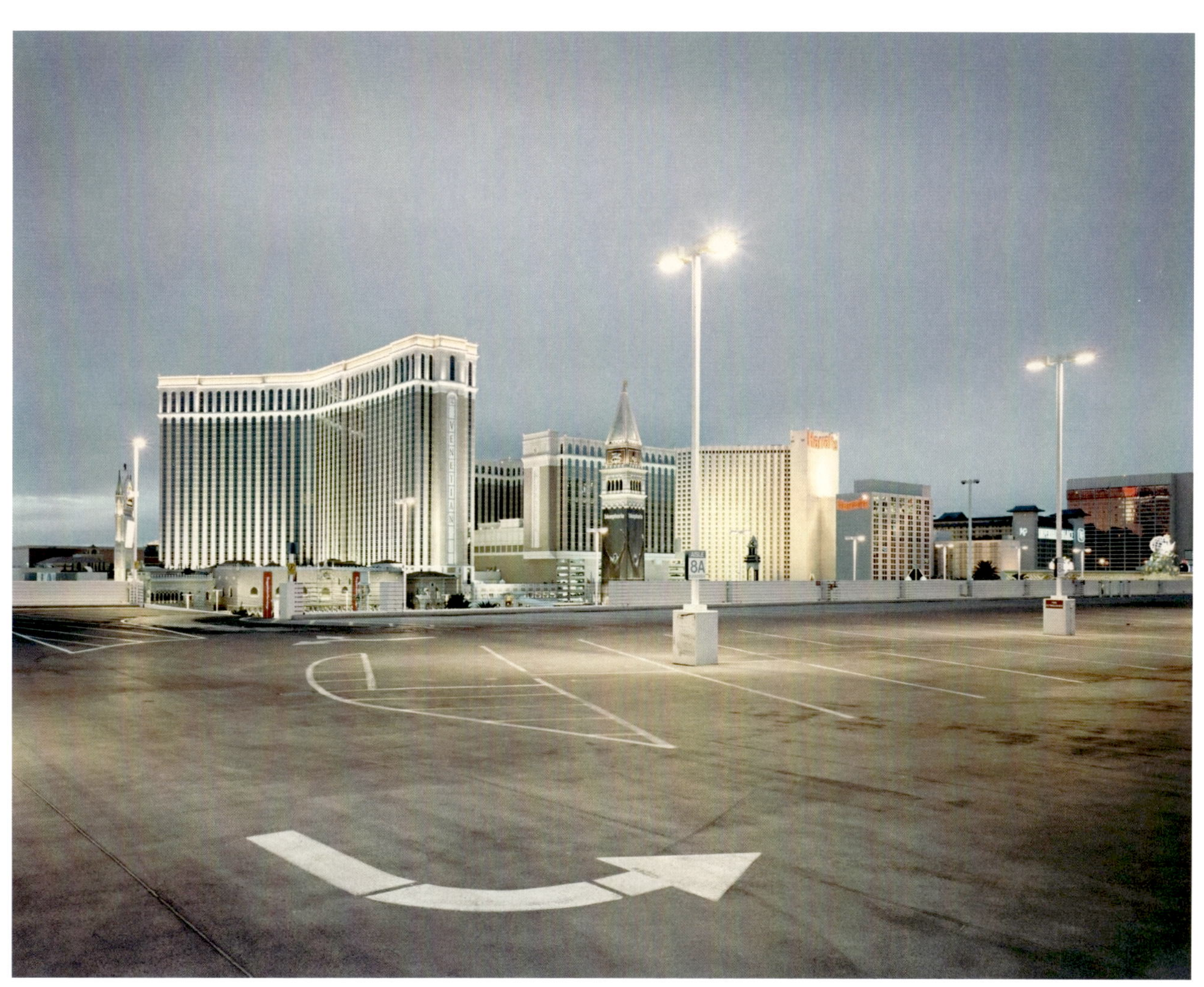

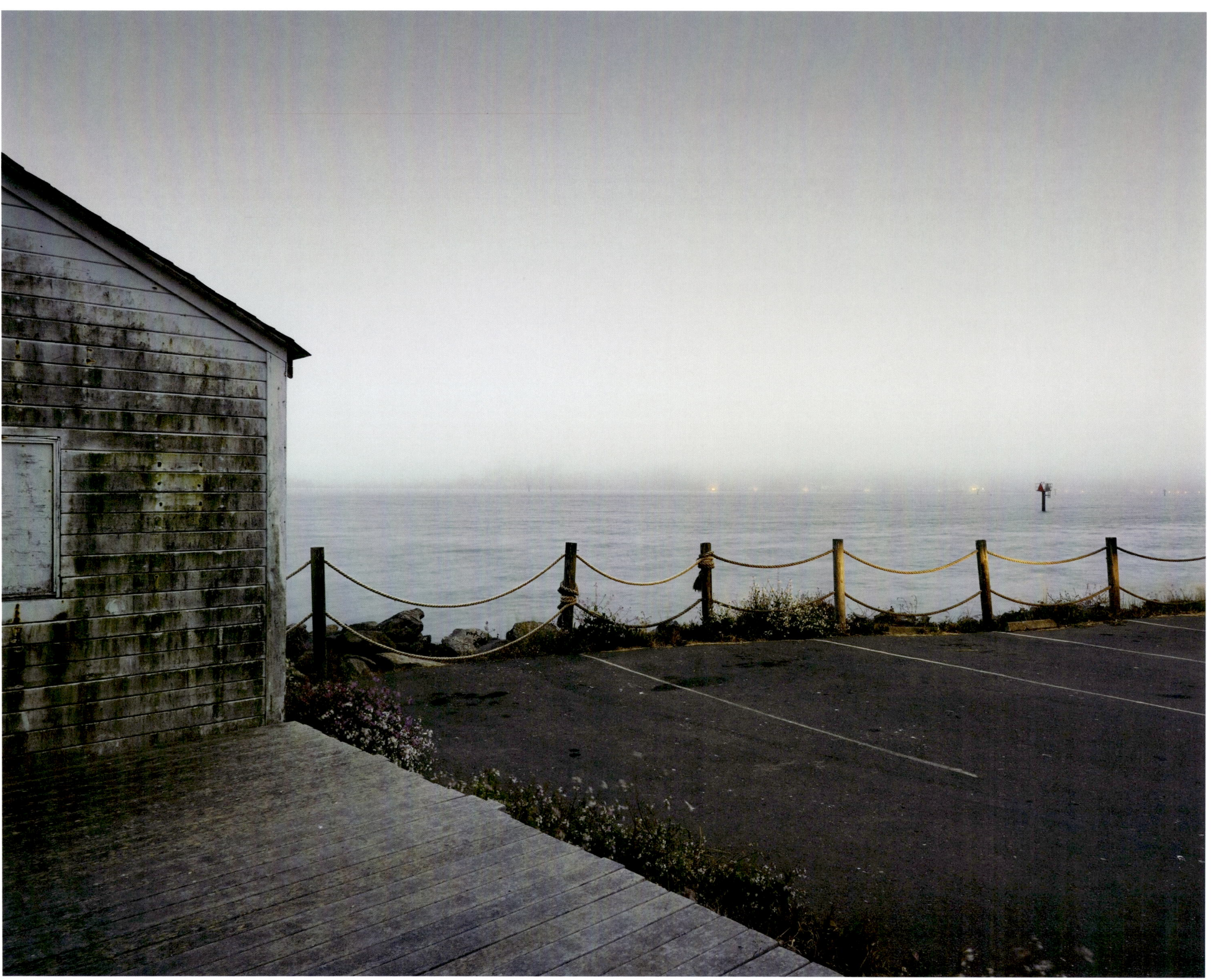

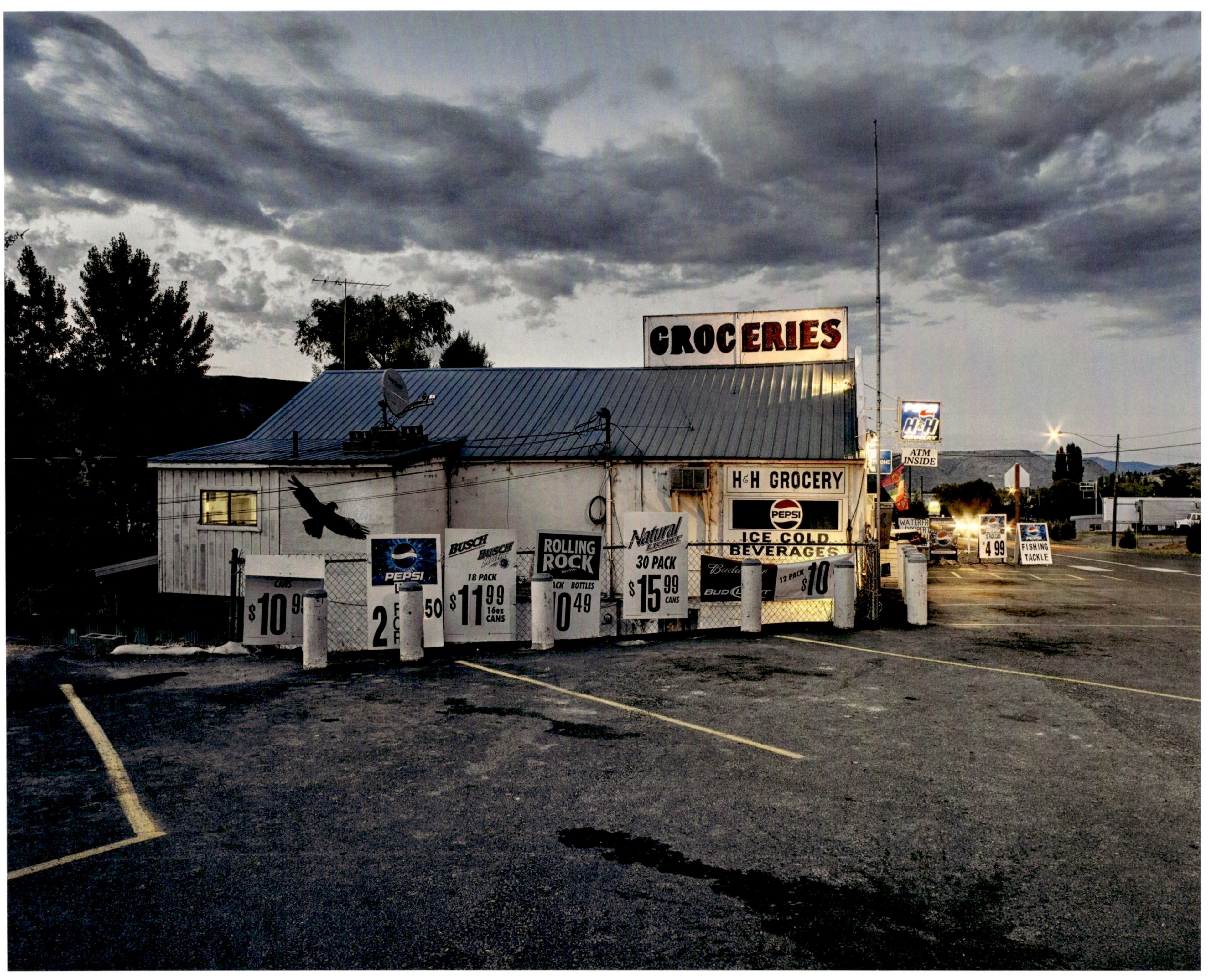
GROCERIES
H&H GROCERY
PEPSI
ICE COLD
BEVERAGES
ATM INSIDE
PEPSI
BUSCH
18 PACK
$11 99
16oz CANS
ROLLING ROCK
Natural LIGHT
30 PACK
$15 99
CANS
12 PACK $10
$4 99
FISHING TACKLE

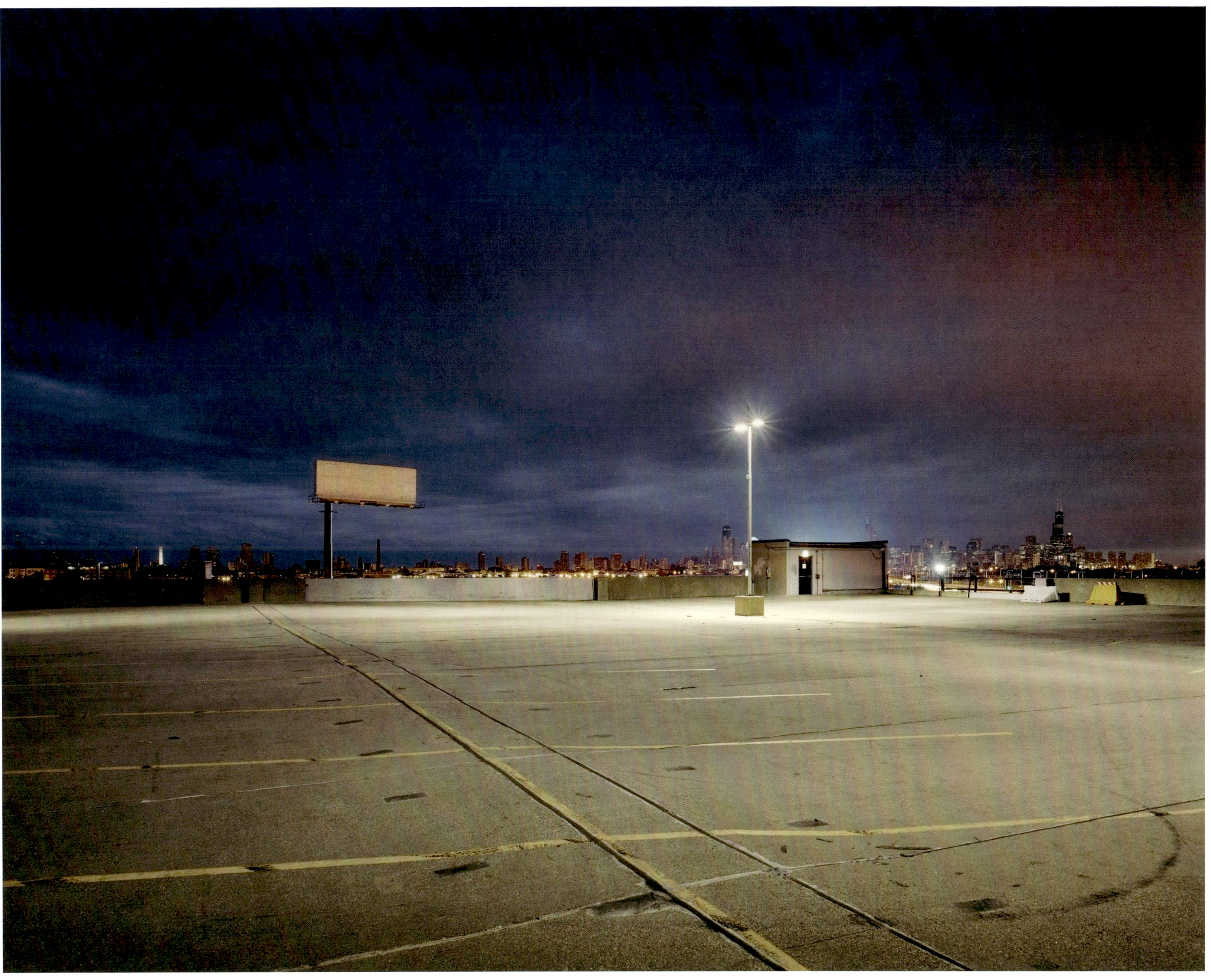

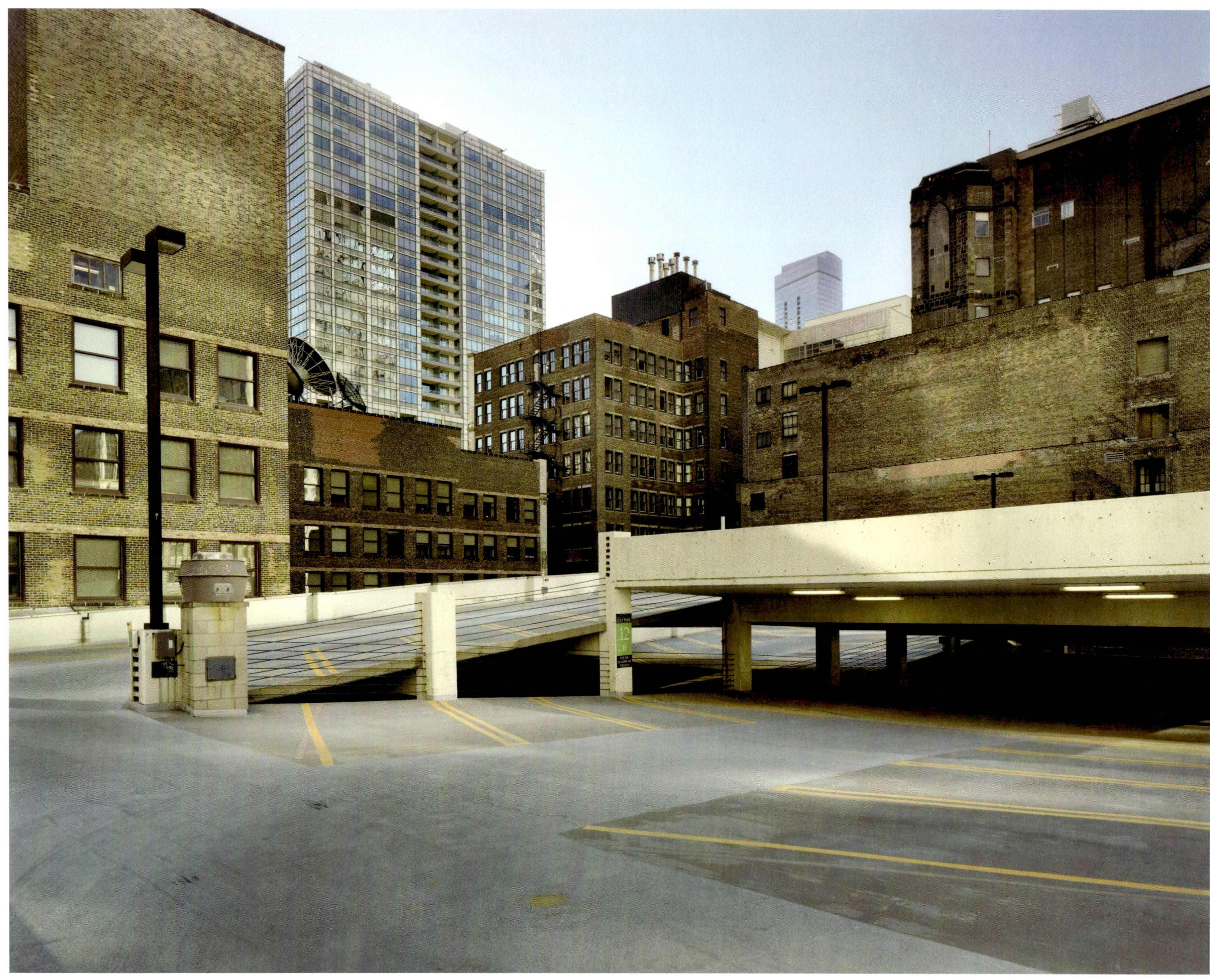
SELF PARK
12
B

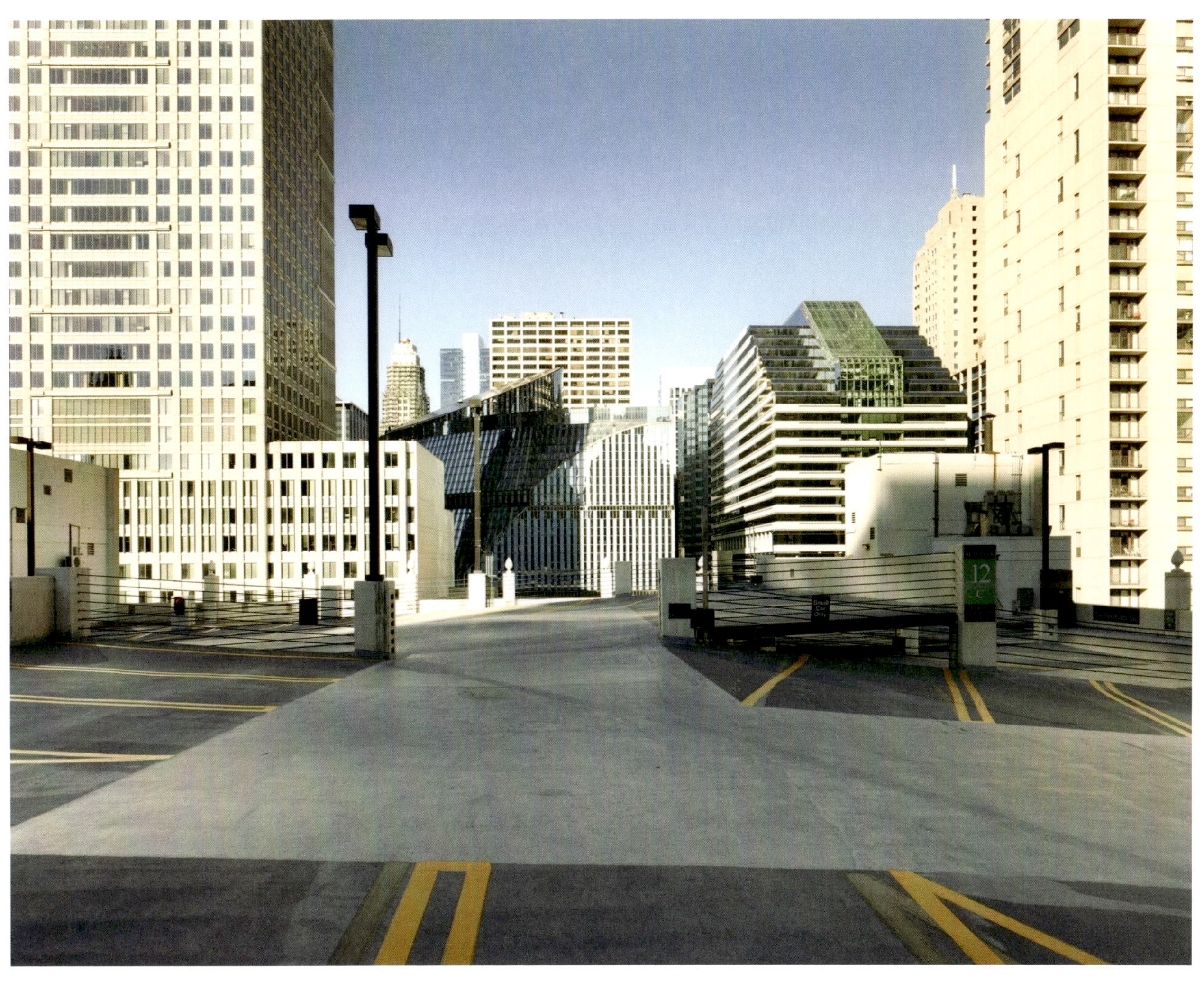

CHICAGO, USA 2012——42
CHICAGO, USA 2012——43

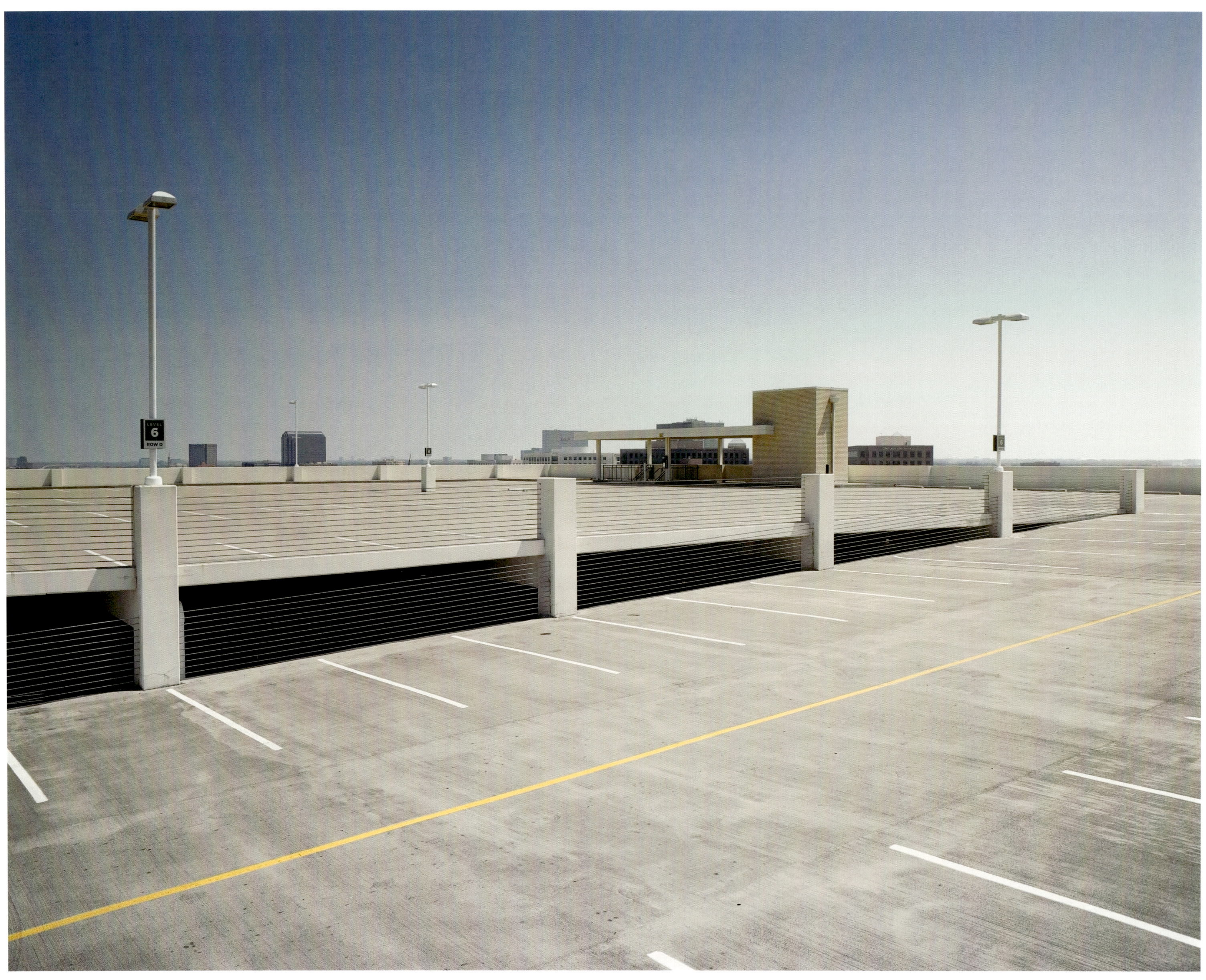
LEVEL
6
ROW D

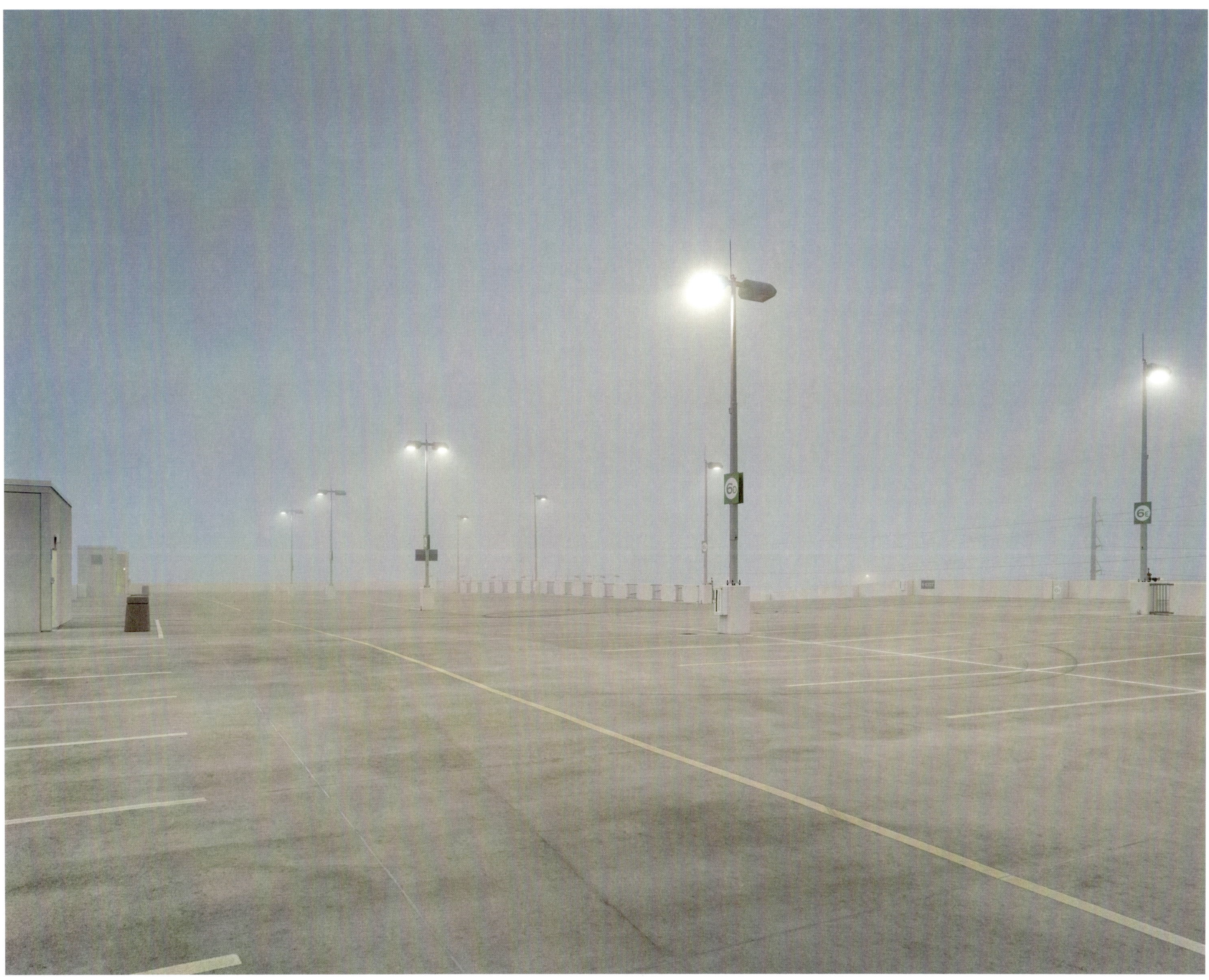
6D
6E

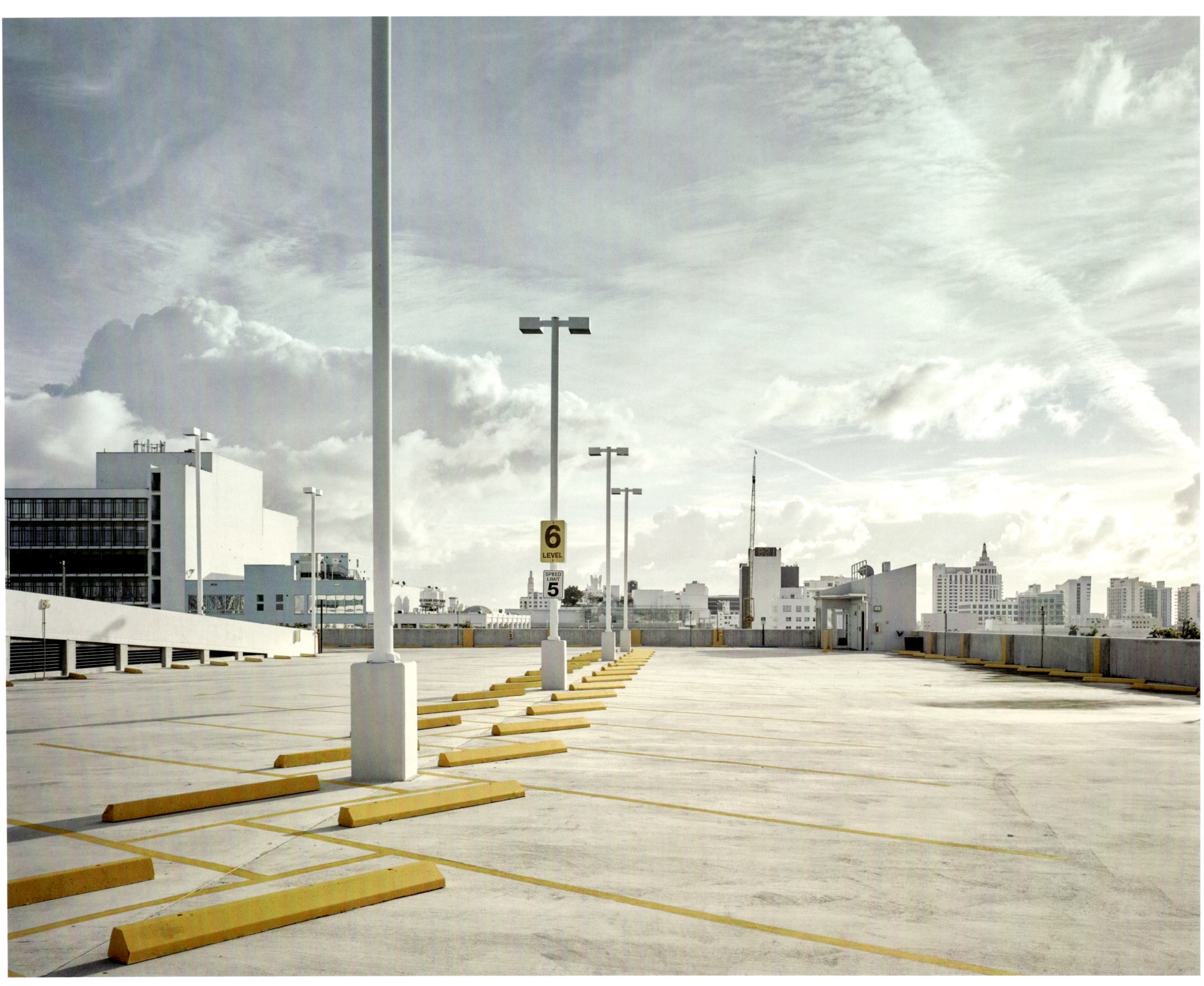
6
LEVEL
SPEED LIMIT
5

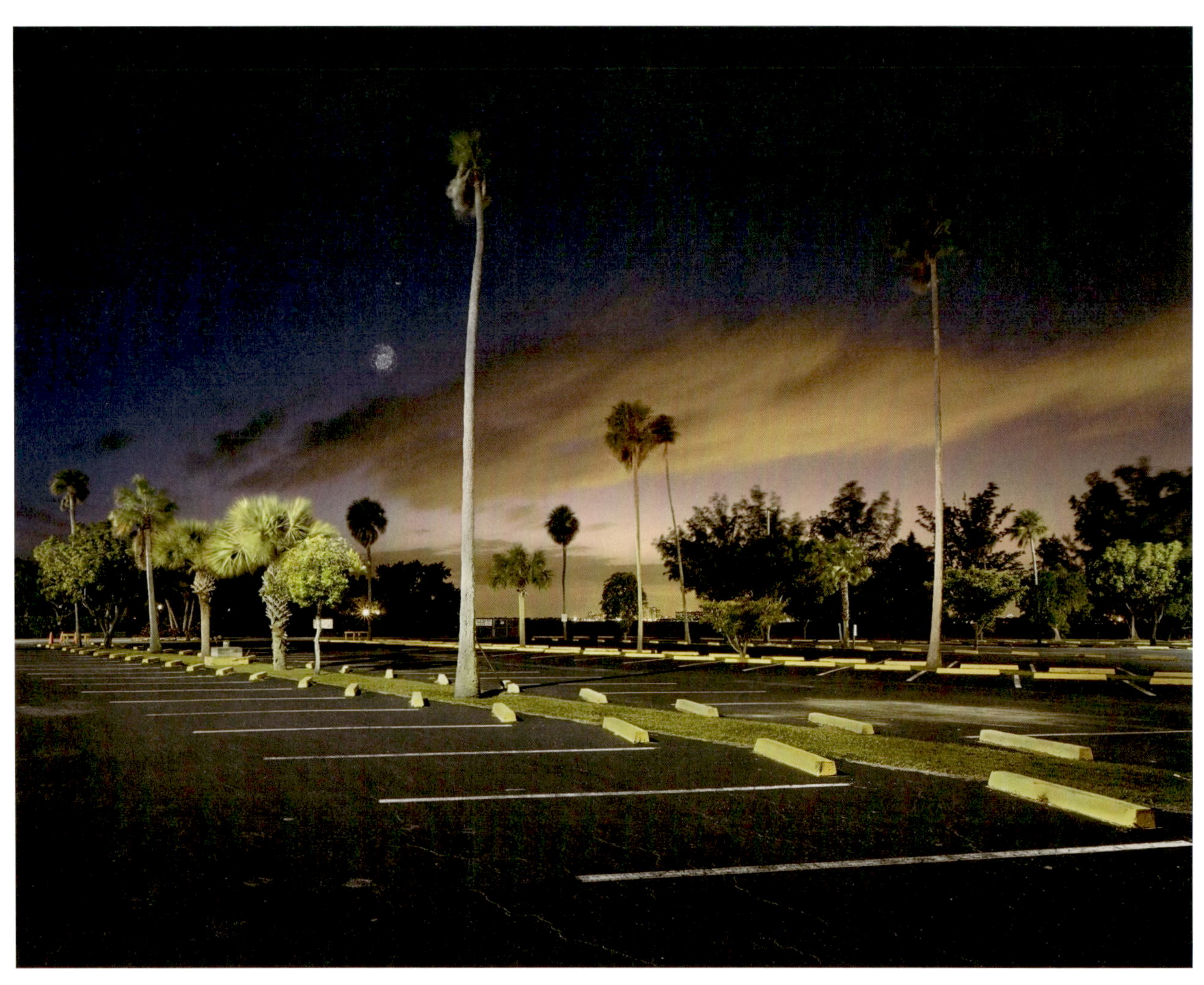

47———2011 MIAMI, USA
48———2011 MIAMI, USA

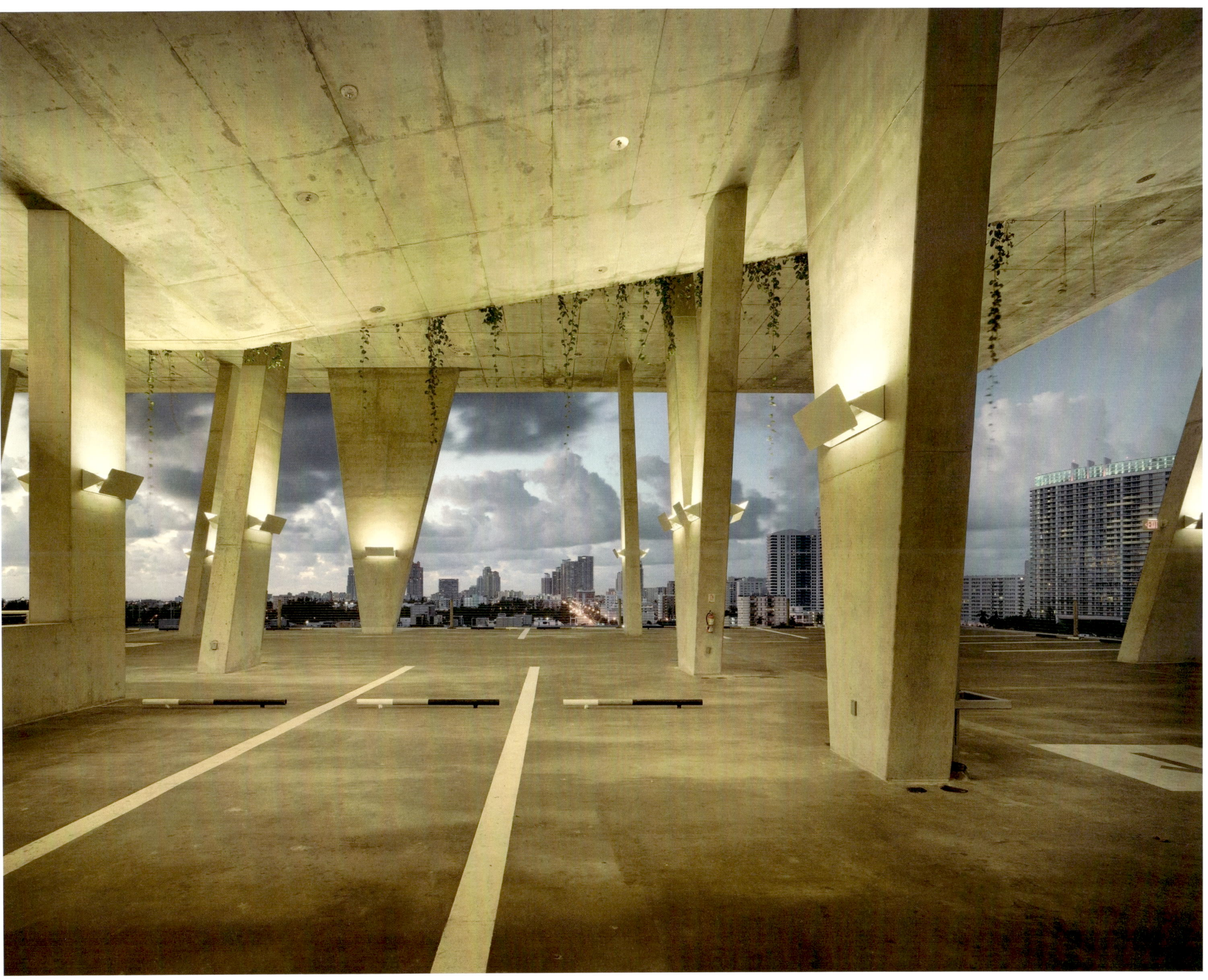

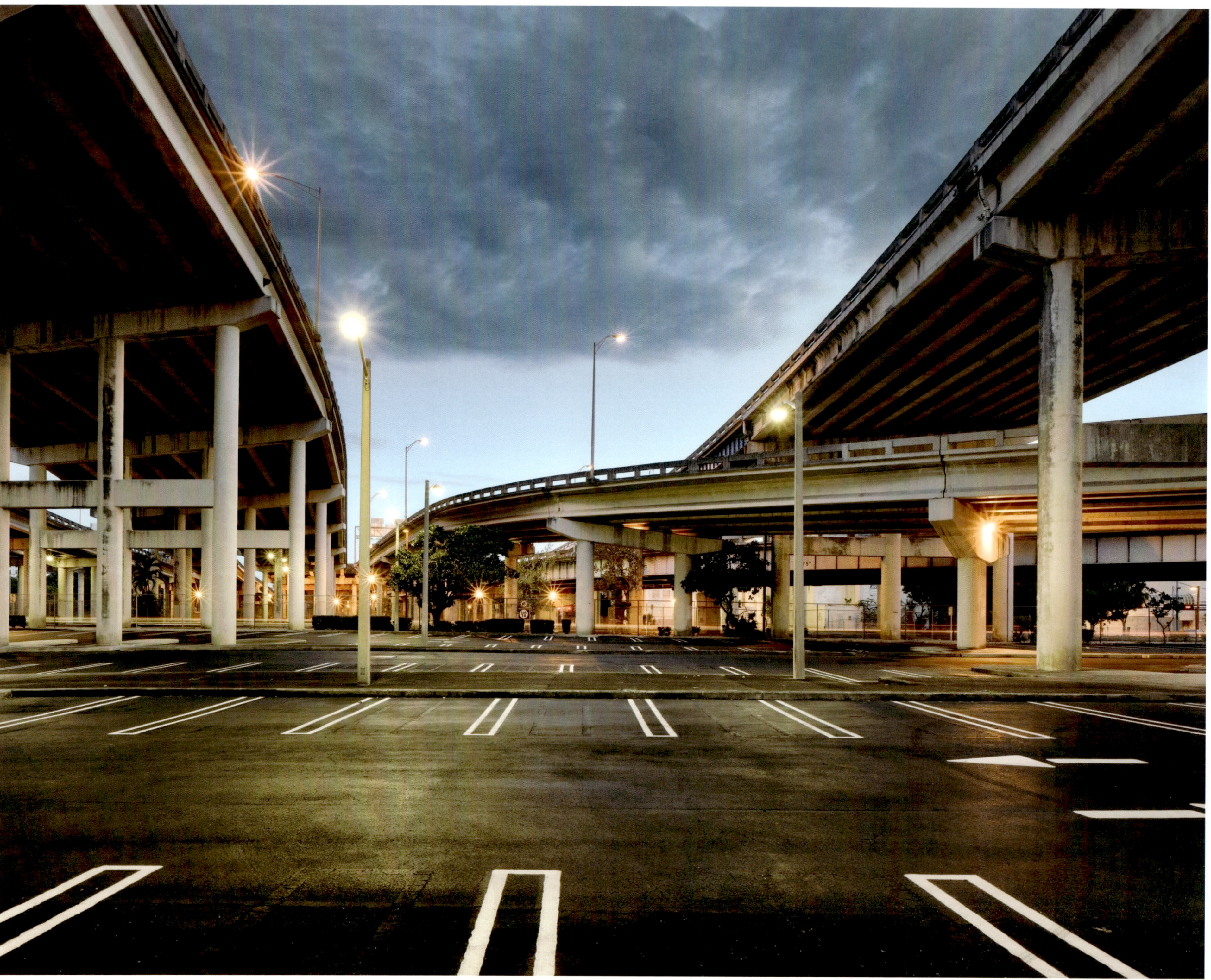

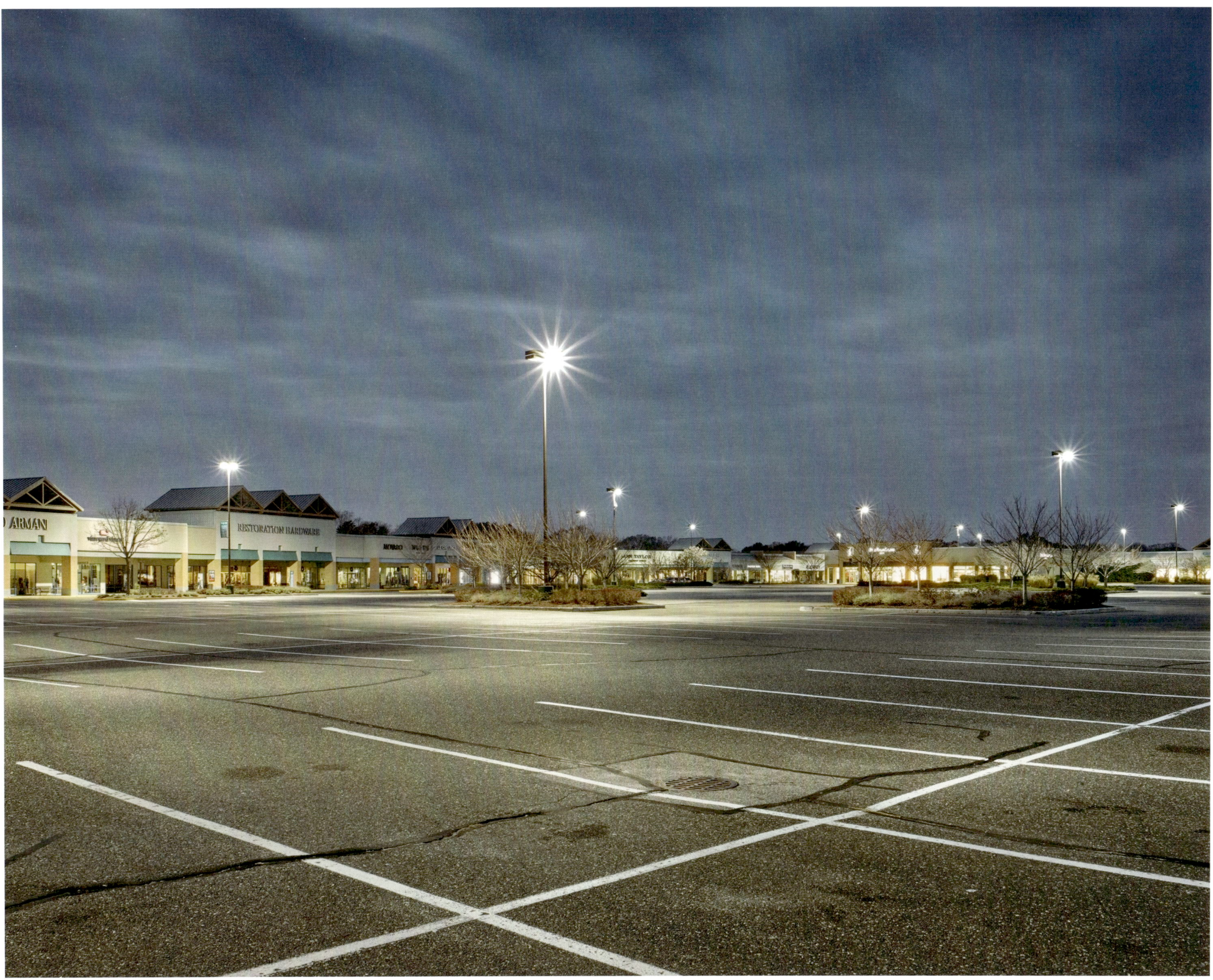
RESTORATION HARDWARE

51———2014 HAMPTON BAYS, USA

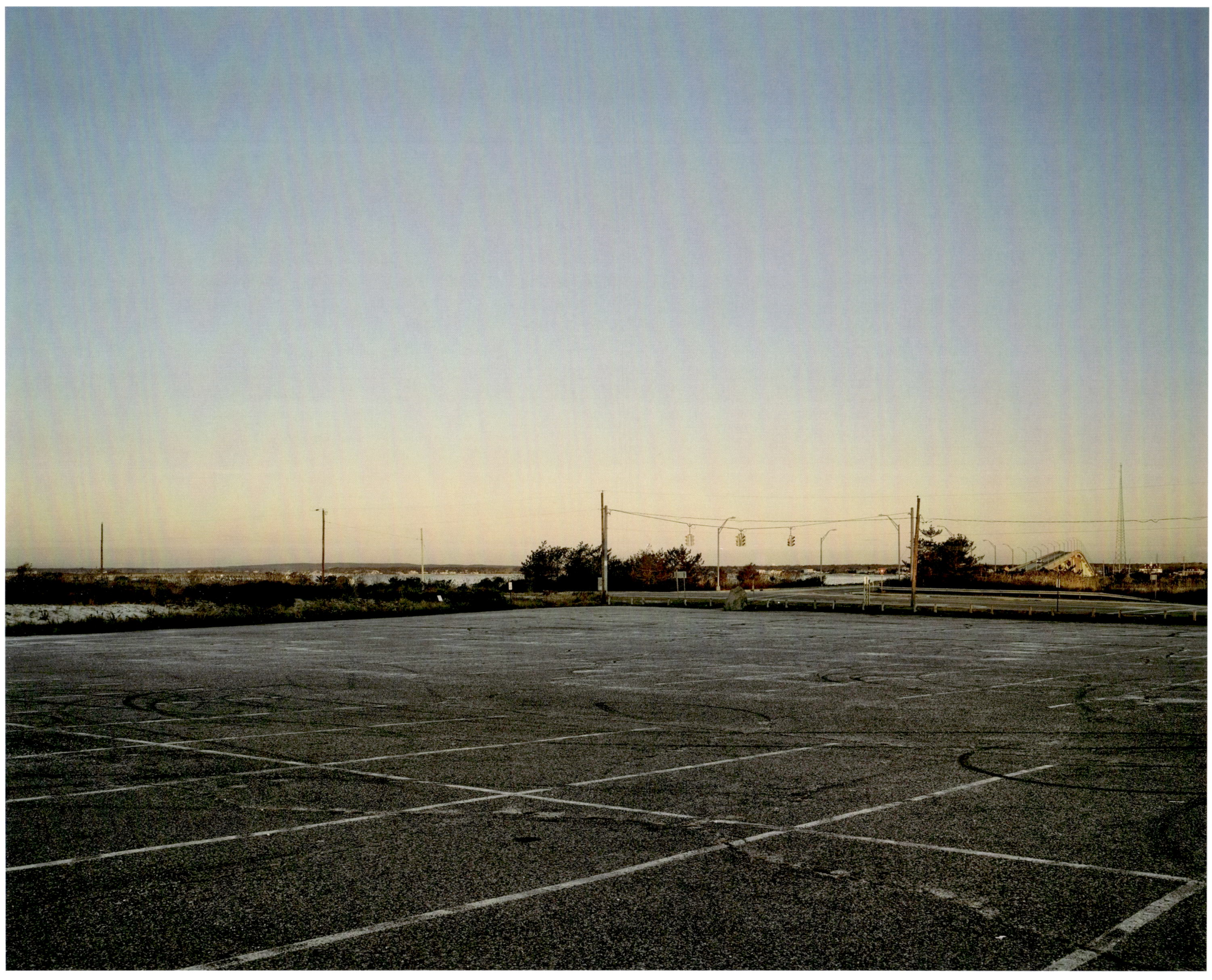

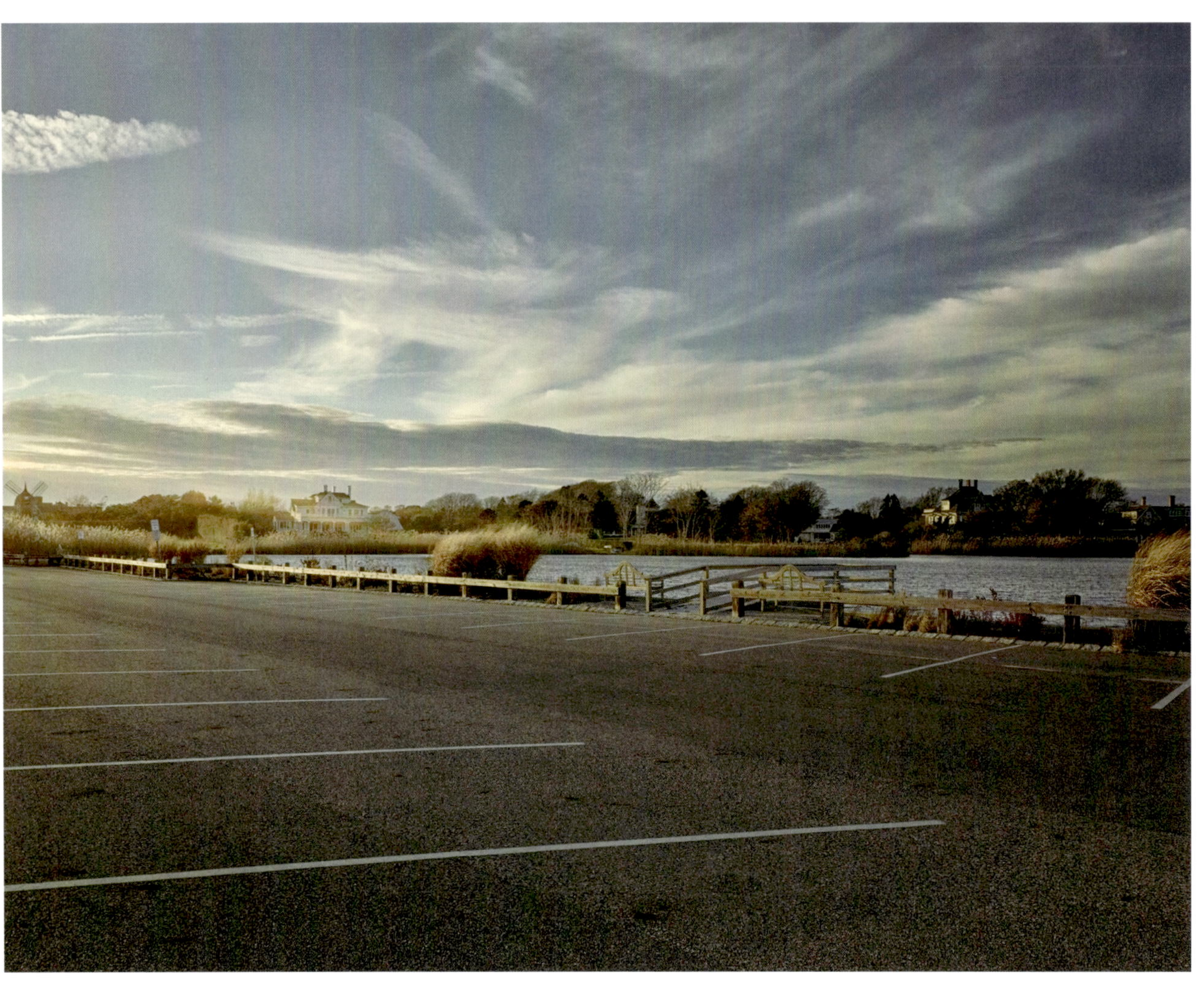

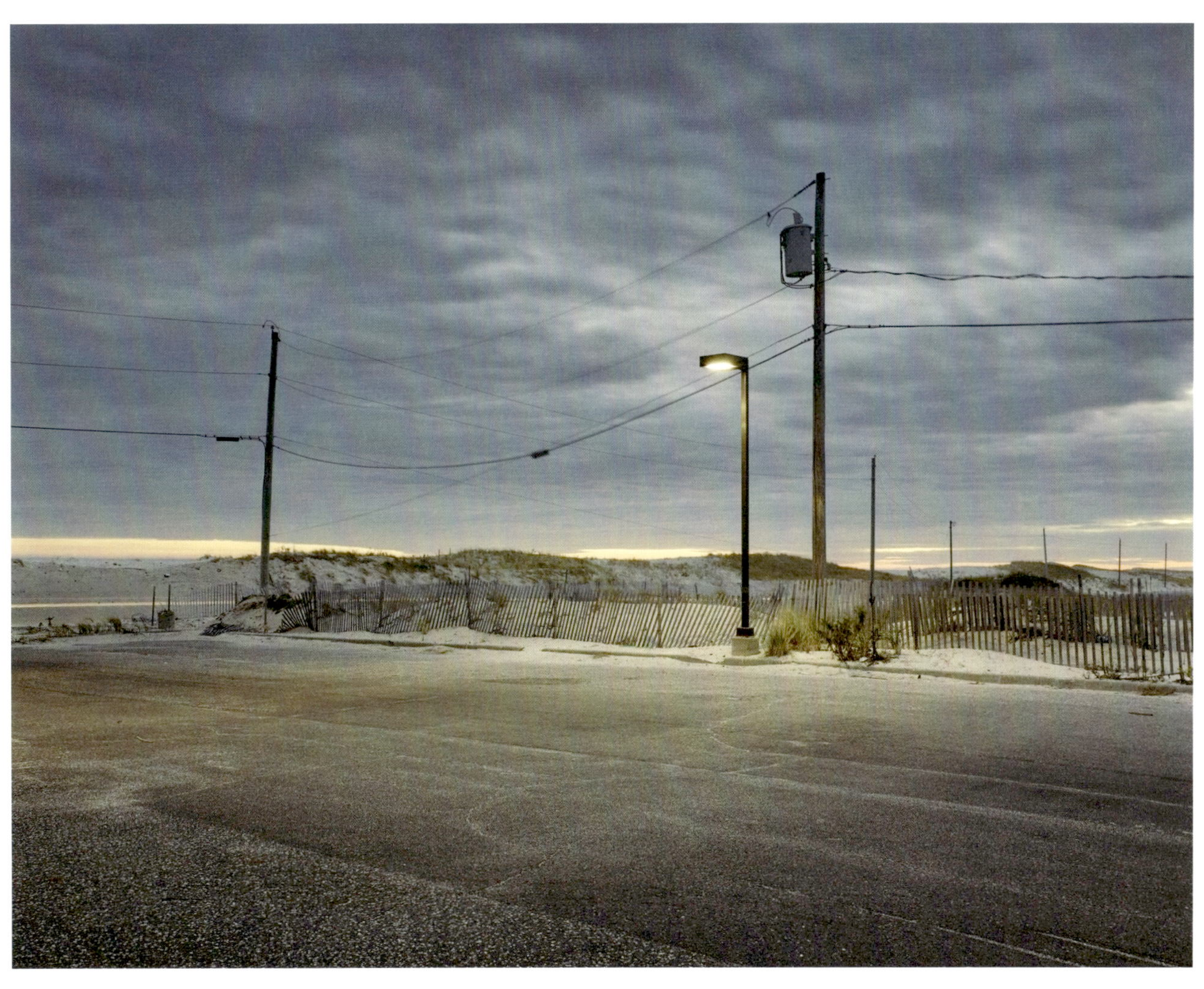

HAMPTON BAYS, USA 2014——52
HAMPTON BAYS, USA 2014——53

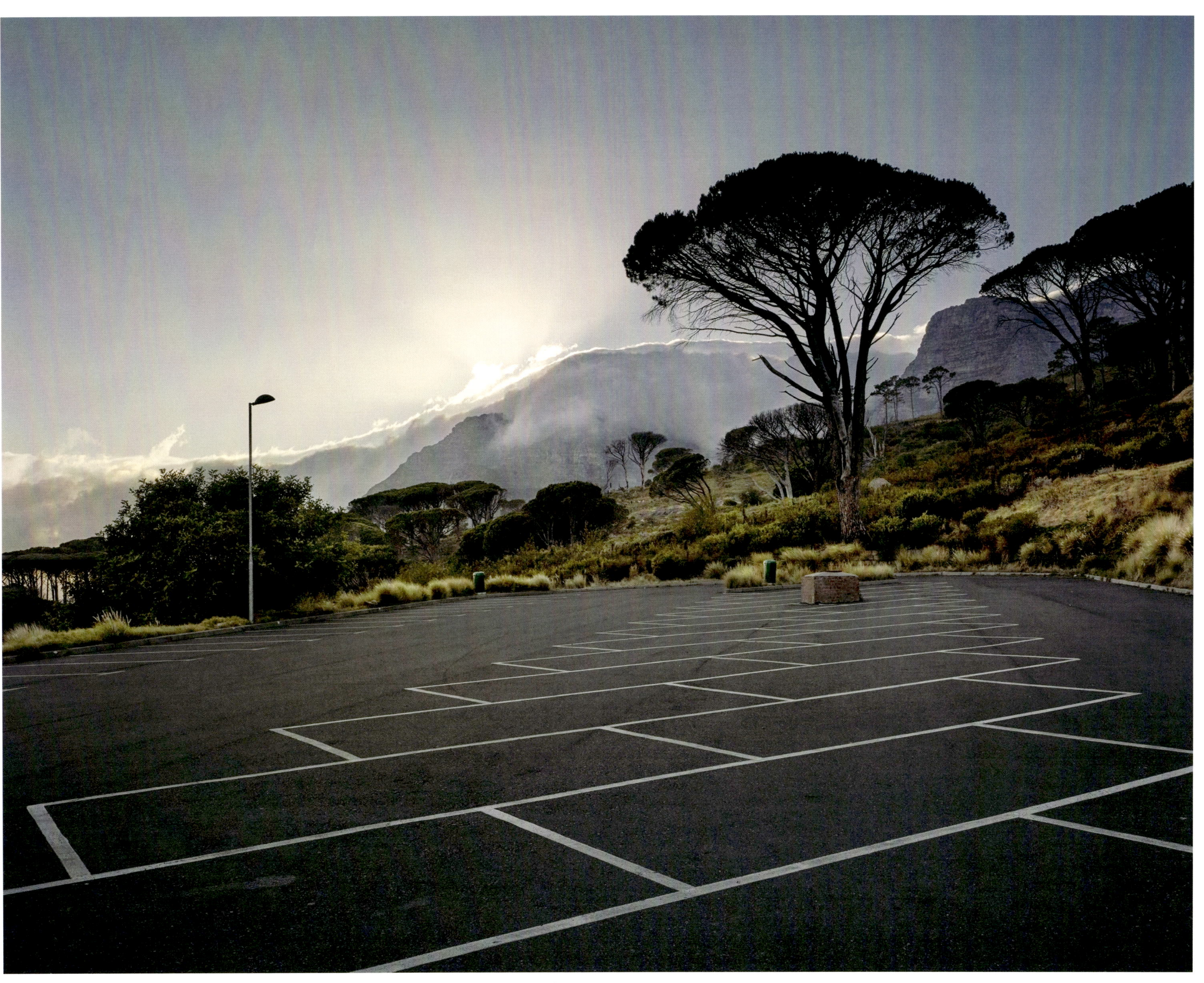

55———2010 AHRWEILER, GERMANY

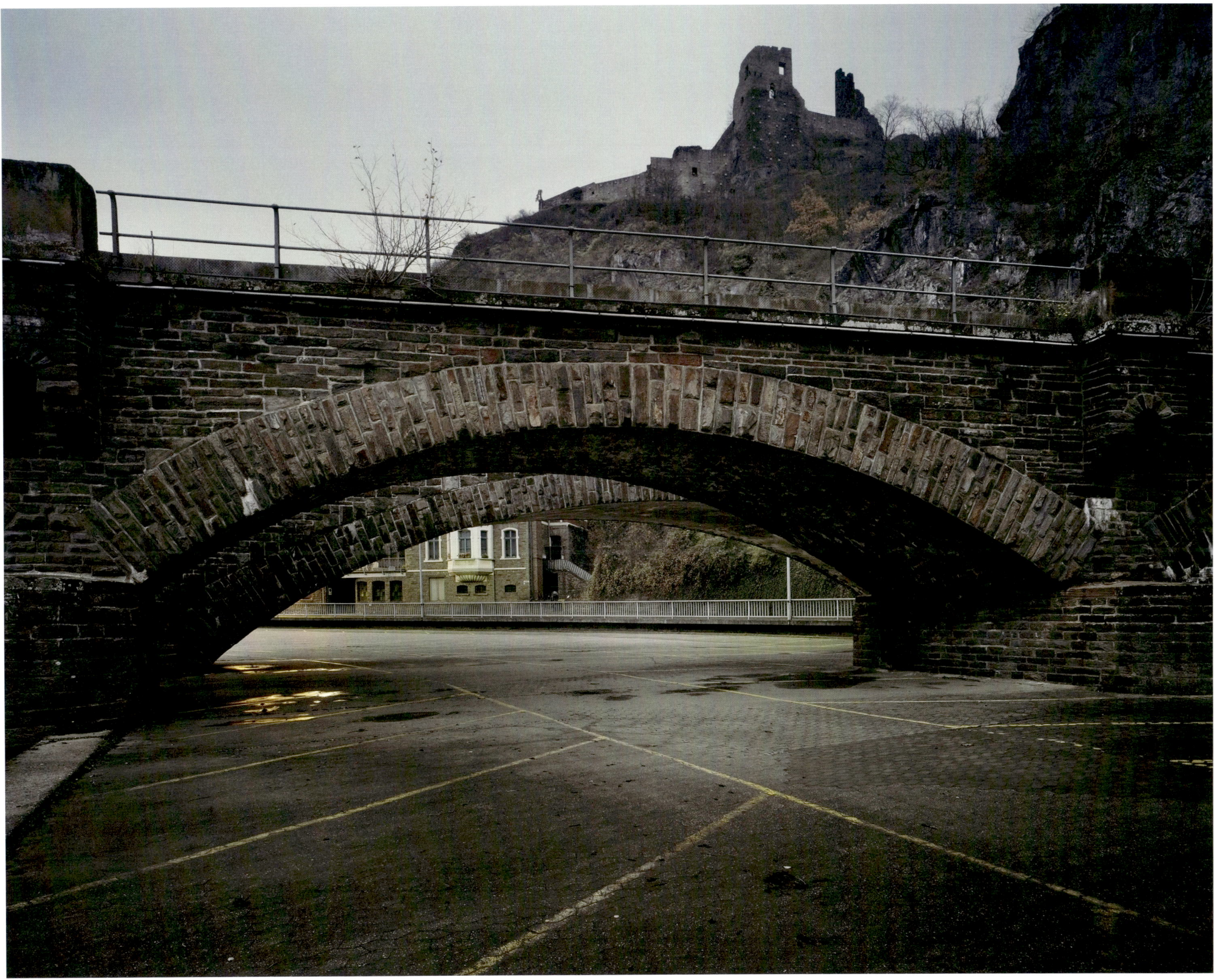

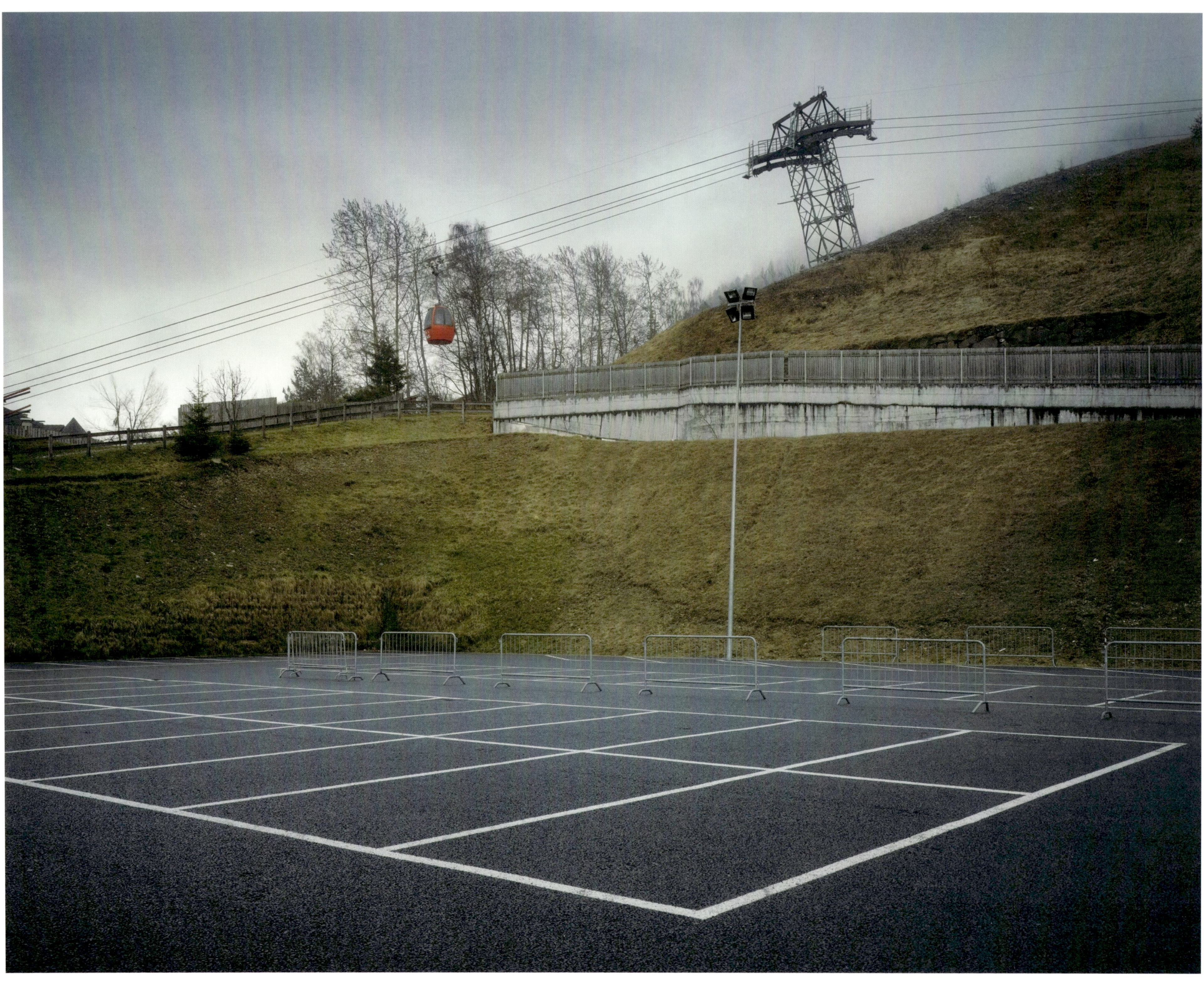

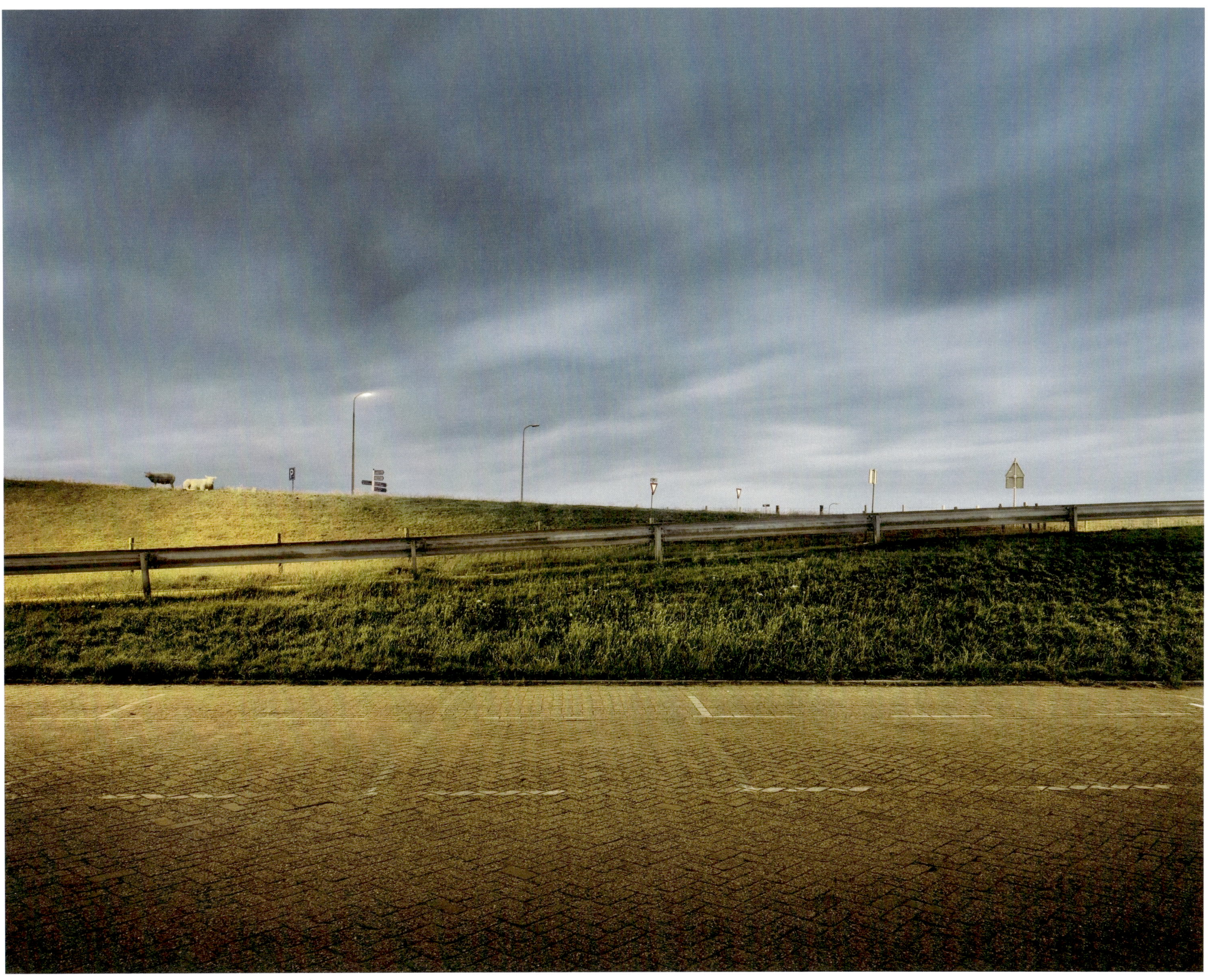

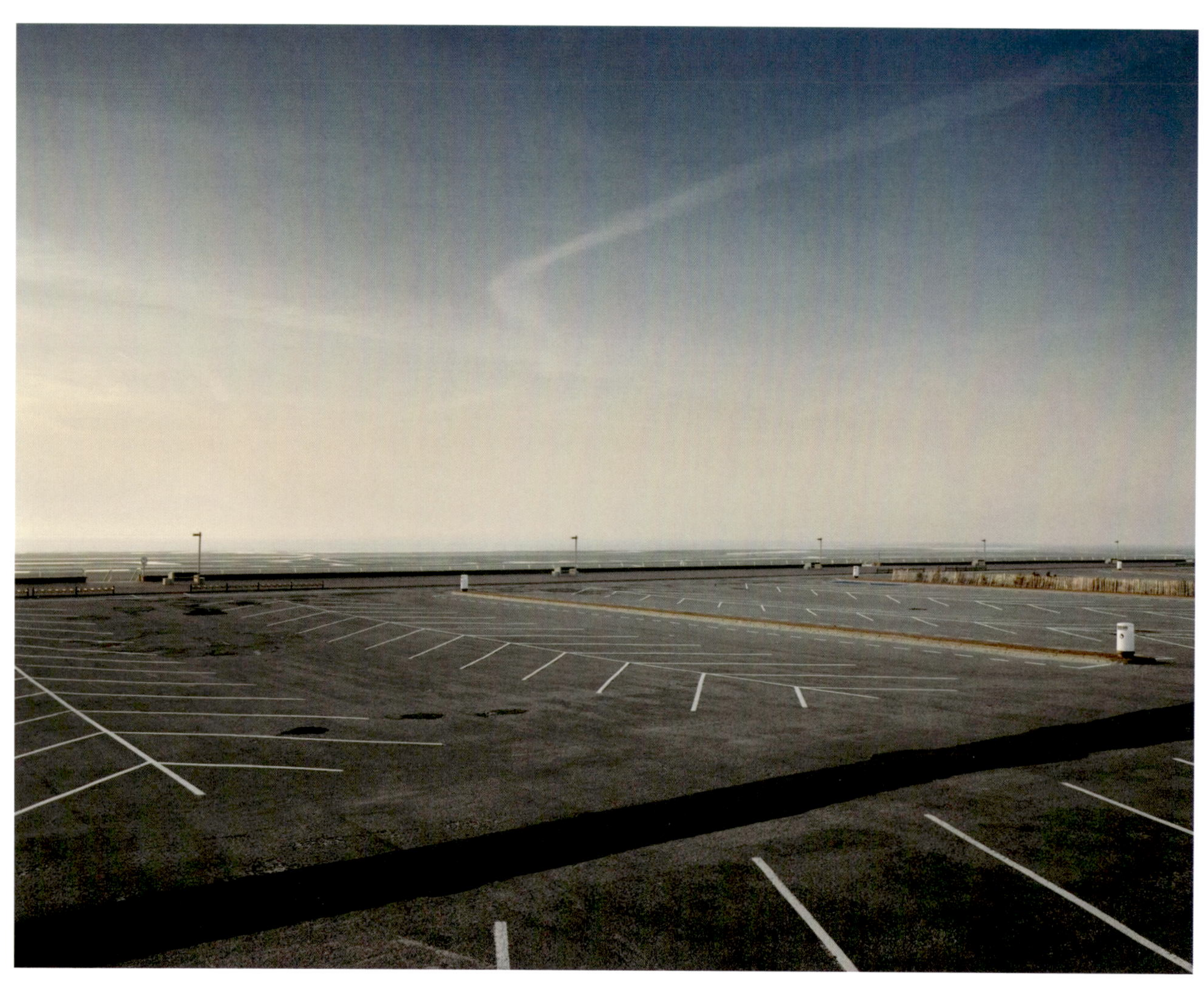

58——2008 LE TOUQUET, FRANCE
59——2008 CALAIS, FRANCE

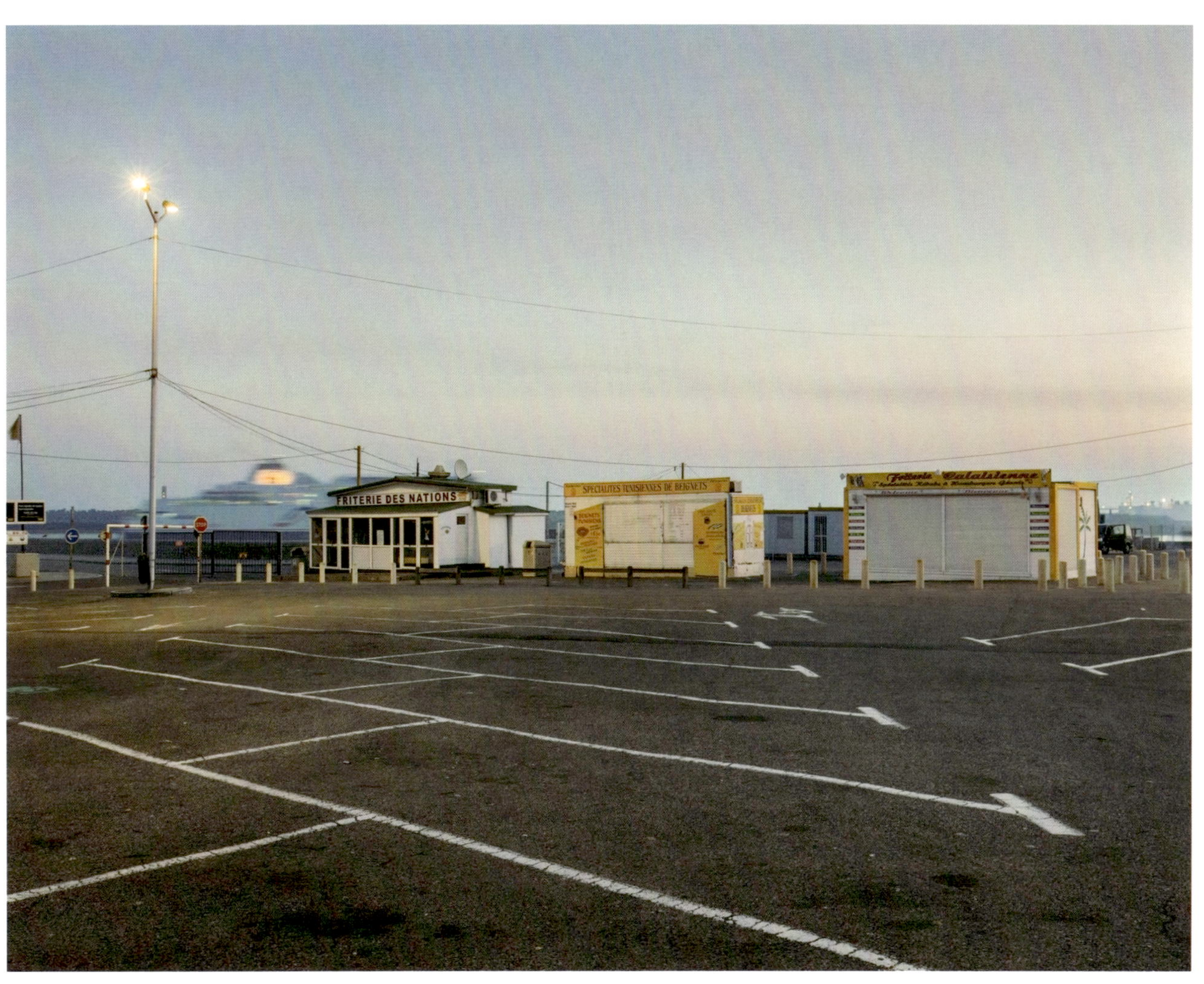
FRITERIE DES NATIONS
SPECIALITES TUNISIENNES DE BEIGNETS
Friterie Calaisienne

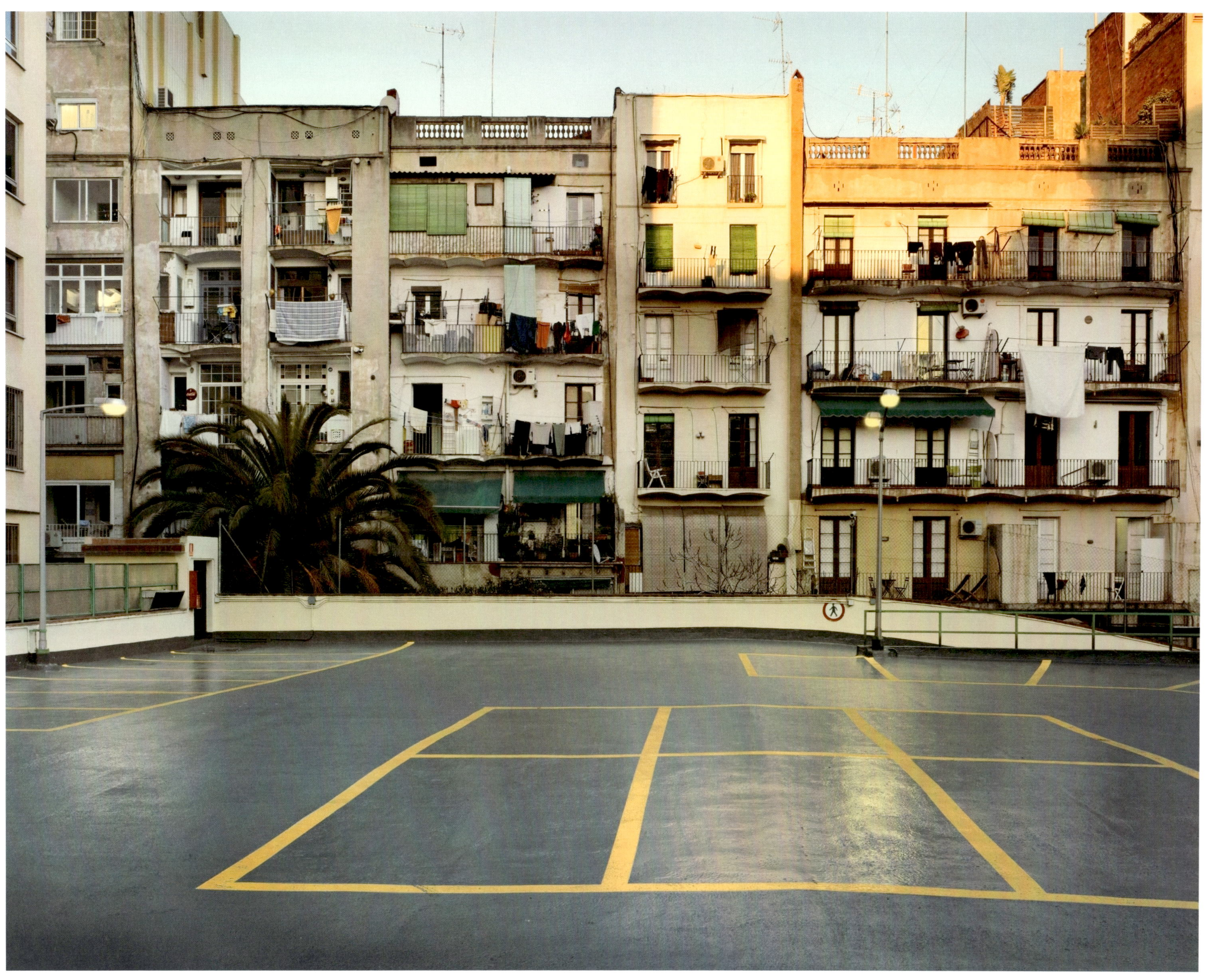

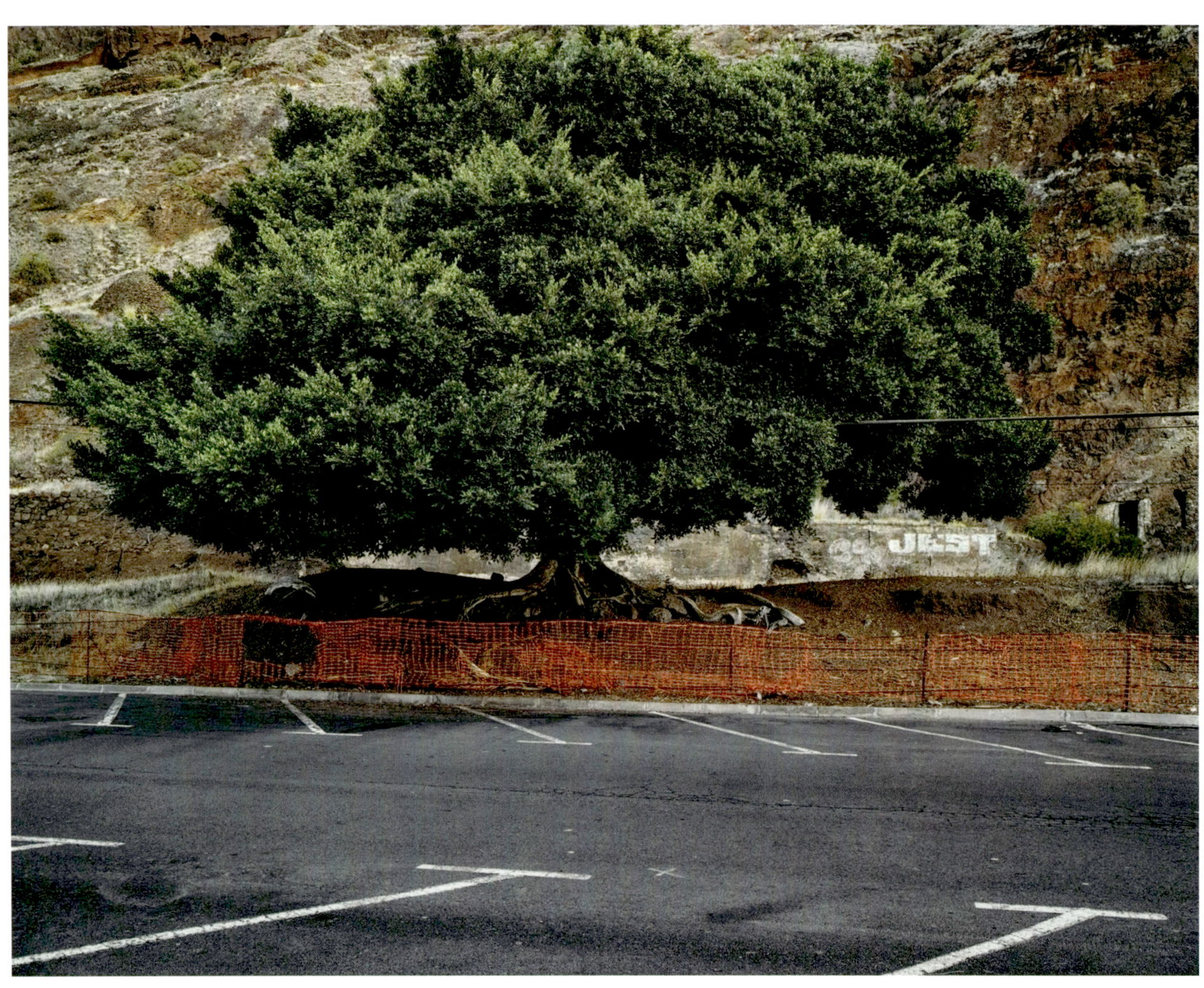
JEST

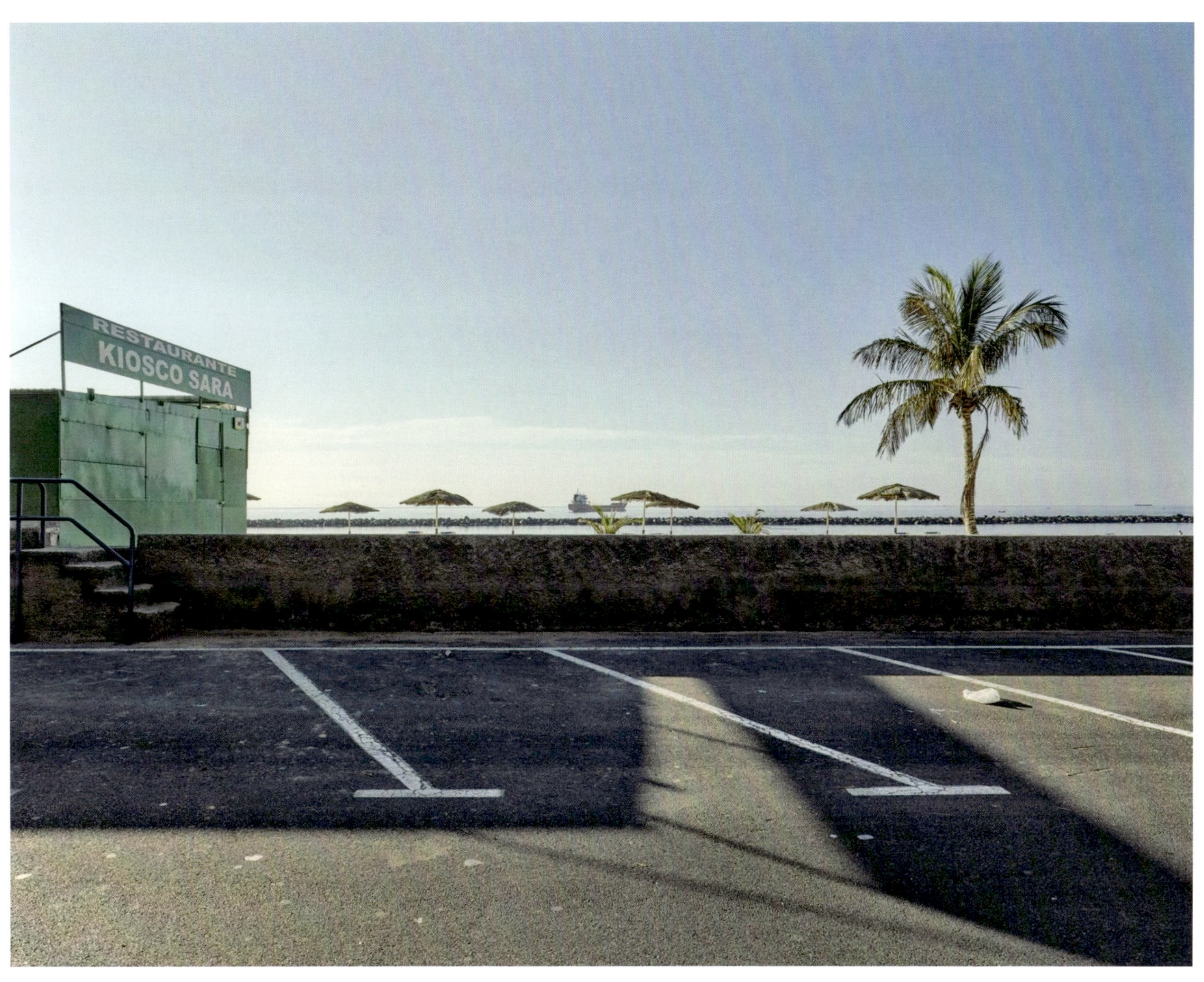

TENERIFE, SPAIN 2013 ——— 61
TENERIFE, SPAIN 2013 ——— 62

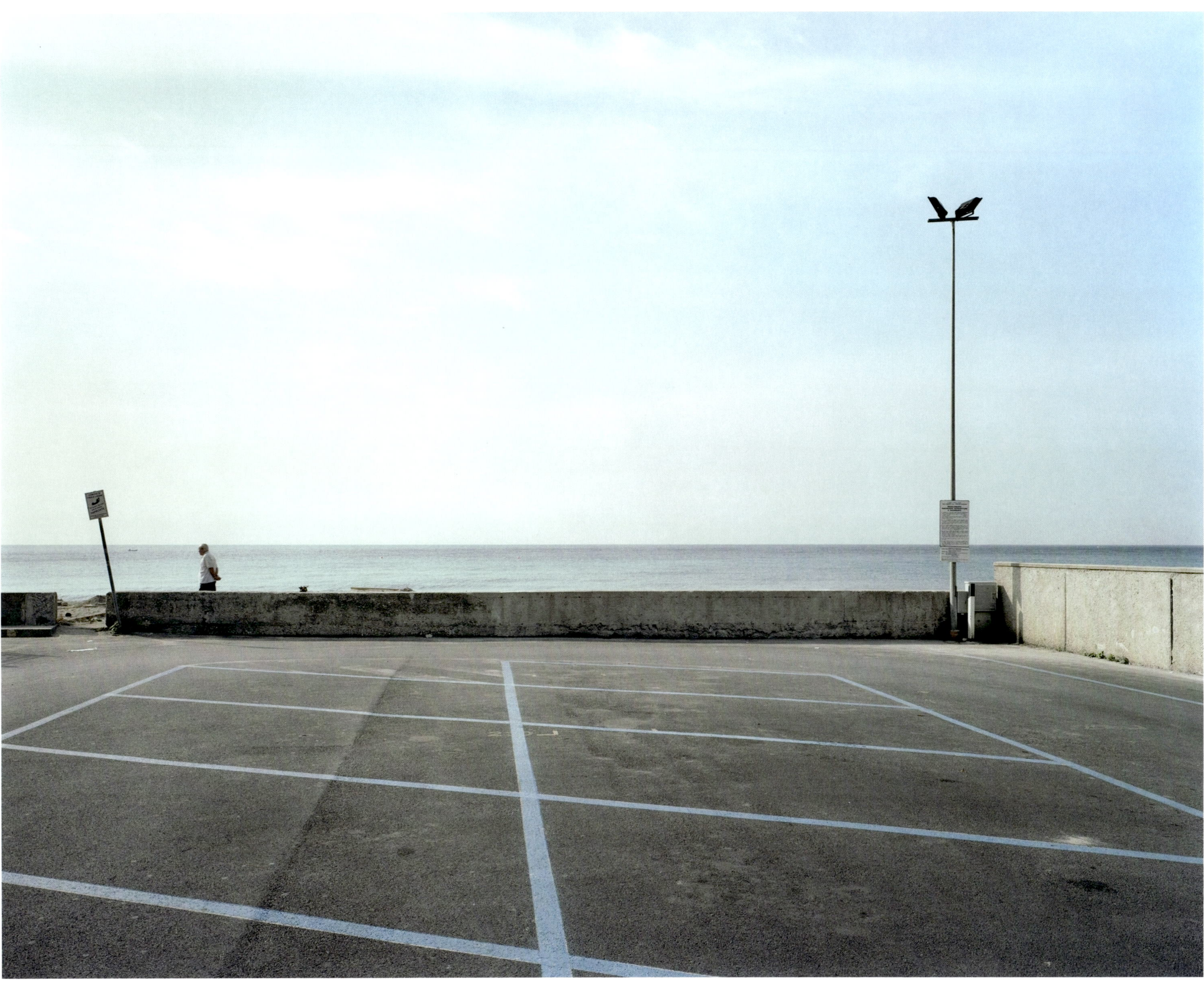

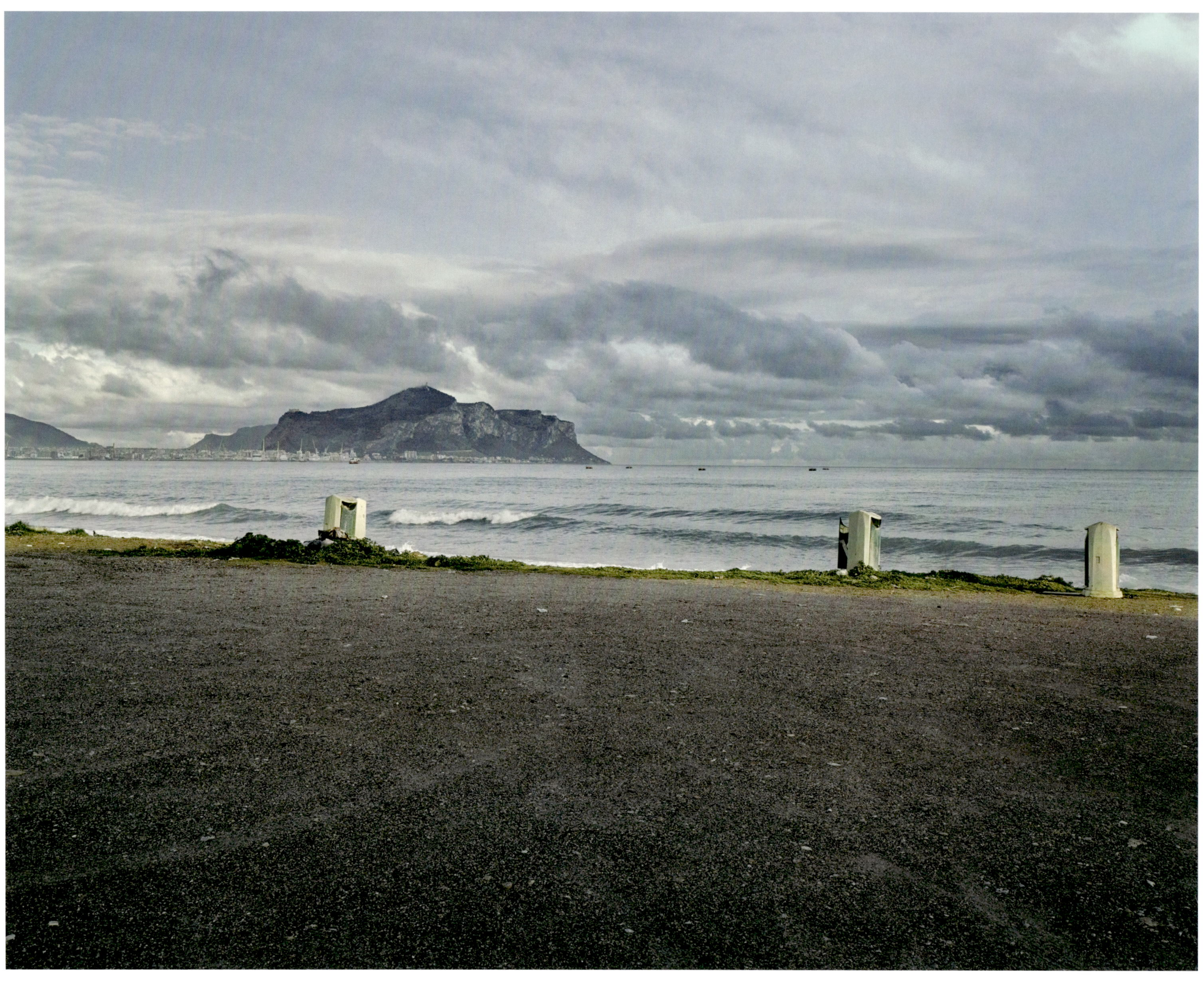

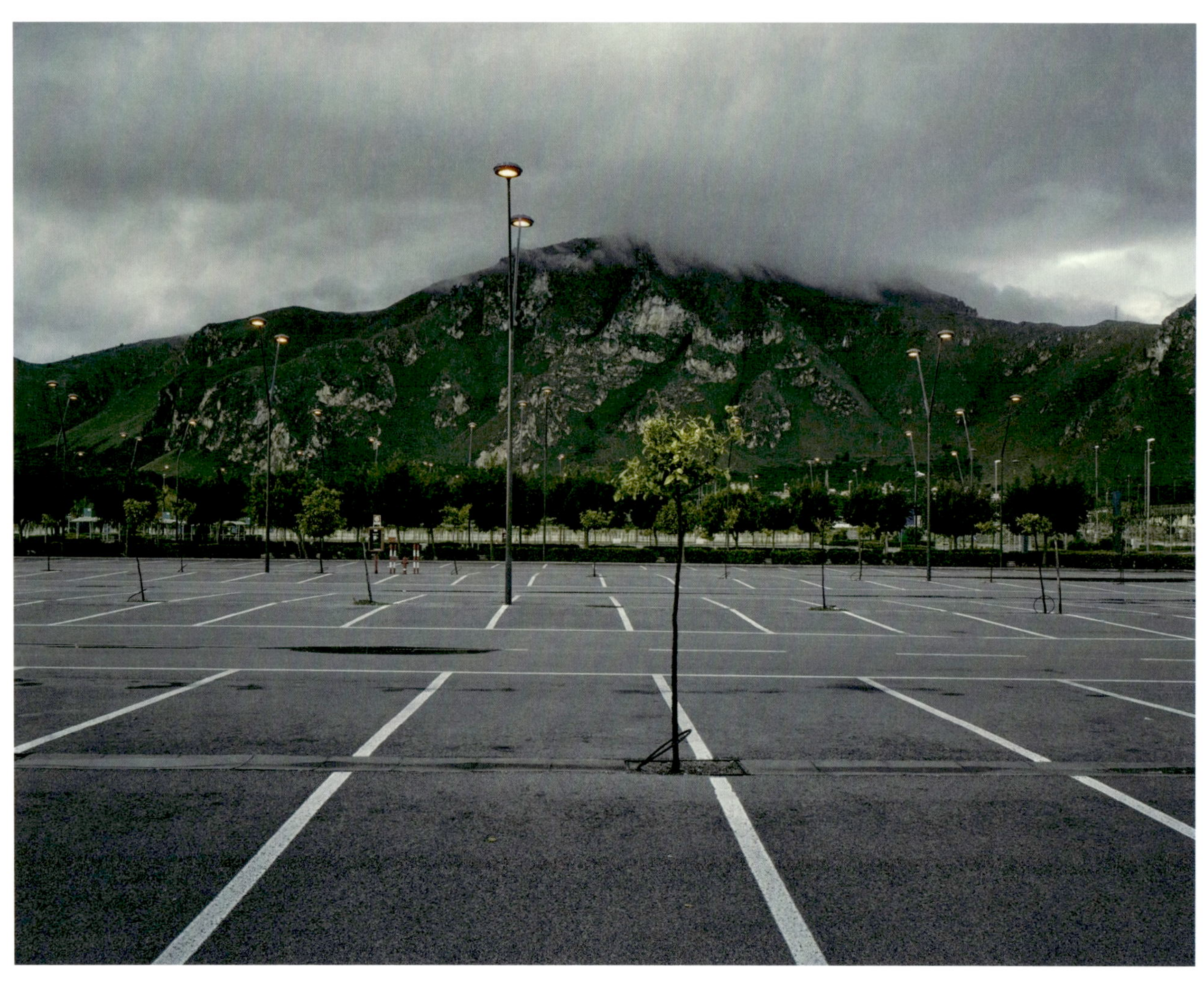

65———2016 PALERMO, ITALY
66———2016 PALERMO, ITALY

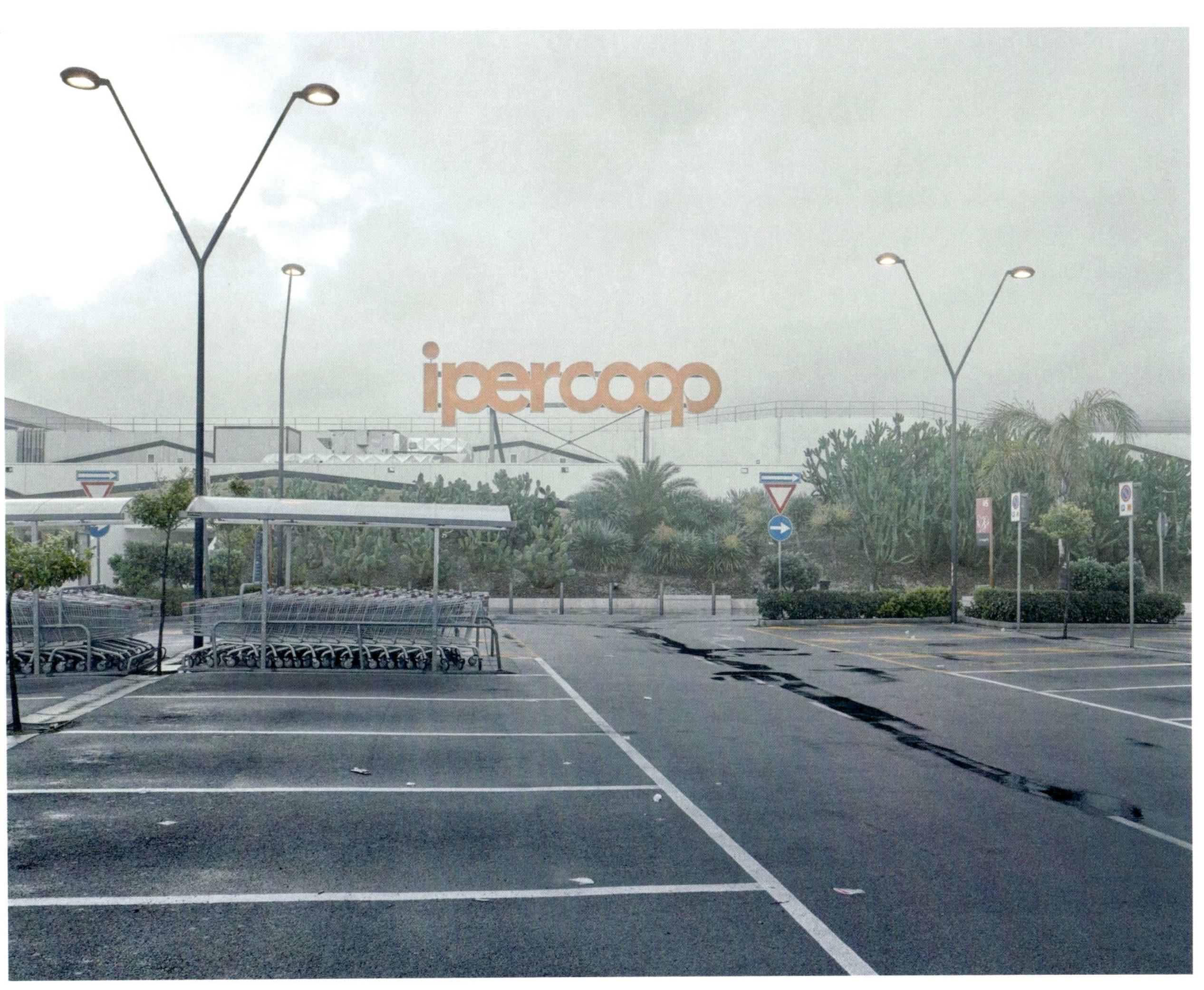
ipercoop

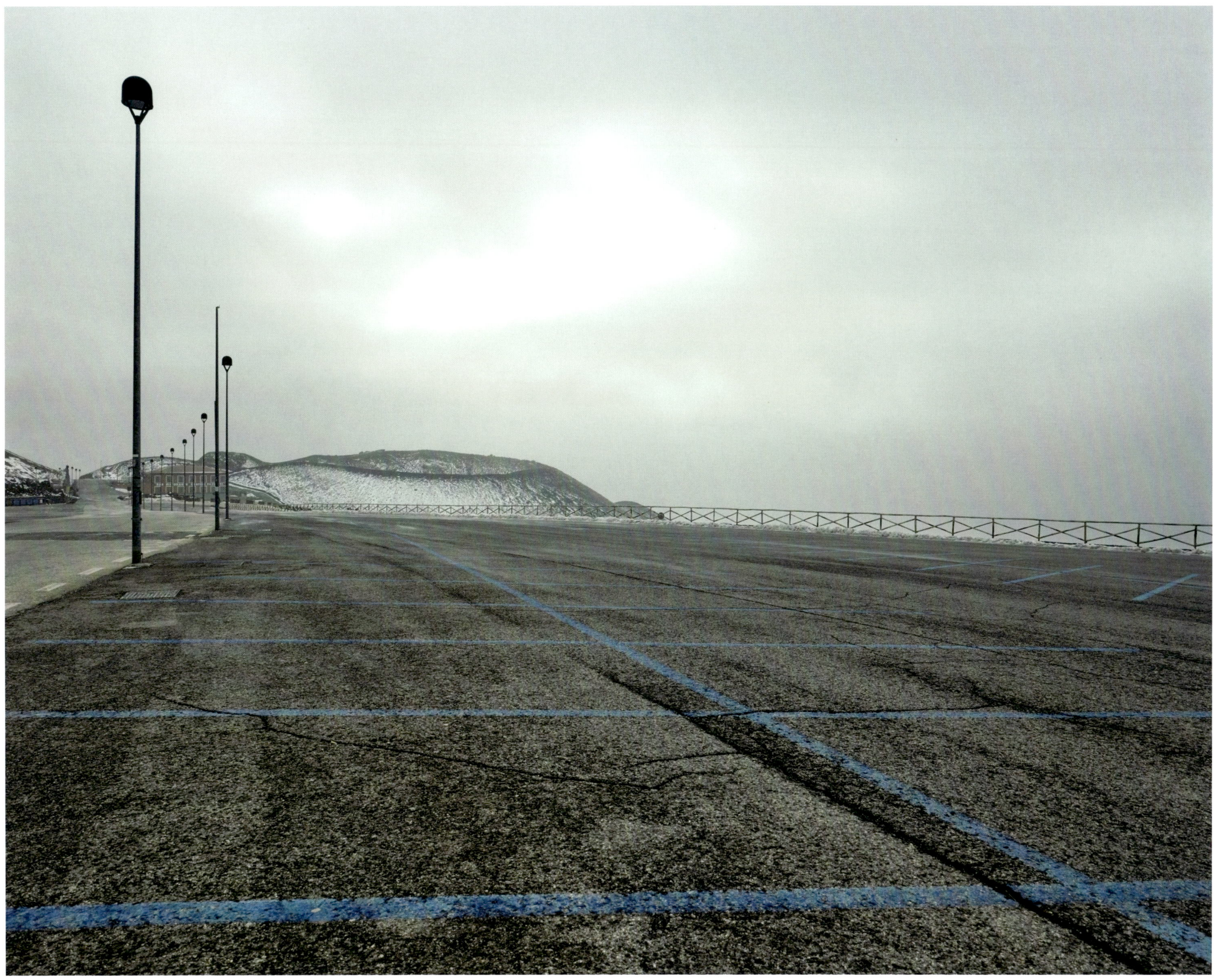

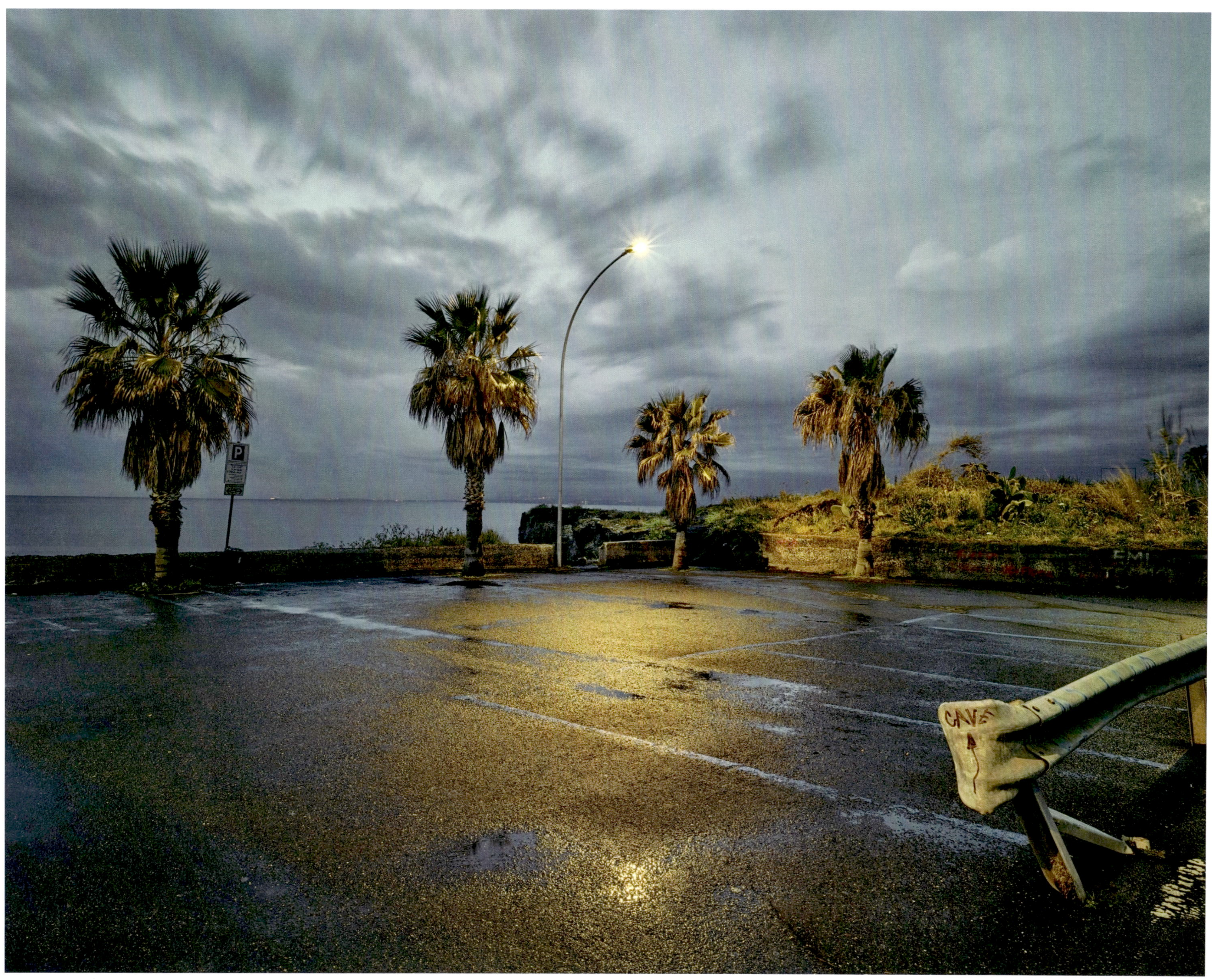
P
CAVE

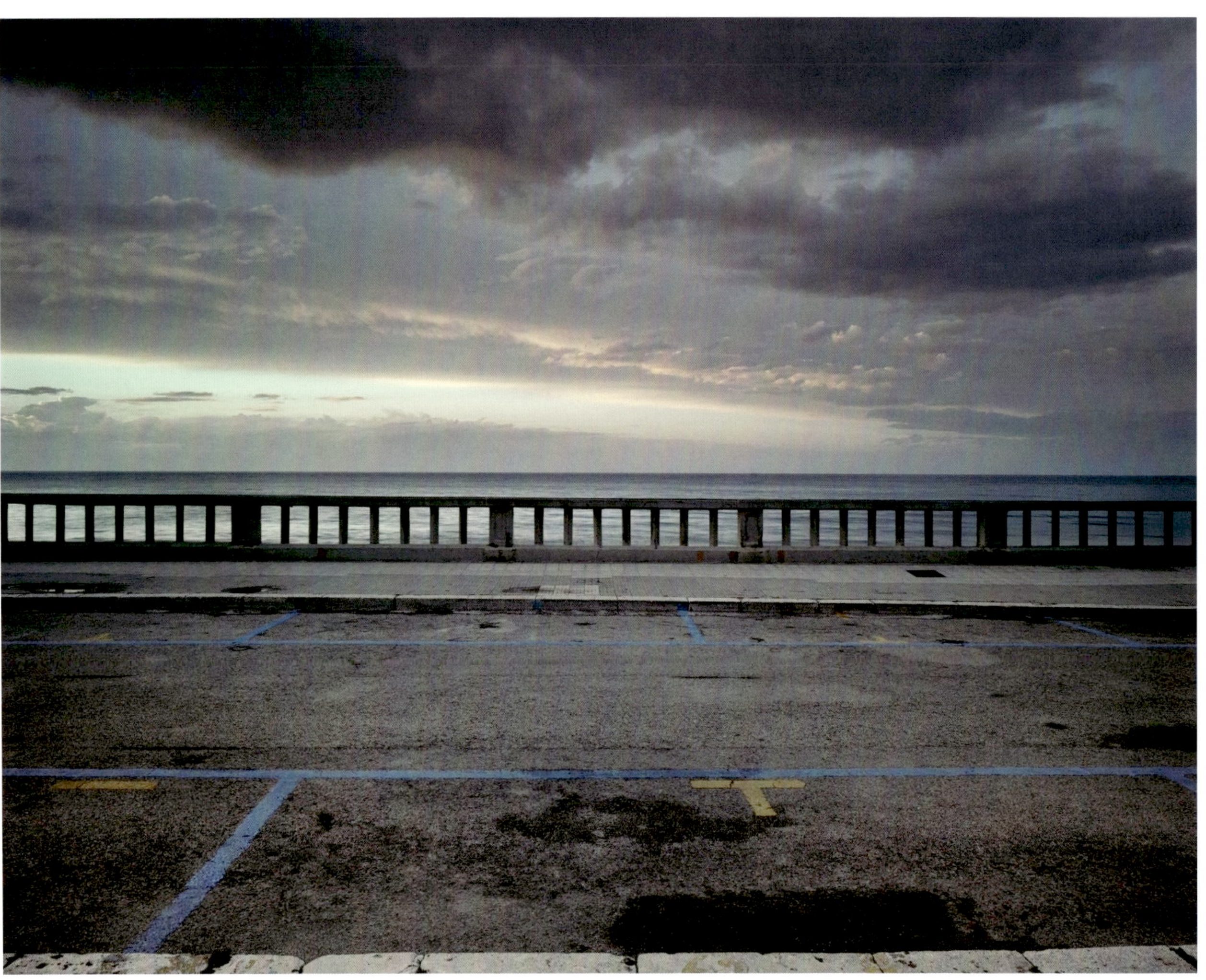

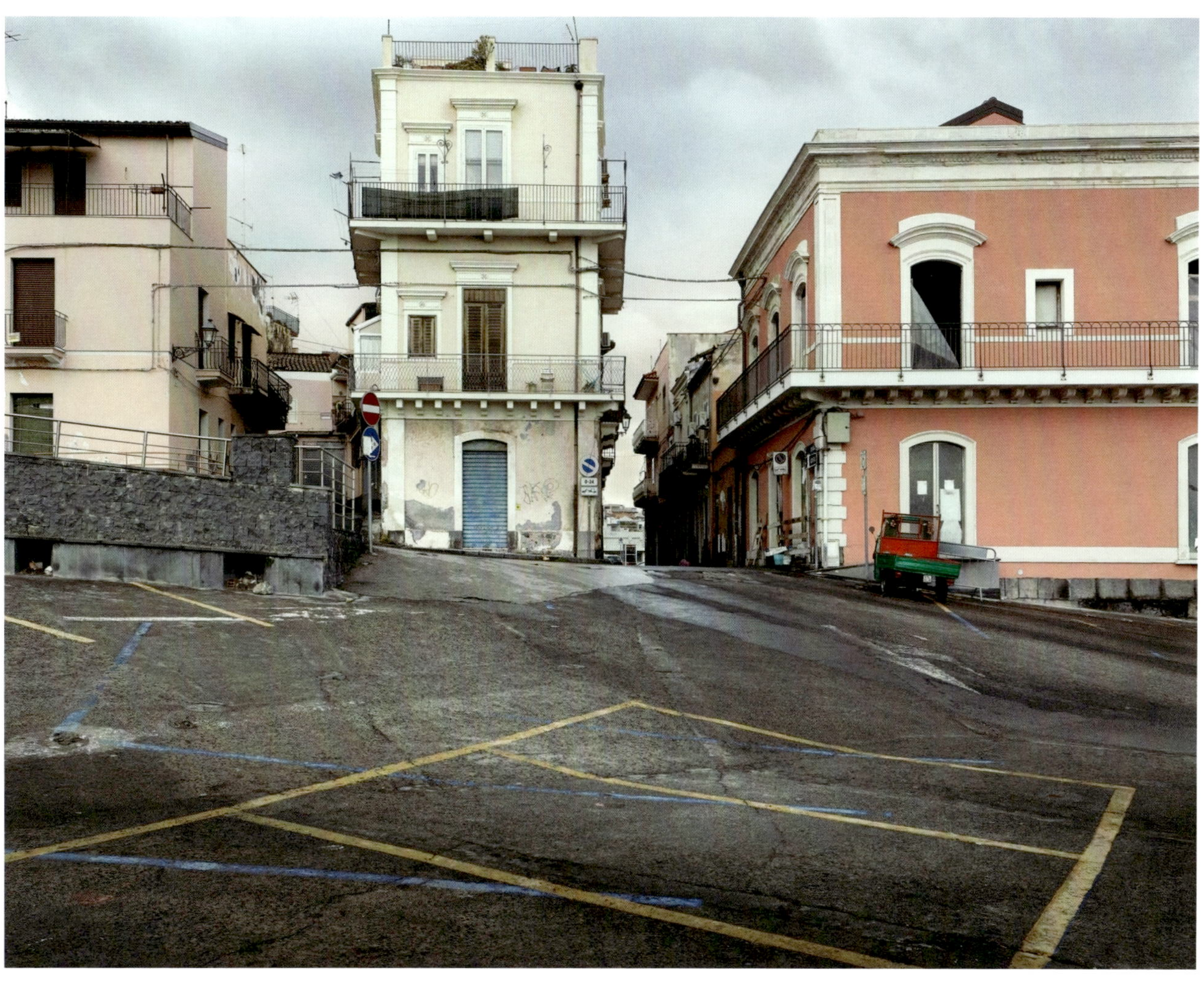

CEFALU, ITALY 2016 — 69
ACI CASTELLO, ITALY 2016 — 70

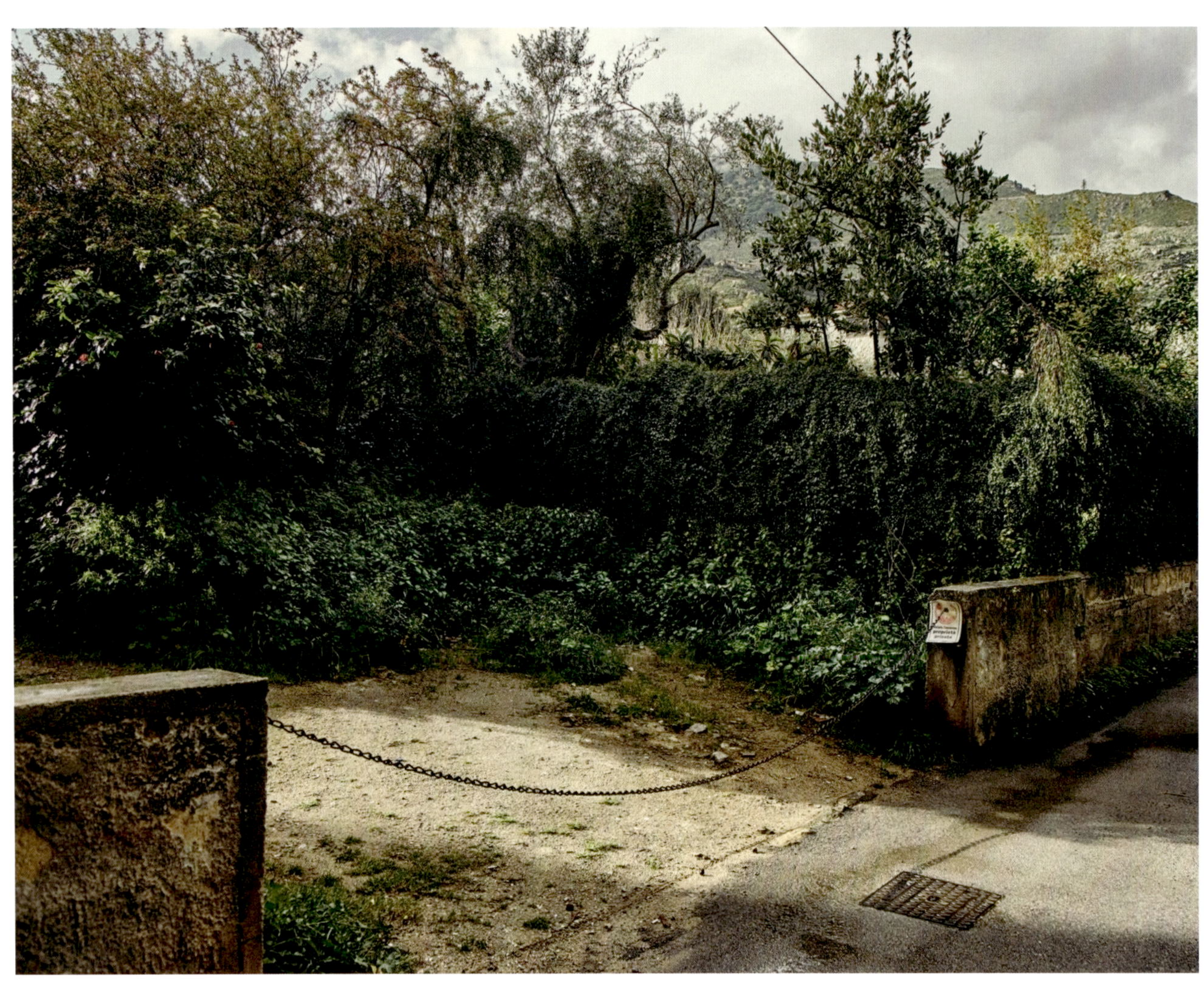

71———2016 PALERMO, ITALY
72———2016 PALERMO, ITALY

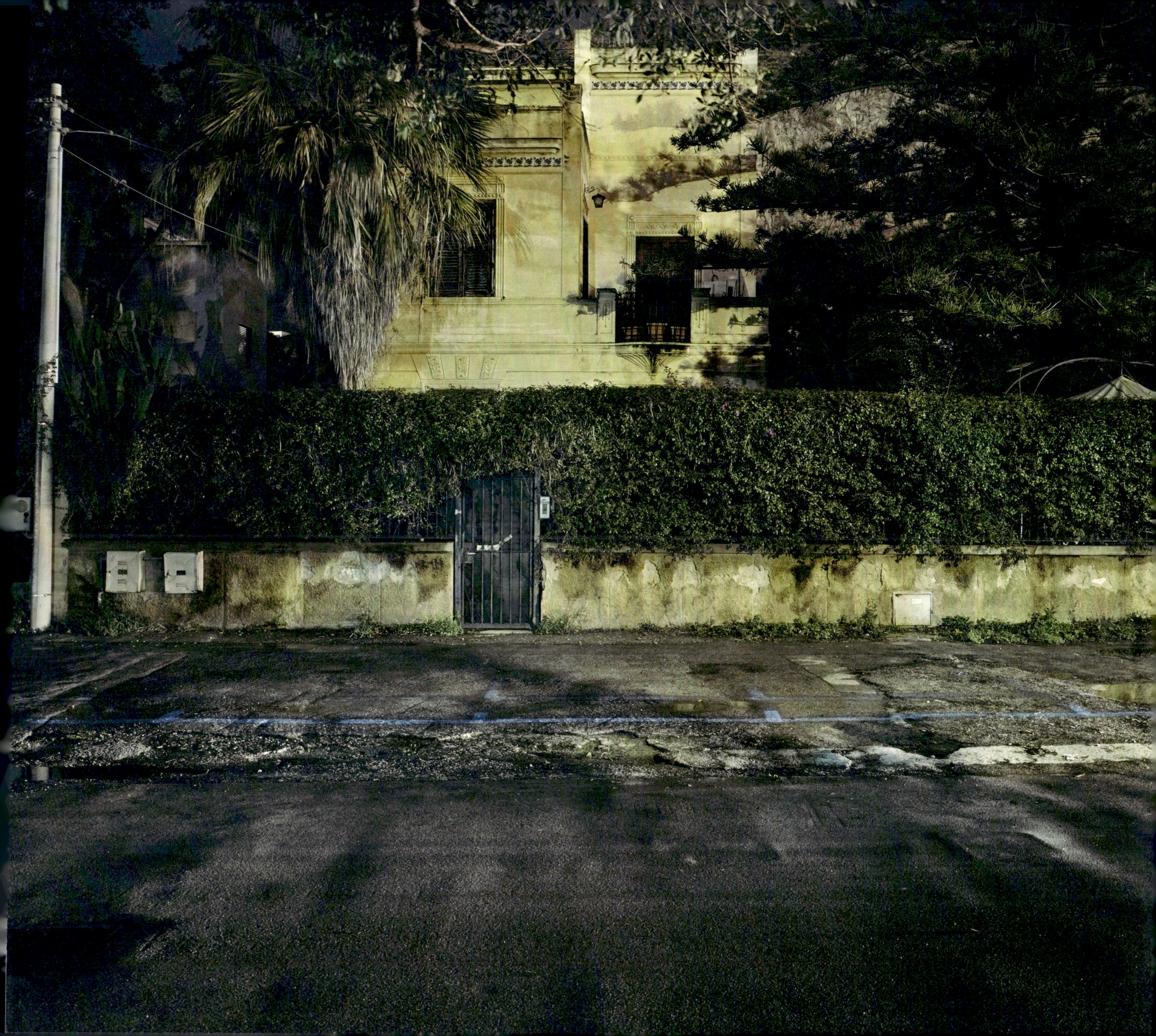

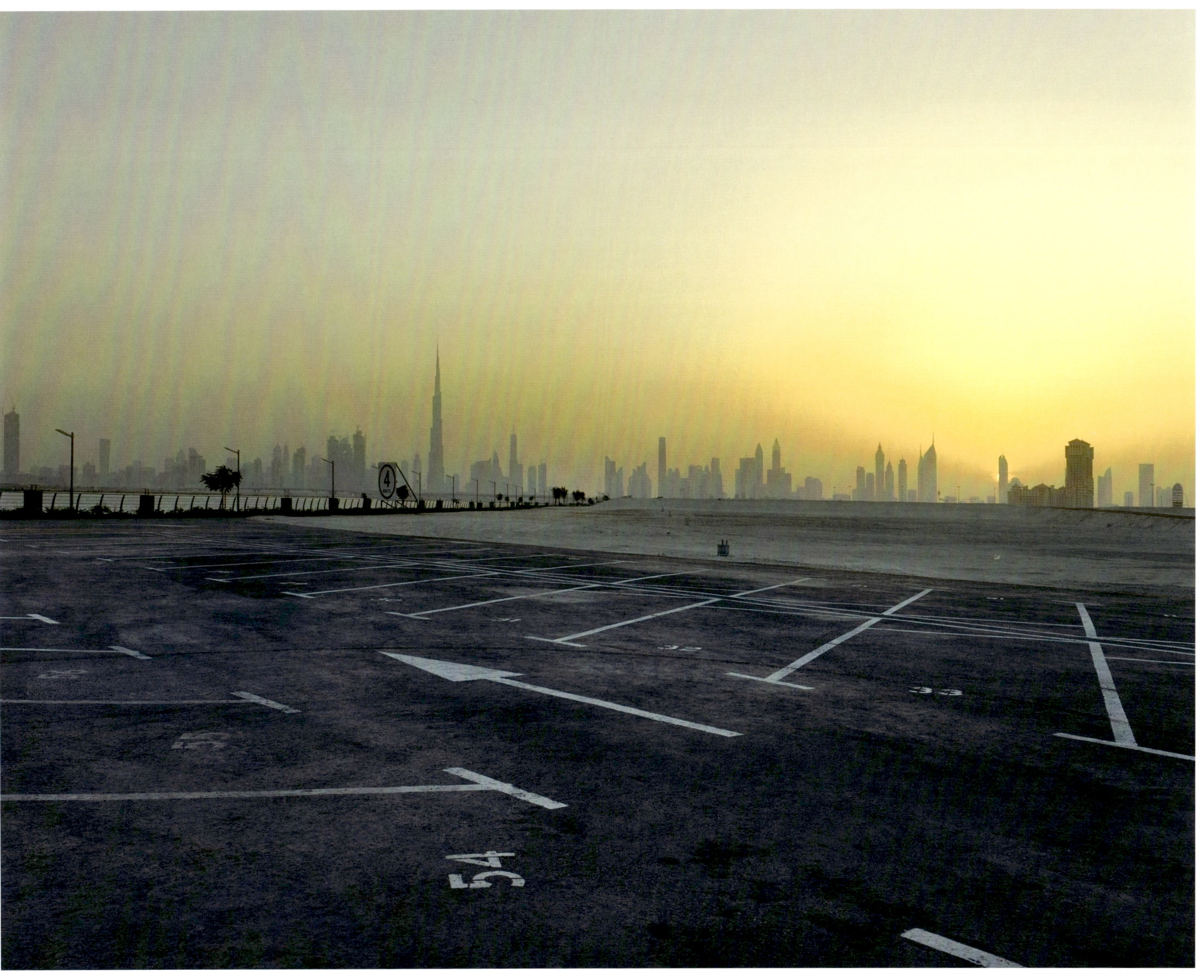
54

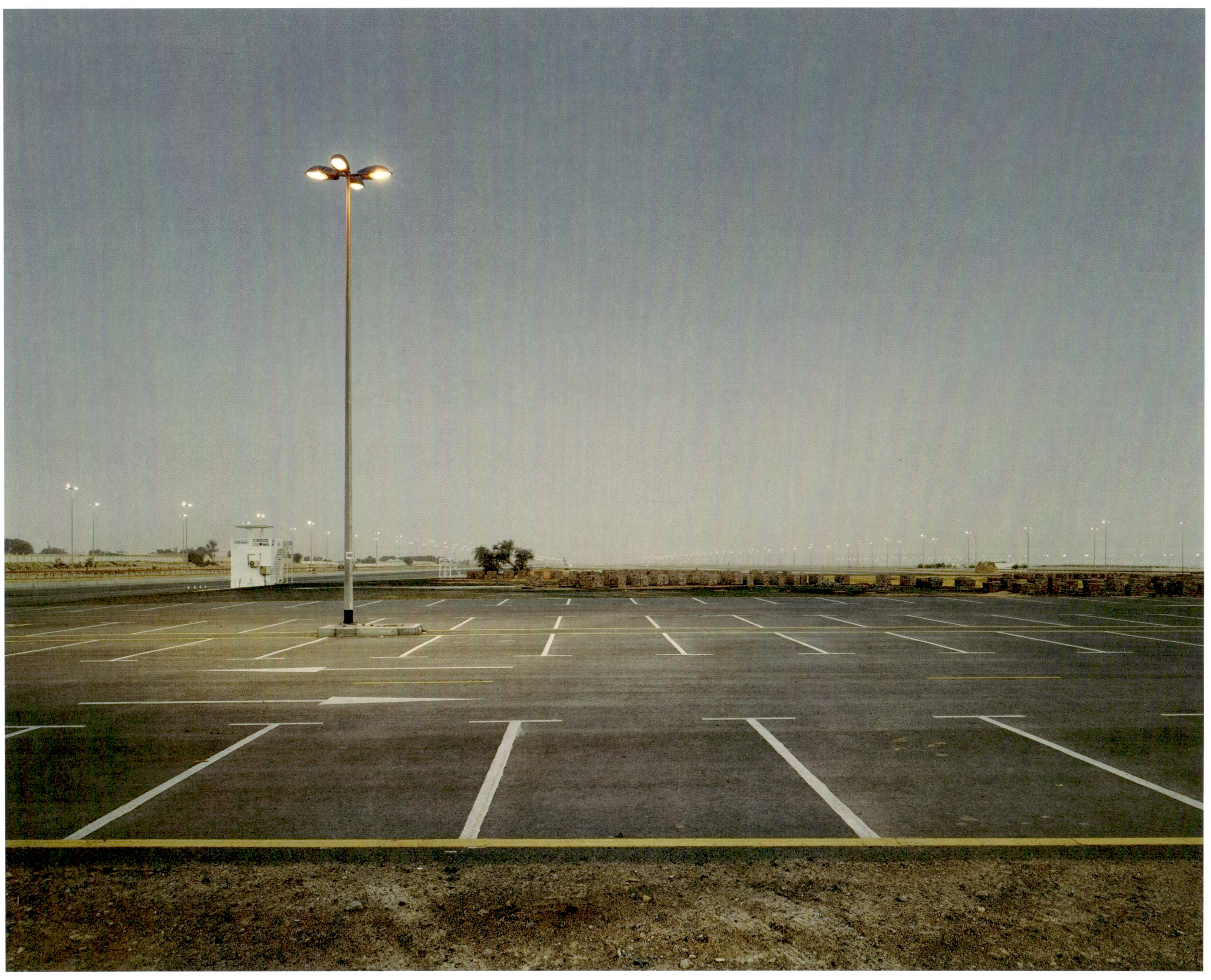

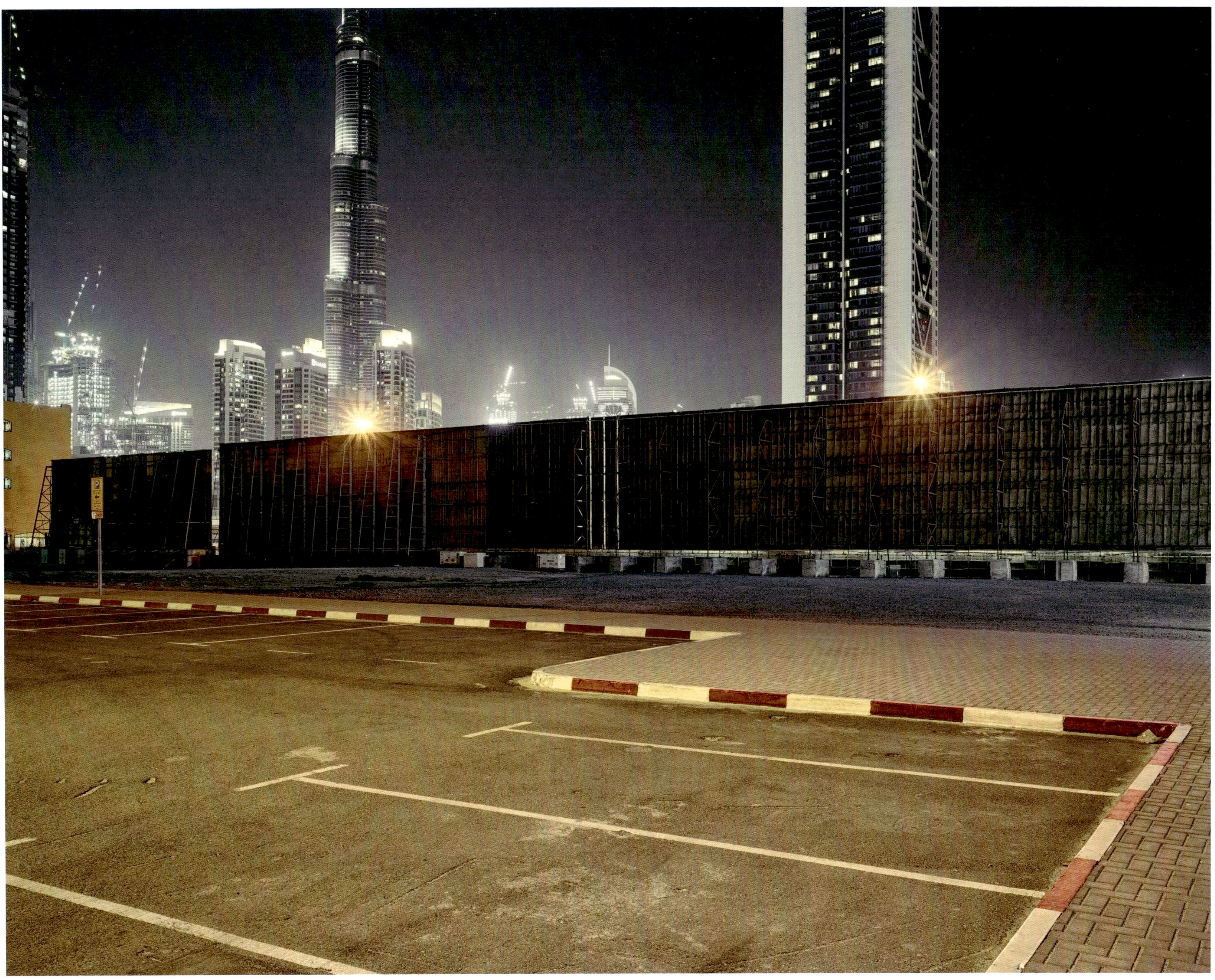

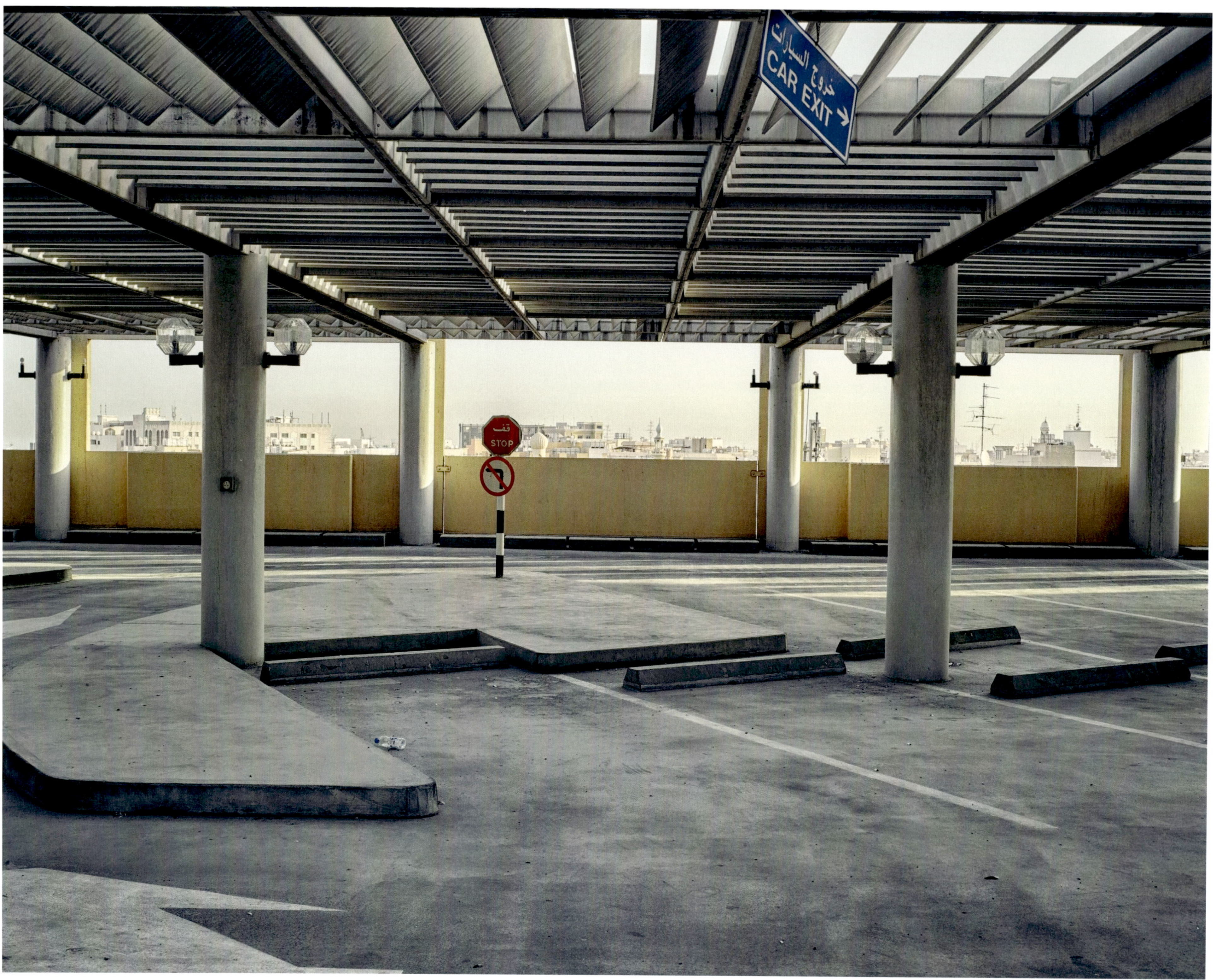

خروج السيارات
CAR EXIT
قف
STOP

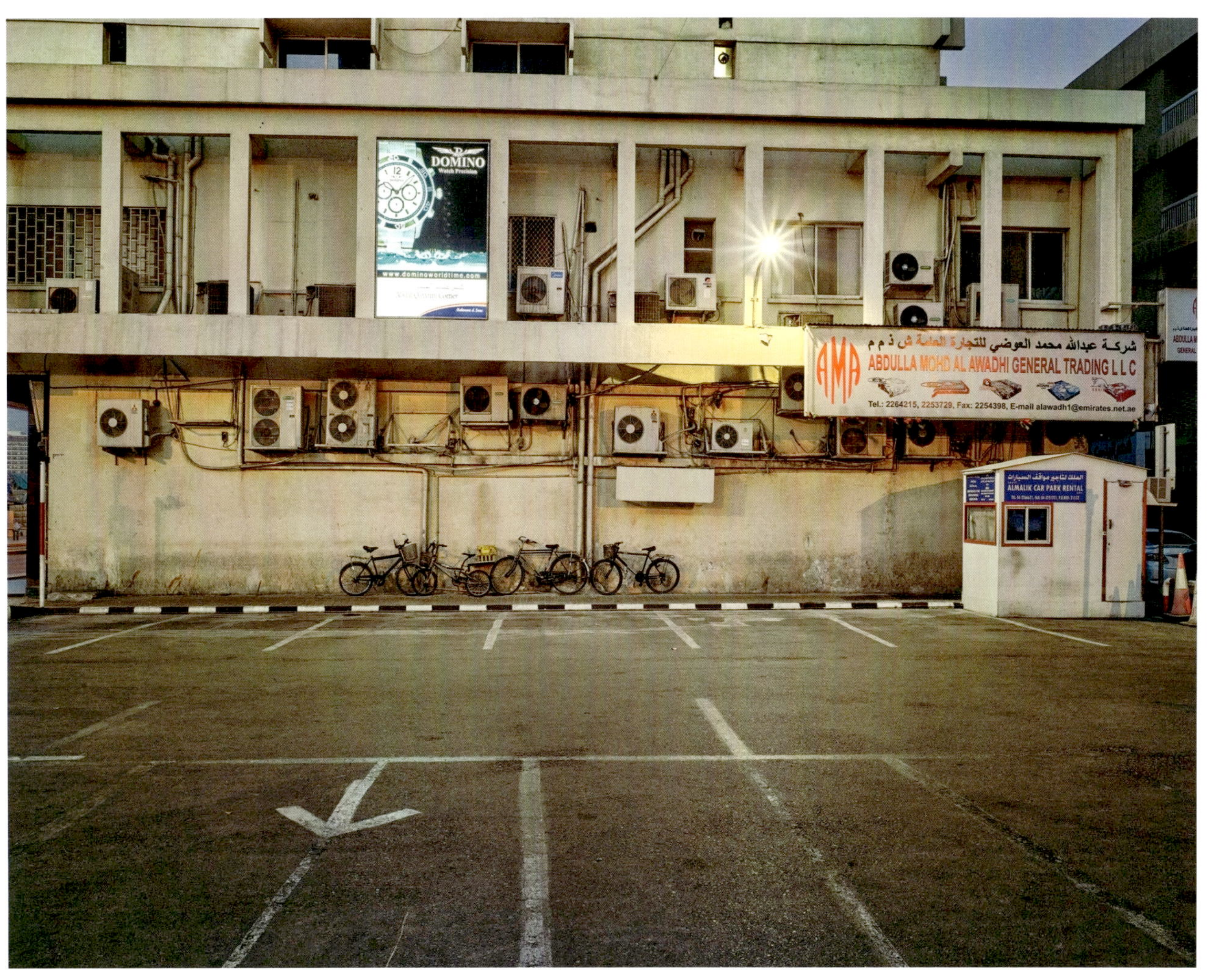

DUBAI, UNITED ARAB EMIRATES 2016 ——— 76
DUBAI, UNITED ARAB EMIRATES 2016 ——— 77

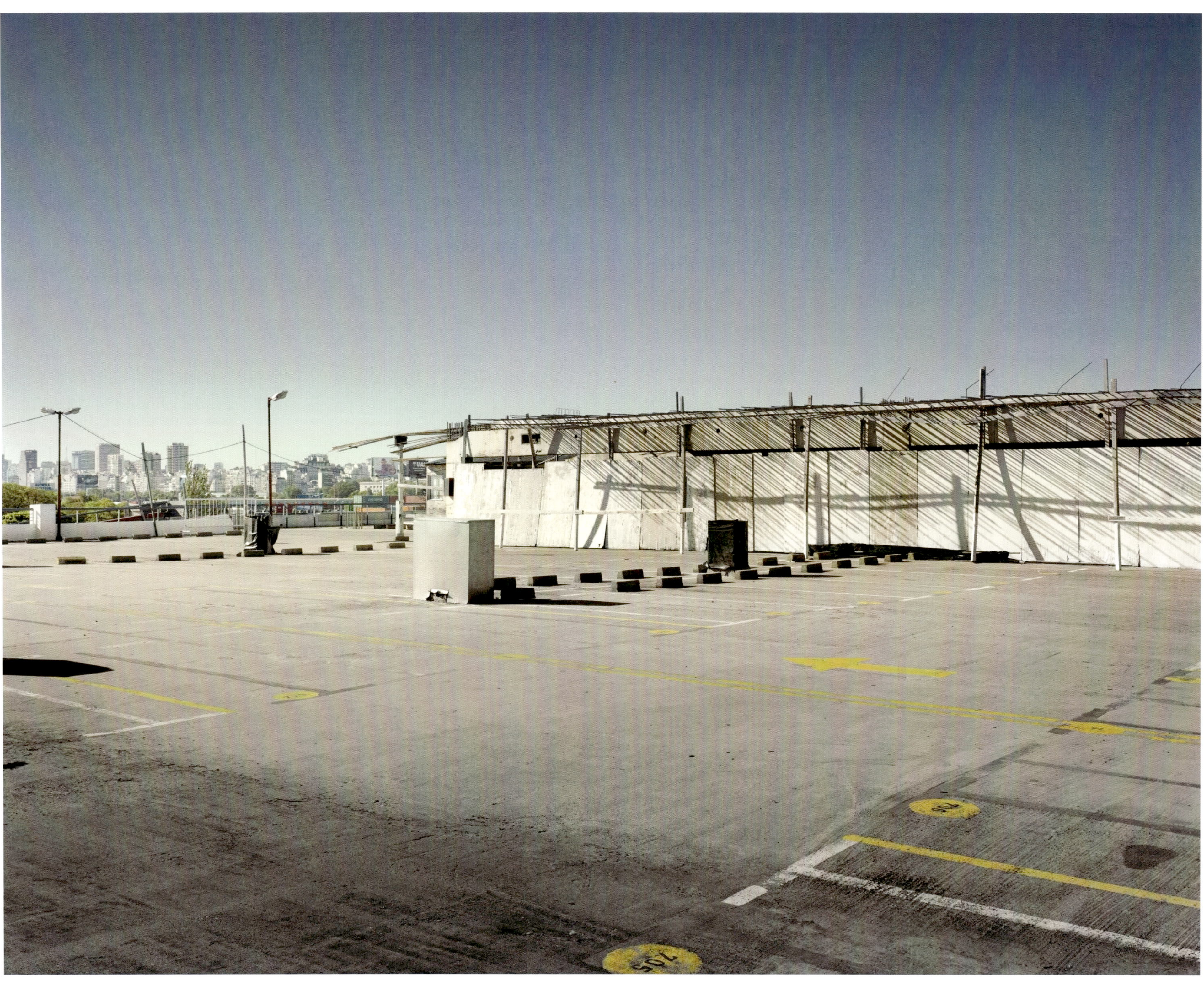

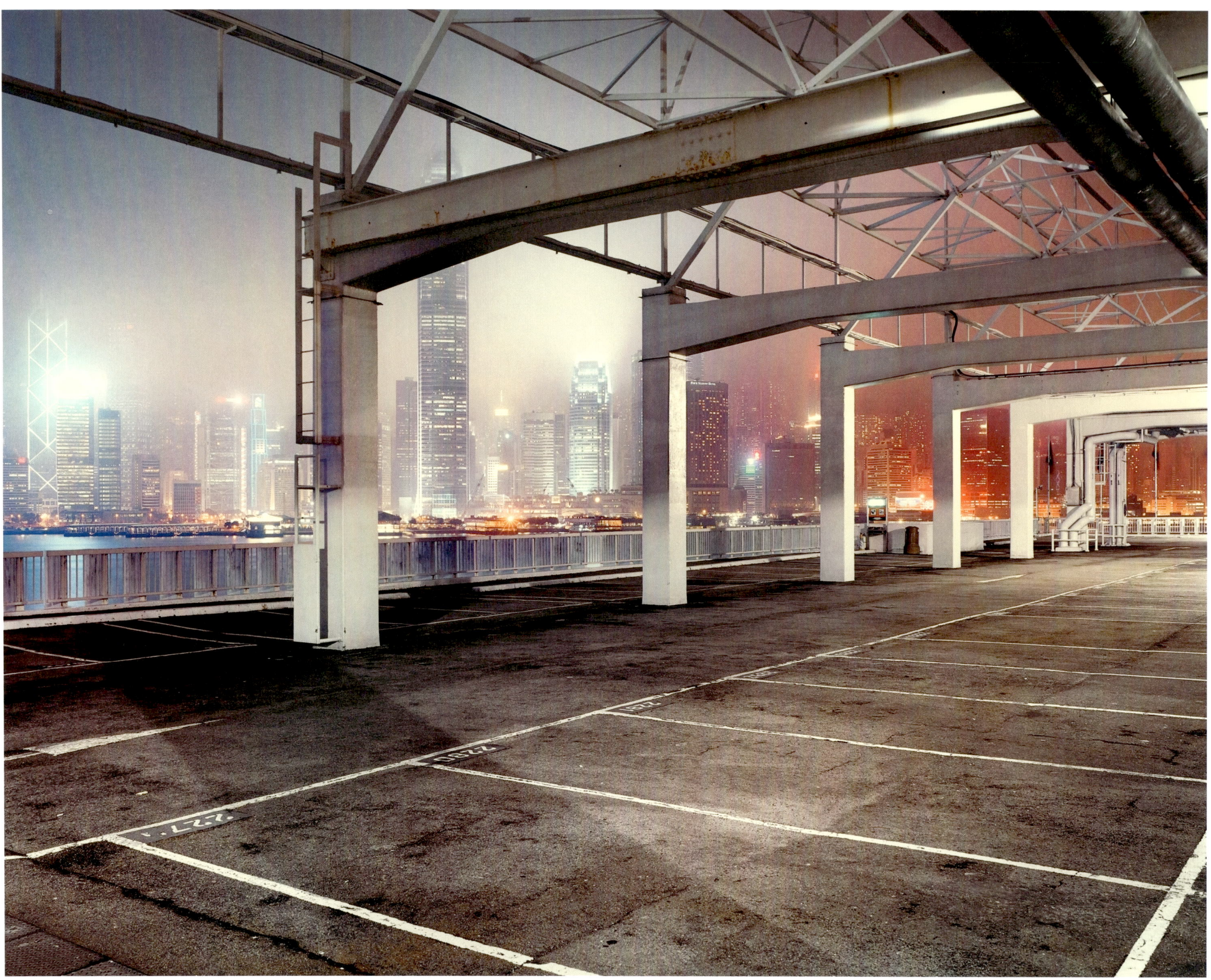

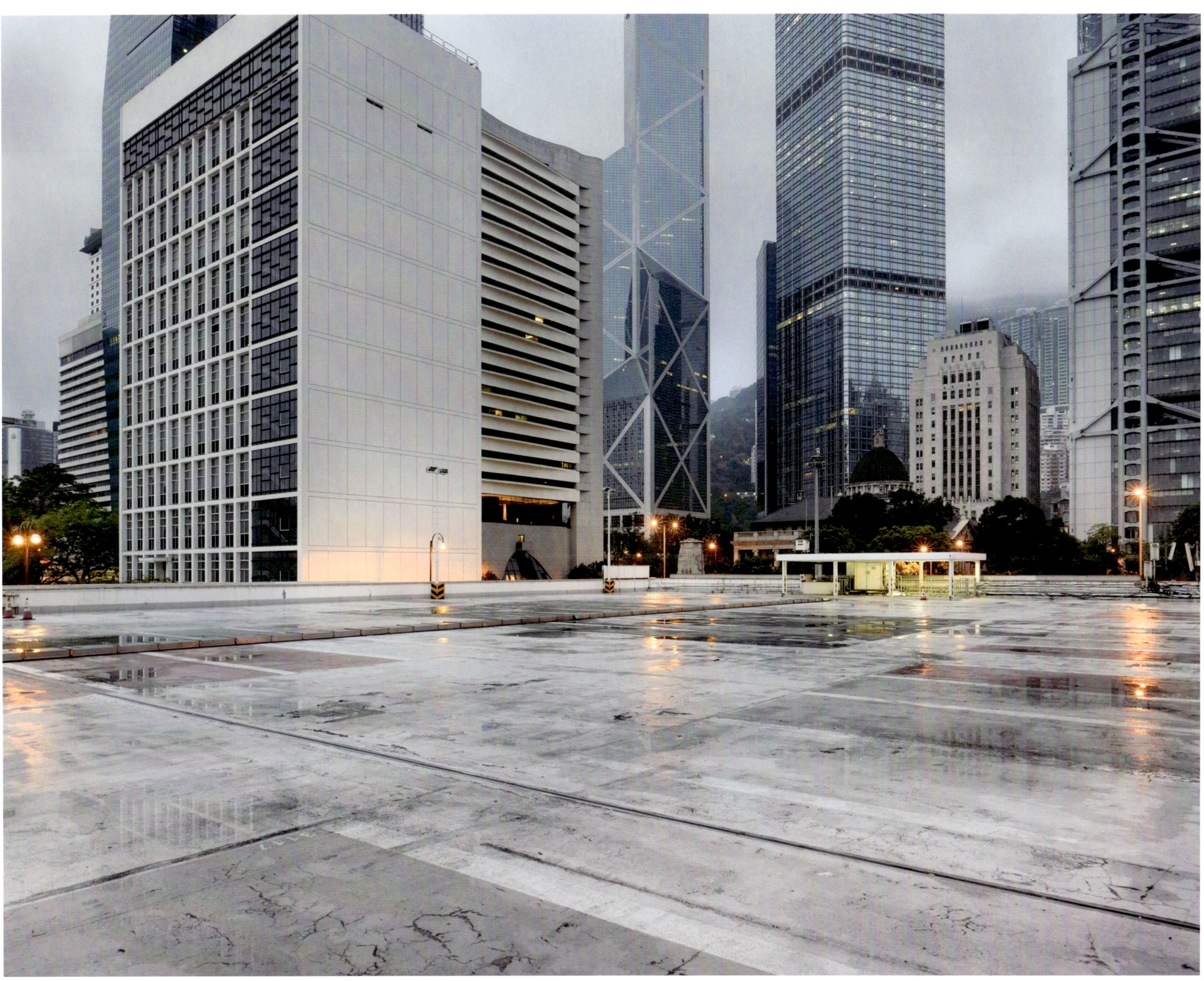

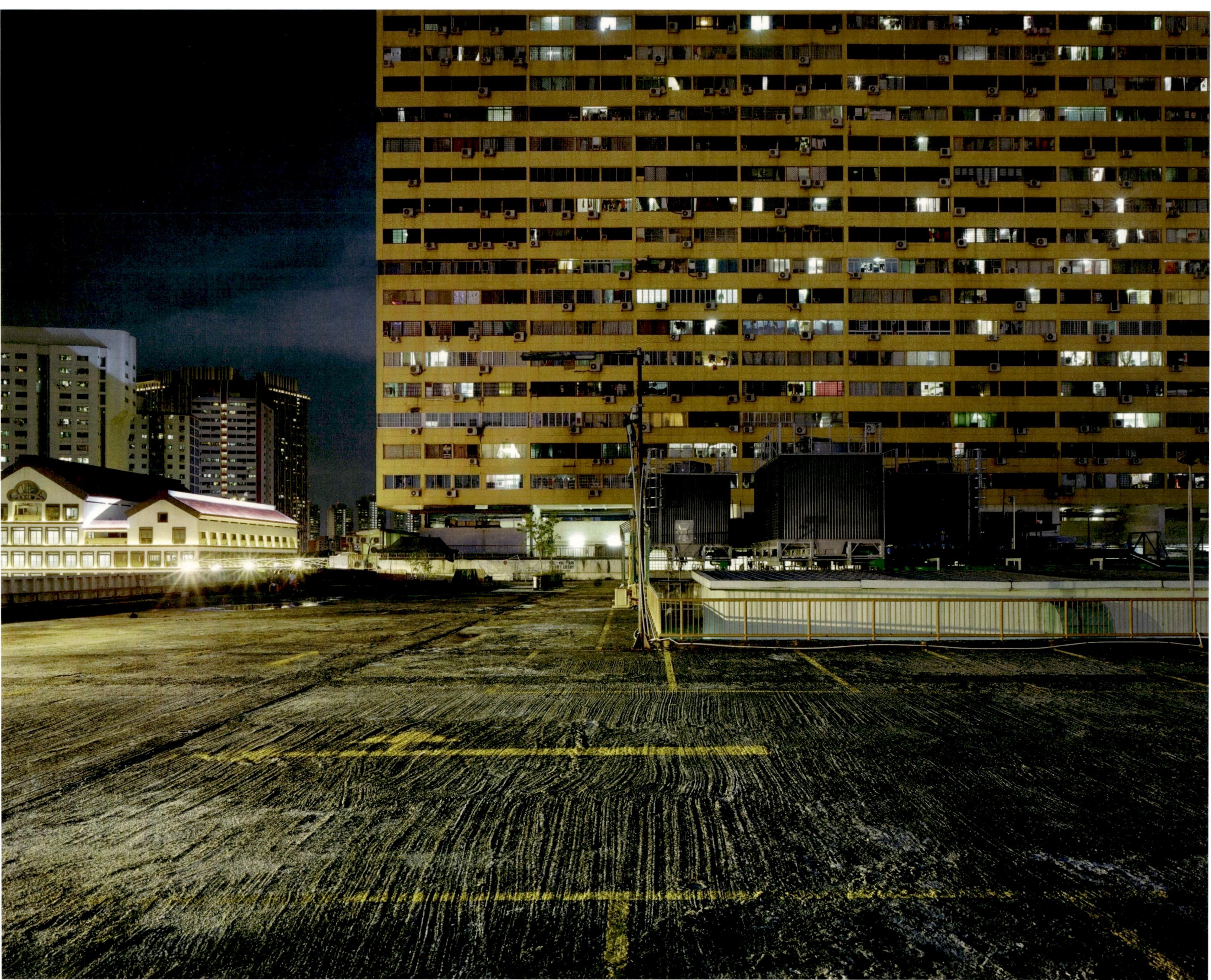

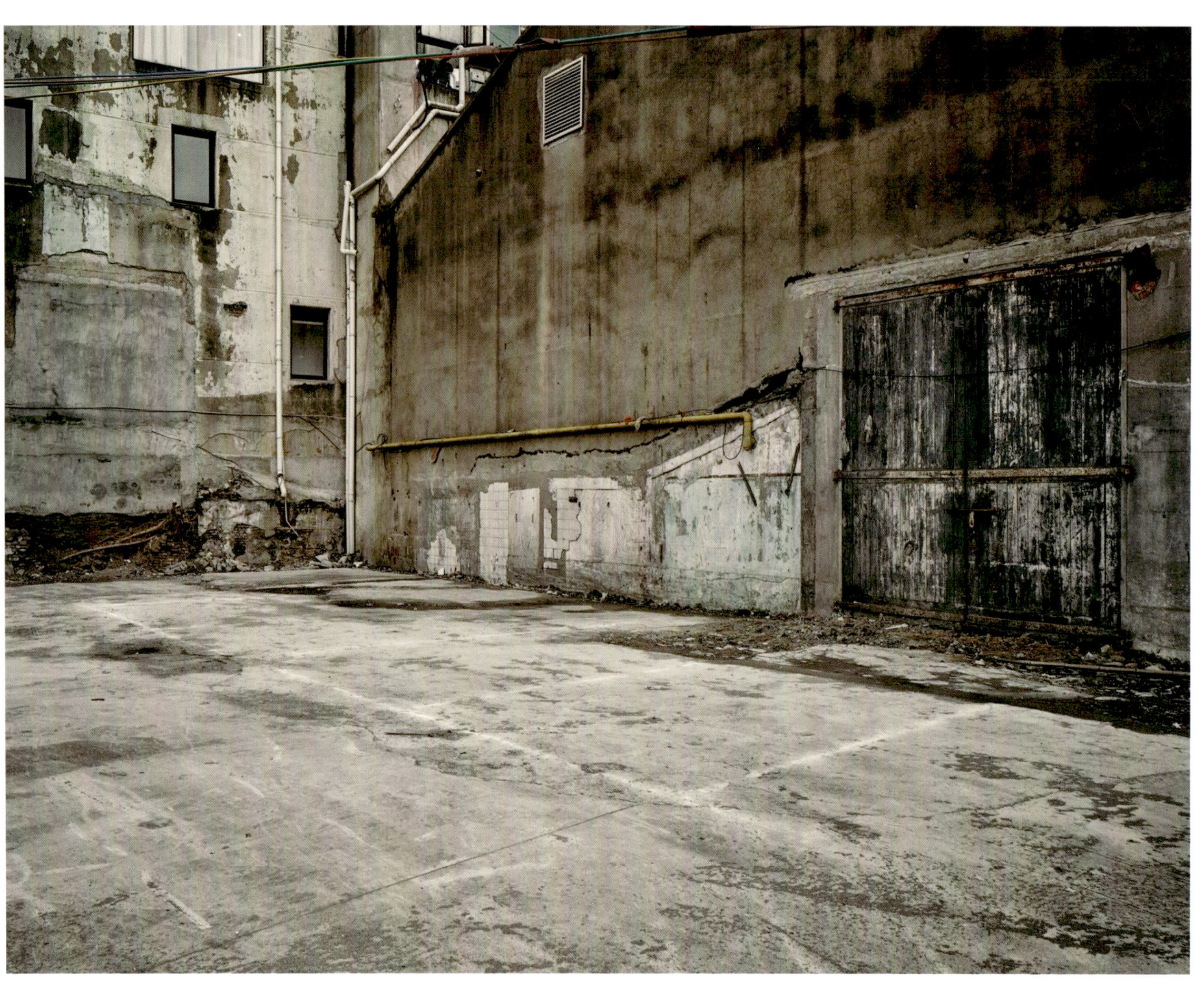

82________2016 SHANGHAI, CHINA
83________2016 SHANGHAI, CHINA

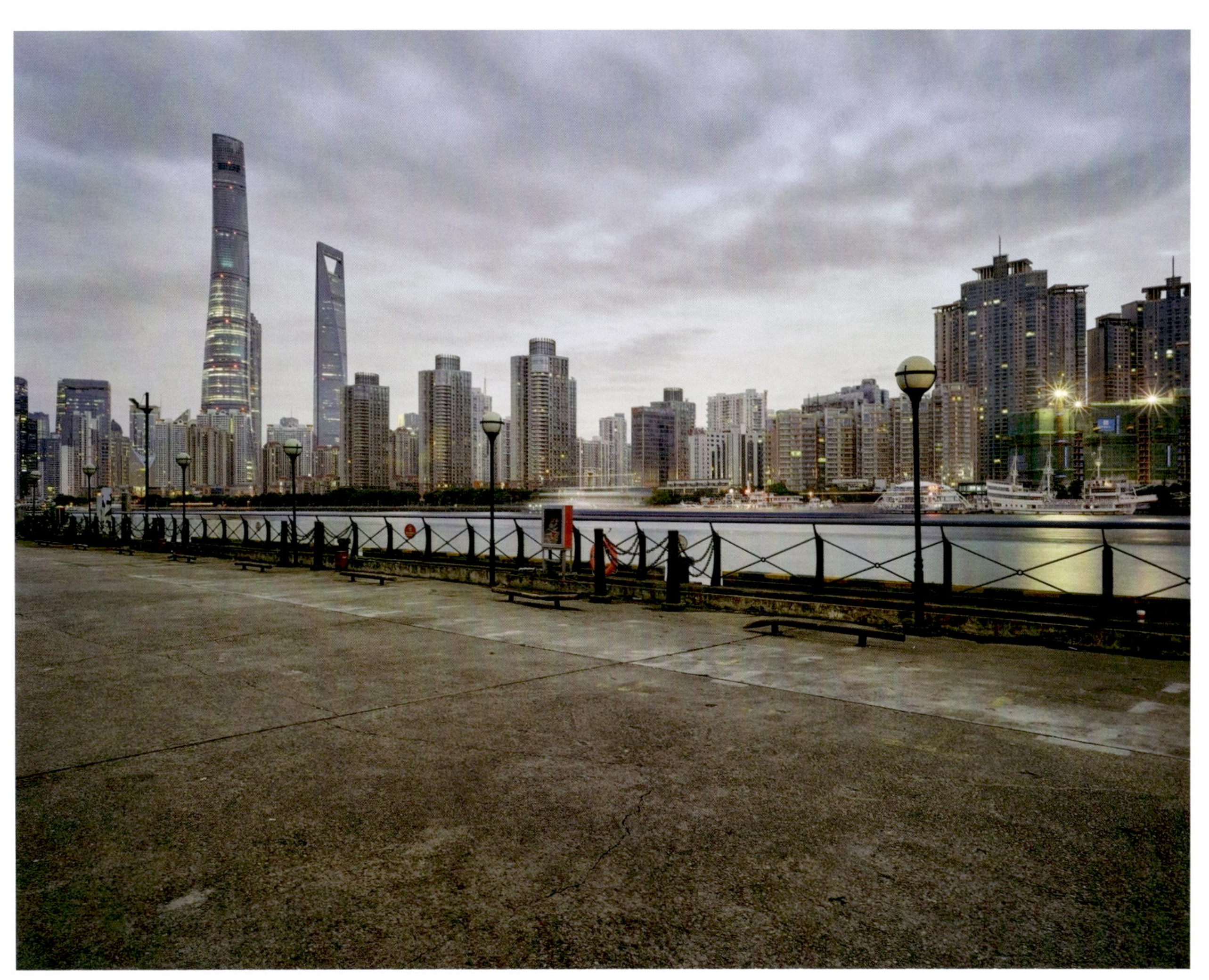

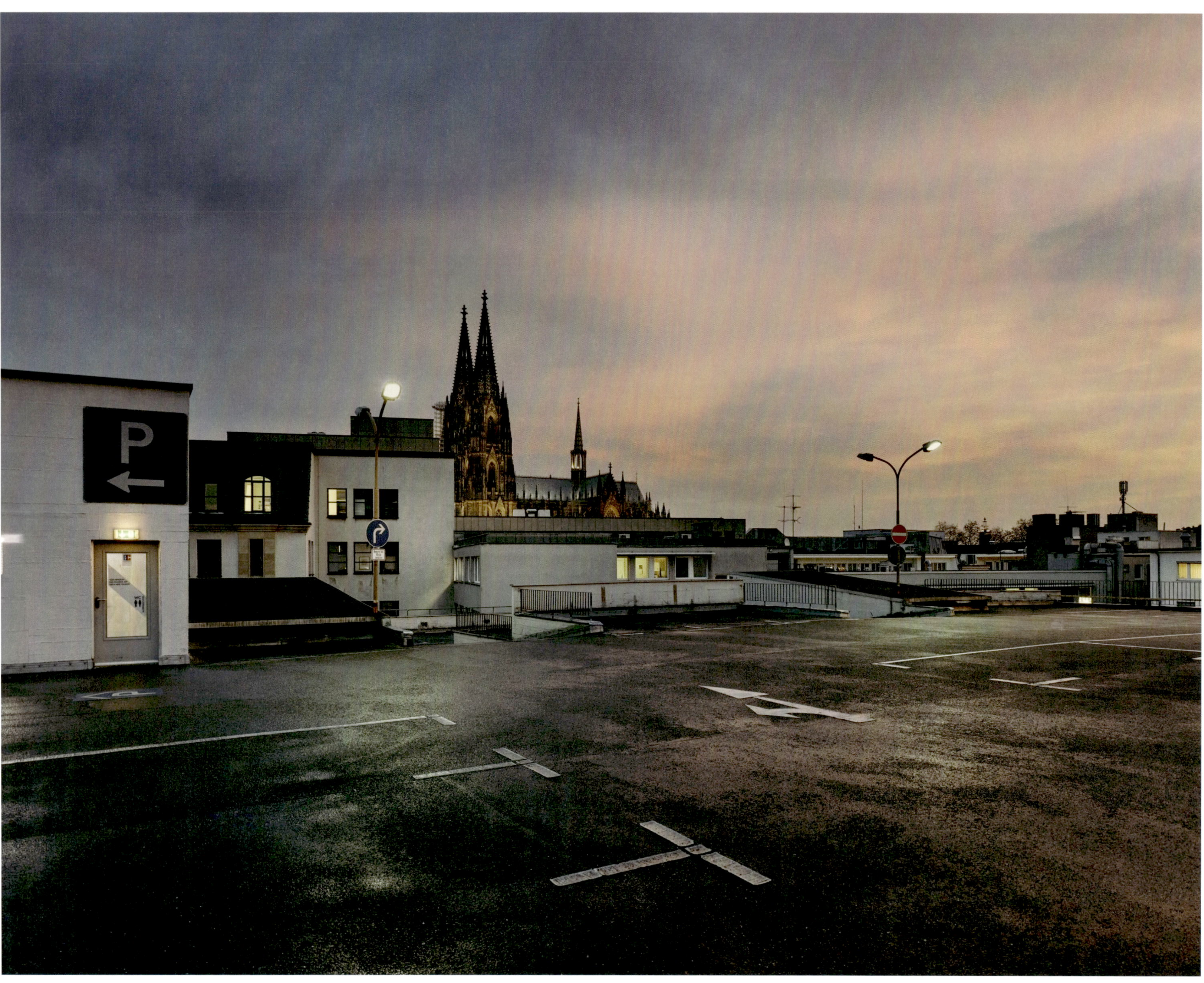
P

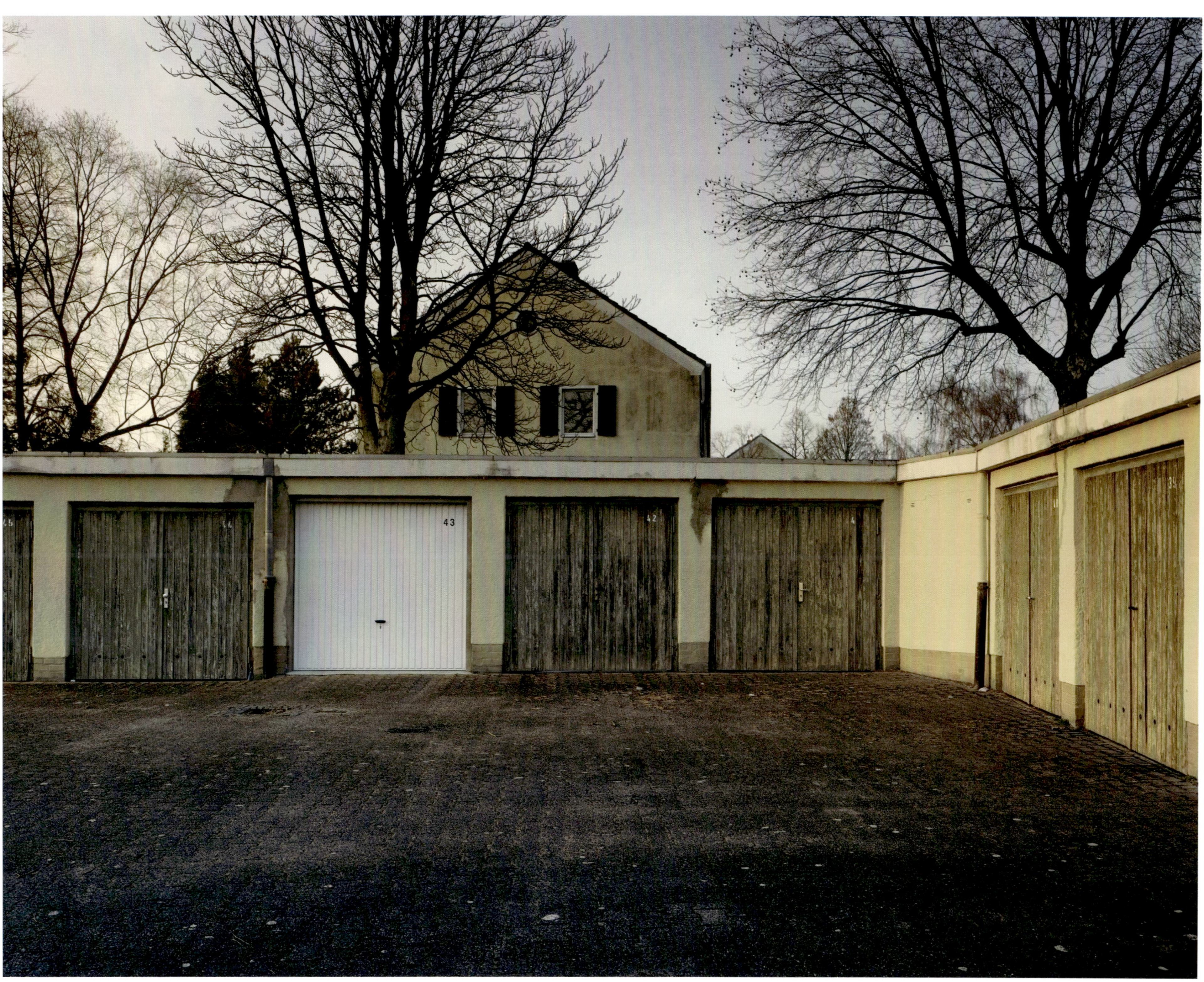
43

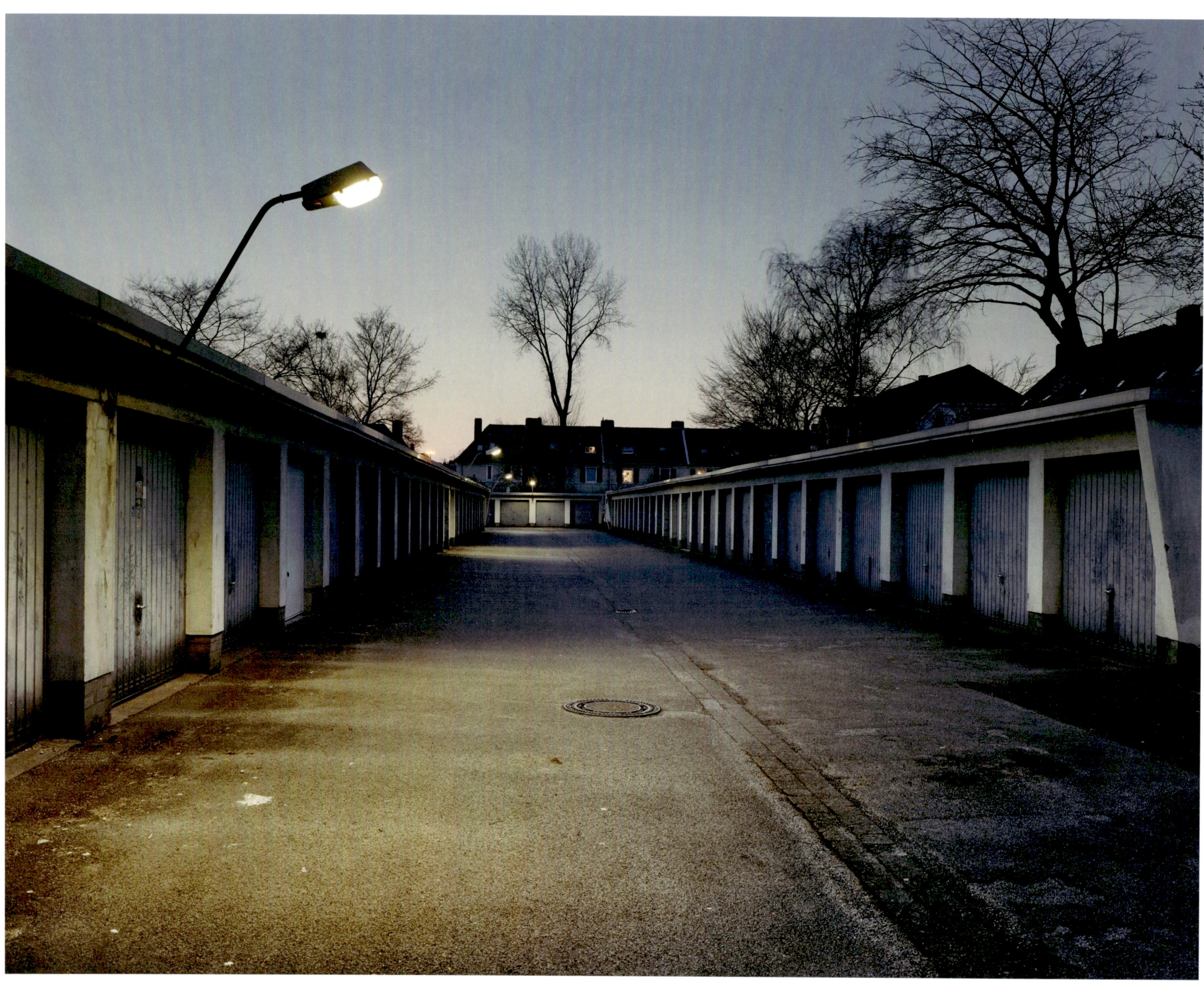

87———2008 POINT REYES, USA

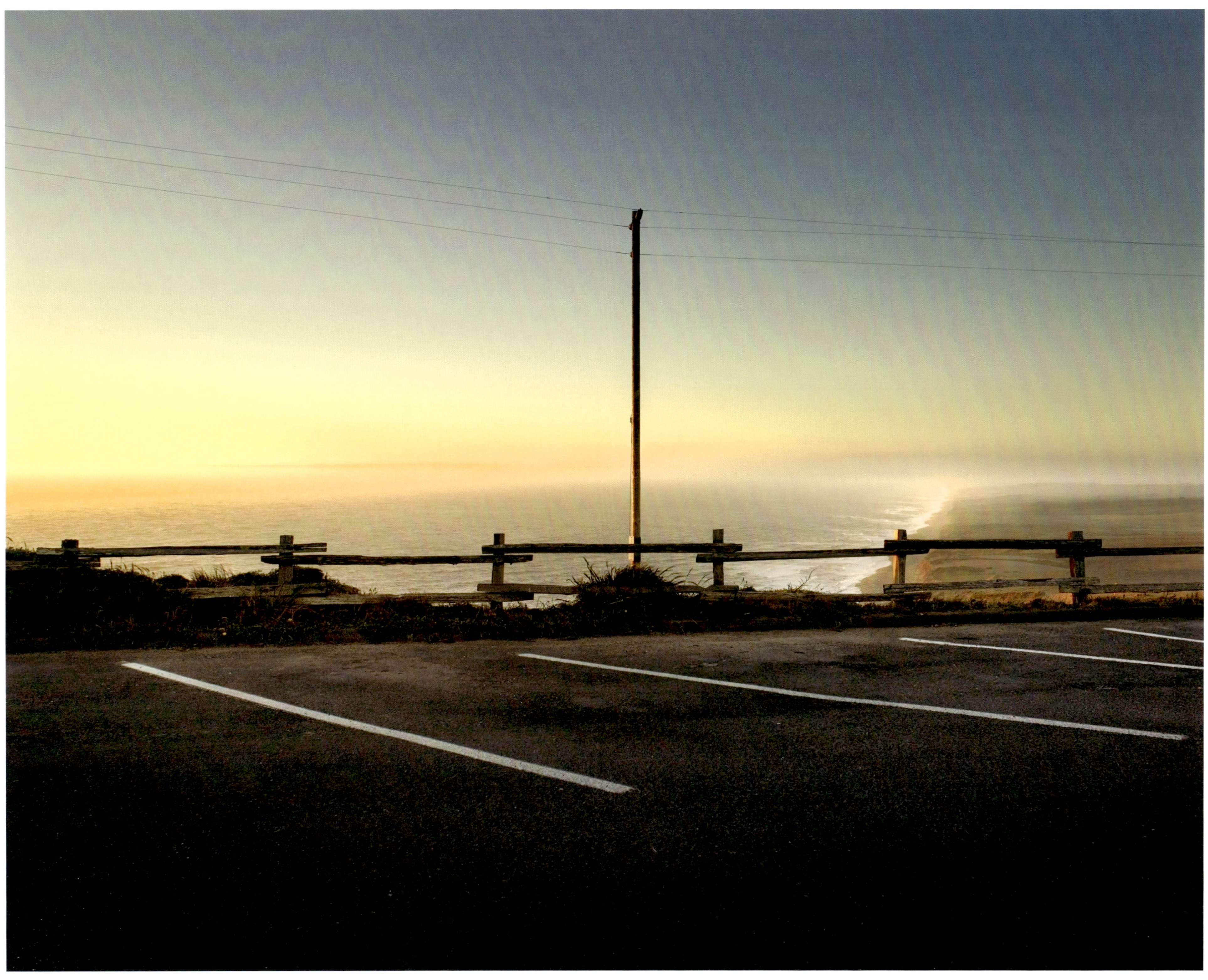

»EIN SCHILD, DAS AUSSICHT ÜBER DIE INSEL VERSPRICHT: OVERLOOK. ES IST SEIN VORSCHLAG GEWESEN, HIER ZU STOPPEN. EIN PARKPLATZ FÜR MINDESTENS HUNDERT WAGEN, ZUR ZEIT LEER; IHR WAGEN STEHT ALS EINZIGER IN DEM RASTER, DAS AUF DEN ASPHALT GEMALT IST. ES IST VORMITTAG.«

Max Frisch, Montauk

Ganz nüchtern gesagt: Ein Parkplatz ist ein Ort, an dem ich mein Auto abstellen darf. Was fasziniert Sie daran?
Parkplätze sind wie Strichcodes in der Landschaft. Eindeutig identifizierbar, überall auf der Welt. Ich würde mich nicht wundern, wenn Außerirdische versuchen würden, diese Codes auszulesen. Als Botschaft sozusagen. Für mich gilt das jedenfalls, und mit »Solitude« habe ich genau diesen Versuch unternommen. Parkplatz ist dabei das Gegenteil von Bewegung. Die andere Seite des Lärms. Mobilität lediglich als Möglichkeit. Aber auch das Angekommensein: auf den Punkt, im Geviert. Frei vom Ziel, wenn man so will. Im Augenblick und ohne Zweck. Also: Kunst.

Viele Ihrer Aufträge bestehen darin, Autos für Werbung in Szene zu setzen. Das Projekt »Solitude« zeichnet sich nun durch deren völlige Abwesenheit aus. Eine ironische Spielerei? Eine ästhetische Inspiration?
Kein bewusster Witz, aber ein wohlgelauntes *Yes!* vielleicht. Ich habe auf diese Weise einfach die Möglichkeit, neben meiner kommerziellen Arbeit für mich zu fotografieren und mir die Freude am Bild zu erhalten. Im Übrigen ist es ja auch so: Auf diesen Reisen bin ich auftragsfrei unterwegs, das heißt, ich entscheide, wie ich etwas mache. Ich kann etwas aus einem anderen Blickwinkel betrachten, ein Anderssein im Bild formulieren – eben nicht das Gemeinte. Darin liegt dann tatsächlich vielleicht auch ein Stückchen Ironie.

Wie entstand die Idee, Parkplätze weltweit zu fotografieren?
Ursprünglich war es ein Nebenprodukt meiner Arbeit als Werbefotograf in den USA, oder sonst wo auf der Welt. Da steht man ja häufig auf Parkplätzen oder Parkdecks, um vor einer Skyline Autos zu fotografieren. Die formale Struktur und auch die schiere Größe haben schon immer Eindruck auf mich gemacht: auf der einen Seite die Skyline, der riesige Himmel – und dann dieses Raster. Zunächst habe ich aus formalästhetischen Gründen begonnen, diese Plätze, die für uns leer geräumt worden waren, zu fotografieren. Das war mehr eine Vorarbeit. Erst nach einiger Zeit habe ich gemerkt, dass da eine Serie entsteht. Schließlich habe ich begonnen, die Orte zu suchen. – Heute ist mir klar, dass das einfach Bilder sind. Ich habe nichts erfunden. Ich habe es gefunden. Eine eigenwillige Begegnung von Job und zweckfreier Inspiration, könnte man sagen.

Was qualifiziert einen Parkplatz zum Fotomotiv?
Das frage ich mich bei jedem Bild aufs Neue! Da ich mich seit 18 Jahren mit dem Thema beschäftige, bekomme ich inzwischen von Kollegen oder Scouts häufig Bilder aus der ganzen Welt zugeschickt, mit dem Zusatz *Das wäre doch einer!* Die schaue ich mir dann an und nicht selten sage ich *Nein*. Zu perfekt, zu irgendwas ... So habe ich festgestellt, dass es mir – abgesehen von der formalästhetischen Struktur – vor allem um die Stimmung geht. Wenn ich aus dem Auto aussteige, muss mir dieser Ort etwas erzählen, das im Wesentlichen mit den Menschen zu tun hat: Trennungen, Vereinigungen, dunkle Geschäfte oder absurde Zufälligkeiten, die das Leben aus oder auch wieder in die Bahn bringen. Genau an diesem einen Ort. Eine Entdeckung ohne Aufdeckung. Sichtbares und Verborgenes halten sich auf stimmungsvolle Weise die Waage. Wenn ich das dort finde, dann mache ich ein Bild.

Wie gehen Sie bei der Suche nach dem passenden Motiv vor?
Es gibt oft Kontakte vor Ort oder Tipps aus dem jeweiligen Team. Hinzu kommen Google Maps und Google Earth, aber auch die zufällige Begegnung.

Daraus entsteht das Material für die vorsortierende Auswahl. – Wenn ich dann unterwegs bin, schaue ich mir die Orte aus meiner Perspektive an: die Möglichkeiten für einen Standort, Hintergründe, Szenerie und nicht zuletzt: Ist das Ding irgendwann auch wirklich leer? Volle Parkplätze interessieren mich irgendwie nicht.

Sie sind gewöhnlich mit einem großen Team unterwegs. »Solitude« ist jedoch etwas für den Einzelgänger. Wie unterscheidet sich die Arbeitsweise?
Ich mag beides. Vom rein Praktischen her konzentriere ich mich bei den Auftragsarbeiten auf das Motiv in *frei geschossener*, also höchst professioneller Weise. Vorbereitung ist alles. Und die leistet das Team. Bei meiner Serie arbeite ich absolut reduziert. Da wird kein zusätzliches Licht gesetzt, keine Straßensperrung, kein großes Set. Nur die Kamera und ich. Das muss auch so sein, weil ich gemerkt habe, dass es immer auch ein Stück weit um die Auseinandersetzung mit mir selbst geht: auf das richtige Licht, das richtige Dunkel zu warten; da stehst du neben dem Stativ und guckst, was da in drei, vier Stunden so passiert – auch mit dir. Aber genau diese Abwechslung ist es wohl, die mir das gibt, was ich als Fotograf und Mensch brauche.

Woher rührt der Wunsch, aus der Stille und Unsichtbarkeit hinauszugehen und das Ergebnis unter anderem in Buchform zu präsentieren?
Das Buch gehört einfach zur Fotokunst. Mir gibt ein solches Projekt die Möglichkeit, die Essenz zu filtern, die dieses Projekt seit 18 Jahren ausmacht. Das ist eine professionelle, eine sehr persönliche Biografie. Ich mag diese Bilder. Viele Leute mögen sie. Ich trage sie für mich und andere zusammen. Dass daraus ein Buch werden würde, war vorher nicht abzusehen. Aus dem Sammeln ist eine Sammlung entstanden. Deshalb ein Buch und sicher werden auch Ausstellungen folgen. Für mich ist das ein Statement zu meiner Arbeit. Allerdings auch keine Festlegung auf immer und ewig. Die Serie kann weitergehen – und es wird Neues kommen. Das ist kein Widerspruch.

Gibt es Vorbilder, die Sie bei diesem Projekt beeinflusst haben?
Das ist eher im Nachklang passiert. Natürlich weiß ich, wer was auf welche Weise festgehalten hat. Ich habe aber die Erfahrung gemacht, dass es notwendig ist, dieses Wissen wieder aus den Augen zu verlieren, um seinen eigenen Weg zu gehen. Inspiriert hat mich jedoch in jedem Fall die amerikanische Westküstenfotografie von Ansel Adams und Edward Weston bis hin zu Stephen Shore und Joel Meyerowitz. Später habe ich mich dann mit Bernd und Hilla Becher und deren Schülern auseinandergesetzt, die seriell gearbeitet haben. Auch wenn ich nie den Vorsatz hatte, ihnen nachzufolgen, habe ich im Nachhinein doch gemerkt, wie sehr mich die Beschäftigung mit ihnen geprägt hat. Zum Beispiel darin, an einem Thema, das an der Oberfläche eigentlich dokumentarisch ist, jahrelang dranzubleiben, und die Varianten der Stimmungen festzuhalten. Schlussendlich bleibt die alles entscheidende Frage: Welche Geschichte erzählt mein Bild? Und die Hoffnung, dass es immer wieder eine neue ist.

Parkplätze sind ein Symbol von Urbanität, eine »Speerspitze« des Urbanen im Naturraum. Spielte das für Sie eine Rolle?
Nein, einen solchen vordergründig intellektuellen Überbau, um der Serie eine Richtung zu verleihen, gibt es nicht. Es ist subtiler. Ich wähle den Weg über die Ästhetik. In dem Buch findet man zum Beispiel Landschaften, in die eine brachiale Steinfläche hineingearbeitet worden ist. Ja, das könnte eine wertende Aussage sein. Aber meine Darstellung strahlt trotz allem eine große Ruhe, Ordnung und Gelassenheit aus, und damit auch Schönheit. Der Betrachter ist überrascht: Auf der einen Seite erfährt er die besondere ästhetische Qualität, auf der anderen Seite wird er mit dem brutalen Hineingrätschen des Asphalts in die Natur konfrontiert. Und das über mein Bild und nicht mit einem Slogan.

Zum Prinzip Ordnung: Selbst auf leerem Parkplatz würde sich jeder brav zwischen die Linien stellen. Sie auch?
Ja, auf jeden Fall (lacht). Obwohl ein Freund von mir, mit dem ich viel unterwegs bin, behauptet, ich hätte eine Parktechnik entwickelt, die keine Parallelen kenne. – Es ist halt eine vorgegebene Ordnung und aus irgendeinem Grund halten wir uns daran. Es gibt ja die Theorie, dass beim Erkennen und Vervollständigen komplexer Ordnungssysteme Glückshormone freigesetzt werden, die ein Gefühl von Schönheit hervorrufen. Vielleicht stehen wir ja gar nicht als angepasster Bürger im Kästchen auf dem Parkplatz, sondern als Freigeister und Ästheten. Wer kann das schon wissen.

Parkplätze »predigen« Vereinzelung. Kollektivität funktioniert über Grenzen. Gibt es eine Philosophie des Parkplatzes?
Schau tiefer! Das ist der erste Satz meiner Parkplatzphilosophie. Und der einzige.

Können Sie mittlerweile am Parkplatz erkennen, in welchem Land Sie sich befinden?
Einiges variiert schon: wie die Linien gezogen sind, wie der Grund sich anfühlt, also die Haptik, oder ob es einen Schlussstein in der Parktasche gibt, wie zum Beispiel in den USA. Da kann man vieles beobachten, klassifizieren und interpretieren. Und sicher gibt es eindeutig identifizierbare *nationale* Merkmale. Aber das ist ja meine Sache nicht. Ich schaue und mache Bilder. Man könnte sagen: Zu viele Worte, Fotograf!

Ist während des Fotografierens schon mal einer gekommen und hat gesagt: *Hallo, der Parkplatz ist doch leer! Was fotografieren Sie da eigentlich?*
Nein, das ist noch nicht passiert. Oft zeigt ja auch die Kamera in eine Richtung, in der vieles plausibel für ein Foto erscheint. Vordergrund und Hintergrund – das liegt immer auch im Auge des Betrachters. Dieser sieht im Zweifel etwas vollkommen anderes als ich, da er das komponierte Bild auf seine eigene Weise vollendet. Mich interessiert vordergründig die Leere, sie wird jedoch flankiert durch Fülle. Das Bild ist also immer ein Widerspruch. Und Details schieben sich in die Betrachtung ein, da sie durch die unausgefüllte Fläche betont werden. Aber eigentlich treffe ich zu der Zeit, zu der ich unterwegs bin, sehr selten jemanden. Und schon gar keinen, der sich für Fotografie interessiert.

Leere und Melancholie scheinen sich durch »Solitude« zu ziehen. Stimmt diese Wahrnehmung?
Ja, das ist so. Genau nach diesen beiden Ausdrücken suche ich auf meinen Reisen. Und an diesen Orten, auf diesen Plätzen kann ich sie finden, da sie mir bewusst sind und ich sie in mir trage. Der Betrachter meiner Bilder sieht den Ort, an dem ich mich im weitesten Sinne erkannt habe. Und er findet ein Bild für seine Melancholie, für das, was er als Leere empfindet. Sein Bild wird nie meins sein. Allerdings wissen wir dann voneinander. Auch ein Grund für dieses Buch.

Gibt es einen Parkplatz Ihrer Träume?
Nein, für mich besteht der Reiz in der Unstetigkeit. Der Offenheit. Da mündet nichts in ein Bild am Ende. Was dem aber vielleicht nahekommt, das zeigt sich in der Beziehung zwischen den Bildern. Dem insistierten Geheimnis der *Sehnsuchtsmotive* und dem Parkplatz meiner Kindheit: ein Garagenhof in der Nähe meines Elternhauses. Da haben wir gekickt. Aber weder die einen noch das andere sind Schlüsselbilder. Sie sind nur die beiden Linien, zwischen denen ich in den vergangenen 18 Jahren immer wieder eingeparkt habe.

Das Interview führte Dipl.-Phil. Jürgen Opel, freier Journalist des NDR, Berlin, 26.4.2017.

»A SIGN PROMISING A VIEW ACROSS THE ISLAND: OVERLOOK. IT WAS HE WHO SUGGESTED STOPPING HERE. A PARKING LOT FOR AT LEAST A HUNDRED CARS, AT THE MOMENT EMPTY; THEIR CAR IS THE ONLY ONE STANDING IN THE GRIDS PAINTED ON THE ASPHALT. IT IS MORNING.«

Max Frisch, Montauk

A parking lot is, to put it prosaically, a place where I can park my car. What do you find fascinating about them?
Parking lots are like barcodes in the landscape: clearly identifiable, throughout the world. I wouldn't be surprised if aliens were to try to read those codes–as a message, so to speak. This is the case for me at least, and it is exactly what I attempted to do with »Solitude«. Parking lots are the opposite of movement. The other side of noise. Mobility merely as a possibility. But also the state of having arrived: on the mark, within the rectangle. Free of a destination, if you will. In the moment and without purpose. In other words: art.

Many of your commissions involve staging cars for advertising. The »Solitude« project, on the other hand, is characterized by their complete absence. Playful irony? Aesthetic inspiration?
Not a deliberate joke, but a lighthearted *yes!* perhaps. This just allows me to take photographs for myself alongside my commercial work and retain the pleasure of the image. Besides, I am on the road without an assignment on these trips. This means that I decide how to do things. I can view something from a different angle, I can articulate an otherness in the image –precisely not what is intended. There may be a bit of irony in that, I guess.

How did the idea come up to photograph parking lots around the world?
Originally, it was a by-product of my work as a commercial photographer in the U.S. and elsewhere in the world. When going about this work you often find yourself on parking lots or parking decks to photograph cars against the backdrop of skylines. The formal structure as well as the sheer scale has always impressed me: on the one hand the skyline, the vast sky, and then this grid. Initially I began photographing these lots, which had been cleared for us, for formal, aesthetic reasons. That was more like preliminary work. Only after a while did I realize that it was developing into a series. Eventually I started seeking out the places. Today I am aware that they are simply pictures. I did not invent anything. They were just something I found. An unconventional encounter of job and purposeless inspiration, you could say.

What qualifies a parking lot as a subject for a photograph?
This is something I ask myself with every new picture! Having worked on the subject for eighteen years, I now often get colleagues or scouts to send me pictures from all over the world, with the words *Isn't this a perfect one?!* I'll take a look at them and more often than not I'll say *No*. Too perfect, too something ... This made me realize that, for me, what it's about, aside from the formal-aesthetic structure, is above all the mood. When I get out of the car, that place has to tell me something basically related to the people: separations, getting together, dark transactions, or absurd coincidences which throw life off course or put it back on track. In this one place. A discovery without uncovering. The visible and the hidden balance one another in a way that is full of atmosphere. If I find this there, I take a picture.

How do you go about searching for the suitable subject?
Often there are local contacts or I get tips from the team in question. Google Maps and Google Earth are also helpful. And then there is the chance encounter. This provides the material for a first selection. Then when I'm on the road, I take a look at the places from my perspective, paying particular attention to possible points of view, backgrounds, scenery and, not least: is

this thing really going to be empty at some point? Full parking lots somehow don't interest me.

You are usually on the road with a large team. »Solitude«, however, is something for the loner. How does the working method differ?
I like both. For purely practical reasons, when I do commissions I focus on the subject in a *free shoot* manner, meaning in a highly professional way. Preparation is everything. And this is done by the team. In the case of the parking lot series I work in a completely pared-down way. No lighting is added; no streets are blocked; no large set. Just the camera and I. And this is really how it has to be, because I noticed that to some extent it is always about reflecting on myself as well. While waiting for the right light or the right level of darkness, you stand there next to the tripod and look at all the things that happen in three, four hours–including what happens to you. But this diversion is probably precisely what I need as a photographer and a human being.

Where did the desire come from to move out of the quiet and the invisible and present the results in the form of a book, among others?
The book is simply part of photo art. Such a book project provides me with an opportunity to filter the essence that has defined this series for eighteen years. It is a professional, a very personal biography. I like these images. Many people like them. I am collecting them for myself and for others. It was not foreseeable that it would result in a book. The collecting has resulted in a collection–hence the book, and exhibitions are sure to follow as well. For me this is a statement on my work, but at the same time not a commitment for ever and ever. The series may continue–and new things will come. There is no contradiction there.

Are there role models that have influenced you in this project?
That happened more in the aftermath. Of course, I know who captured what in what way. But I have learned that it is necessary to lose sight of this knowledge again, in order to find one's own way. Still, I was definitely inspired by American West Coast photography from Ansel Adams and Edward Weston to Stephen Shore and Joel Meyerowitz. Later, I was preoccupied with Bernd and Hilla Becher and their students who worked in a serial manner. Even when it was never my intention to follow their examples, I did realize afterwards how much this preoccupation has influenced me: for instance, in sticking for years with a subject that, superficially, is really a documentary subject, and recording the varying moods. In the end, the all-important question remains: what story does my picture tell? And the hope that, every time, it is a new one.

Parking lots are a symbol of urbanity, a »spearhead« of the urban in the natural environment. Did this play a role for you?
No, there is no such ostensibly intellectual superstructure giving the series a direction. It's more subtle. I prefer to take the aesthetic approach. For instance, there are landscapes in the book that have a paved surface brutally set into them. This could indeed be an evaluative statement. But my image nevertheless exudes great tranquility, order, and serenity–and therefore beauty, too. The viewer is surprised: on the one hand, he experiences the aesthetic quality and, on the other, he is confronted with the violent intrusion of asphalt into nature. And he does so through my picture rather than based on a slogan.

Regarding the principle of order: even in an empty parking lot everyone would dutifully park between the lines. Does that apply to you, too?
Yes, absolutely (laughs). Although a friend of mine, with whom I am on the road a lot, claims I have developed a parking technique that is without parallel. It is a prescribed order and for some reason we abide by it. There is this theory that when we recognize and complete complex systems of order, our bodies release endorphins that induce a sense of beauty. Perhaps it is, in fact, as free spirits and aesthetes, rather than as conformist citizens, that we stand in the parking bay. Who knows.

Parking lots »preach« isolation. Collectivity functions across borders. Is there a philosophy of the parking lot?
Look more deeply! This is the first theorem of my parking lot philosophy–and the only one.

Are you by now able to tell by the parking lot in which country you are?
Some things do vary: the way the lines are drawn; the way the ground feels–in other words, the haptics. Whether the parking bay has a concrete curb, as is common in the U.S. There is a lot to observe, classify, and interpret. And surely there are clearly identifiable *national* features. But that is not my thing. I look and take pictures. You could say: too many words, photographer!

Has anyone ever come up to you while you were photographing and said: *Hello, this parking lot is empty! What are you really photographing here?*

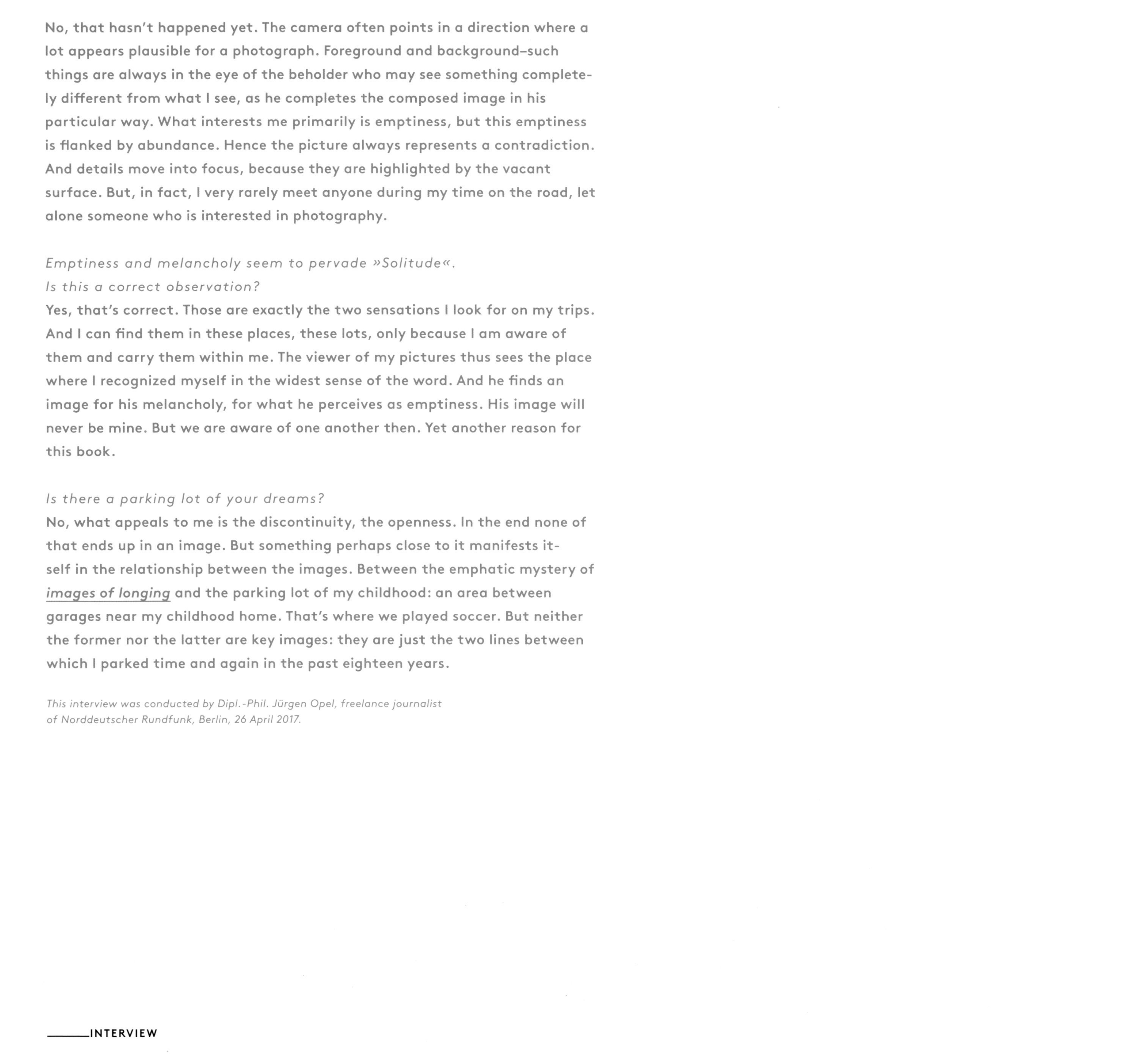

No, that hasn't happened yet. The camera often points in a direction where a lot appears plausible for a photograph. Foreground and background–such things are always in the eye of the beholder who may see something completely different from what I see, as he completes the composed image in his particular way. What interests me primarily is emptiness, but this emptiness is flanked by abundance. Hence the picture always represents a contradiction. And details move into focus, because they are highlighted by the vacant surface. But, in fact, I very rarely meet anyone during my time on the road, let alone someone who is interested in photography.

Emptiness and melancholy seem to pervade »Solitude«.
Is this a correct observation?
Yes, that's correct. Those are exactly the two sensations I look for on my trips. And I can find them in these places, these lots, only because I am aware of them and carry them within me. The viewer of my pictures thus sees the place where I recognized myself in the widest sense of the word. And he finds an image for his melancholy, for what he perceives as emptiness. His image will never be mine. But we are aware of one another then. Yet another reason for this book.

Is there a parking lot of your dreams?
No, what appeals to me is the discontinuity, the openness. In the end none of that ends up in an image. But something perhaps close to it manifests itself in the relationship between the images. Between the emphatic mystery of *images of longing* and the parking lot of my childhood: an area between garages near my childhood home. That's where we played soccer. But neither the former nor the latter are key images: they are just the two lines between which I parked time and again in the past eighteen years.

This interview was conducted by Dipl.-Phil. Jürgen Opel, freelance journalist of Norddeutscher Rundfunk, Berlin, 26 April 2017.

VITA
ERIK CHMIL

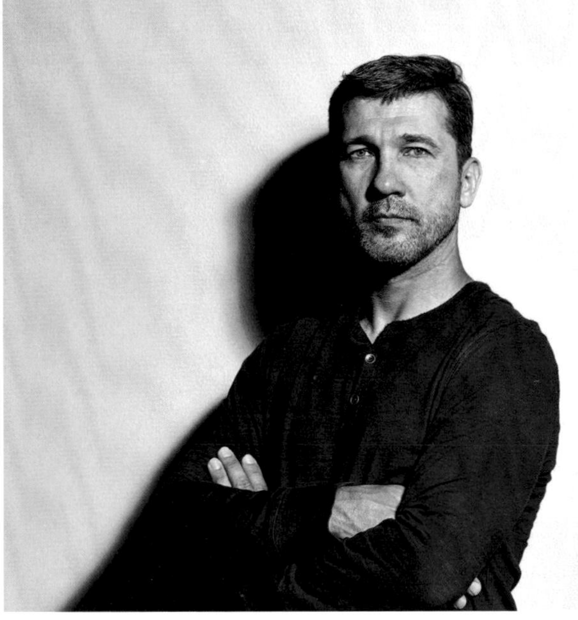

Porträt/Portrait Robert Eikelpoth

- Geboren 1968 in Leverkusen
- Studium der Visuellen Kommunikation in Düsseldorf & Dortmund
- Studienaufenthalte Frankreich & Finnland
- Selbstständiger Fotograf seit 1993 in Köln
- *Portfolio* Automobile und Architektur, Orte und Menschen, Werbung und Editorial
- *Projekte* Joachim Wissler, Food (Kochbuch + Website)
- *Kunden* BMW, Hyundai; Lexus; Porsche, Renault, RTL, VW
- *Preise* red dot award: communication design, World Cookbook Award 2010, ausgezeichnet vom Bund Freischaffender Fotografen BFF, vom World Design Guide iF, dem Art Directors Club und der Association of Photographers AOP

- Born in Leverkusen in 1968
- Studied visual communication in Düsseldorf & Dortmund
- Study visits in France and Finland
- From 1993 freelance photographer in Cologne
- *Portfolio* automobiles and architecture, places and people, advertising and editorial
- *Projects* Joachim Wissler, Food (cook book + website)
- *Clients* BMW, Hyundai, Lexus, Porsche, Renault, RTL, VW
- *Awards* red dot award: communication design, World Cookbook Award 2010, honored by the BFF Professional Association of Freelance Photographers and Film Creators, the iF World Design Guide, the Art Directors Club and the Association of Photographers (AOP)

Erik Chmil
Schanzenstr. 23
51063 Köln / Cologne
www.erik-chmil.de

DANKSAGUNG
ACKNOWLEDGEMENTS

Meine hier gezeigten Fotografien, die meist menschenleer erscheinen, leben von der Kraft, mit der Menschen vor oder nach dem Entstehen des Bildes am Werk gewesen sind. Genauso verhält es sich mit diesem Buch. Ich möchte mich herzlich bei allen bedanken, die »Solitude« entschieden mitgestaltet haben.

Ich bedanke mich zuallererst und ganz herzlich bei Vroni und Carmen von hw.design für ihren sensiblen Umgang mit meinen Bildern und die wunderbare Gestaltung des Buches. Einen erheblichen Anteil an der Entstehung hatte auch mein Freund Frank, dem ich unseren Austausch über meine Fotografie sowie die Unterstützung seiner Agentur verdanke. Ein herzliches Dankeschön geht auch an Thomas und Johannes für einen Teil der Bildbearbeitung und der Produktionsbegleitung. Ganz besonders möchte ich mich bei Tom für seinen unermüdlichen Einsatz und den sensiblen Feinschliff bedanken; ebenso bei Robert für seine unterstützende Arbeit und das, wie ich finde, sehr gelungene Porträt. Vielen Dank auch an Petra Giloy-Hirtz für den gegenseitigen Austausch und den Essay, Jürgen Opel für die Idee und Umsetzung des Interviews und natürlich Thomas Zuhr, der die Aussage und Kraft der Serie gespürt hat und ohne den das Buch nie entstanden wäre. Natürlich gilt mein Dank auch allen Wegbereitern und Wegbegleitern, die ich in den vielen Jahren bei Aufträgen und auf meinen Reisen getroffen habe und über die das ein oder andere Foto eine Geschichte in sich trägt.

Mein besonders herzlicher Dank gebührt natürlich Petra, die es mir erlaubt, meiner Berufung und Leidenschaft nachzugehen und trotzdem ein von Liebe geprägtes Familienleben mit unseren Kindern Antonia und Matteo ermöglicht. Danke!

The photos which I have presented here are mostly devoid of people, and yet they live from the strength of people either before or after the picture was taken. And this book is the same. I should like to express my thanks to all those who have played an important part in the creation of »Solitude«.

First of all, I should like to offer my sincere thanks to Vroni and Carmen of hw.design for their sensitive treatment of my pictures and the wonderful design of this book. My friend Frank was also involved in its development to no small degree. I am grateful for our discussions about my photography and for the support of his agency. Thank you, too, to Thomas and Johannes for some of the picture processing and for accompanying the production. My special thanks go to Tom for his untiring efforts and for the sensitive finishing touches–and to Robert for his support and for the portrait, which I find very successful. I should like to thank Petra Giloy-Hirtz for our discussions and for her essay; Jürgen Opel for the idea behind and execution of the interview; and of course Thomas Zuhr, who sensed the statement and strength of the series. Without him, this book would never have been produced. I also thank all those who have smoothed my path and accompanied me on my journey; whom I have met over the past years during my work and when travelling; and for whom one or the other photo represents a story.

Above all I should like to thank Petra, who allows me to live out my vocation and my passion and who nonetheless makes a loving family life with our children Antonia and Matteo possible. Thank you!

IMPRESSUM
IMPRINT

Erschienen im
Hirmer Verlag GmbH
Nymphenburger Straße 84
80636 München

Alle Fotografien © Erik Chmil

Deutsches Lektorat und Korrektorat Stefanie Adam, München
Übersetzung Bram Opstelten, Richmond, Virginia
Englisches Lektorat und Korrektorat Jane Michael, München

Hirmer Projektmanagement Rainer Arnold
Gestaltung und Satz hw.design, München
Bildbearbeitung Zerone Personal, Tom Stein; Der Postbote, Thomas Lison
Lithografie Reproline Genceller, München

Druck und Bindung Passavia Druckservice, Passau
Papier Luxo Art Samt New 150g/m²
Gedruckt in Deutschland

Bibliografische Information der Deutschen Nationalbibliothek
Die Deutsche Nationalbibliothek verzeichnet diese Publikation in der Deutschen Nationalbibliografie; detaillierte bibliografische Daten sind im Internet über http://www.dnb.de abrufbar.

Published by
Hirmer Verlag GmbH
Nymphenburger Straße 84
80636 Munich

All photographs © Erik Chmil

German copy editing and proof reading Stefanie Adam, Munich
Translation into English Bram Opstelten, Richmond, Virginia
English copy editing and proof reading Jane Michael, Munich

Hirmer project management Rainer Arnold
Layout and typesetting hw.design, munich
Image editing Zerone Personal, Tom Stein; Der Postbote, Thomas Lison
Lithography Reproline Genceller, Munich

Printing and binding Passavia Druckservice, Passau
Paper Luxo Art Samt New 150g/m²
Printed in Germany

Bibliographic information published by the Deutsche Nationalbibliothek
The Deutsche Nationalbibliothek lists this publication in the Deutsche Nationalbibliografie; detailed bibliographic data is available on the Internet at http://www.dnb.de.

ISBN 978-3-7774-2928-1
www.hirmerverlag.de
www.hirmerpublishers.com